ACCOUNTING

Basic Principles and Applications

ACCOUNTING

Basic Principles and Applications

Donald J. Guerrieri, PhD

F. Barry Haber, PhD, CPA

William B. Hoyt, MBA

Robert E. Turner, MS

GLENCOE

McGraw-Hill

New York, New York   Columbus, Ohio   Woodland Hills, California   Peoria, Illinois

Send all inquiries to:
Glencoe/McGraw-Hill
936 Eastwind Drive
Westerville, OH 43081

Printed in U.S.A.

Student's Edition ISBN: 0-02-800772-7

5 6 7 8 9 10   027/043   03 02 01 00 99

Contents

Preface   ix

Unit **1**   **Introduction to Accounting**   1

1   Accounting in a Private Enterprise Economy   2
    The United States Private Enterprise Economy   3
    The Role of Accounting   6
    Career Opportunities in Accounting   9
    Organizations that Influence Accounting Practice   10
    Summary of Key Points   11
    Review and Applications   13
    Focus on Computers: Automation: A Business's Life Support System   16

2   Business Transactions and the Basic Accounting Equation   17
    Property and Property Rights   18
    Financial Claims in Accounting   20
    Business Transactions   21
    Effects of Business Transactions on the Basic Accounting Equation   22
    Using a Computer in Accounting   30
    Summary of Key Points   31
    Review and Applications   33
    Focus on Accounting Careers: Accounting: A Mobile Profession   38

Unit **2**   **The Basic Accounting Cycle**   39

3   Analyzing Transactions Affecting Assets, Liabilities, and Owner's Equity   41
    The Basis of an Accounting System   42
    The T Account   42
    The Rules of Debit and Credit   42
    Applying the Rules of Debit and Credit   46
    Summary of Key Points   53
    Review and Applications   54
    Focus on Computers: U.S. Forestry Service Fights Fires with Computers?   59

4   Analyzing Transactions Affecting Revenue, Expenses, and Withdrawals   60
    The Need for Specific Accounting Information   61
    The Relationship of Revenue, Expenses, and Withdrawals
      to Owner's Capital   61
    The Rules of Debit and Credit for Temporary Capital Accounts   62
    Analyzing Transactions Involving Revenue, Expenses, and Withdrawals   67
    Summary of the Rules of Debit and Credit   75
    Testing for the Equality of Debits and Credits   76
    Summary of Key Points   76
    Review and Applications   77
    Focus on Computers: Home Is Where the Office Is   82

5	Recording Transactions in a General Journal	83
	The Accounting Cycle	84
	The General Journal	87
	Journalizing Business Transactions	88
	Correcting Errors in Journal Entries	96
	Recording Transactions in a Computerized Accounting System	96
	The Chart of Accounts	98
	Summary of Key Points	100
	Review and Applications	101
	Focus on Computers: Passwords to Computer Security	106
6	Posting Journal Entries to General Ledger Accounts	107
	The Fourth and Fifth Steps in the Accounting Cycle	108
	The General Ledger	108
	The Posting Process	111
	Proving the Equality of the Ledger	117
	Finding Errors	118
	Correcting Entries	119
	Summary of Key Points	121
	Review and Applications	122
	Focus on Accounting Careers: Accounting Clerks: Patient, Persistent, Good with Figures	127
	Application Activity 1: Setting Up Accounting Records for a Sole Proprietorship	128
7	Preparing a Six-Column Work Sheet	130
	The Sixth Step of the Accounting Cycle	131
	Preparing a Work Sheet	131
	A Review of the Steps in Preparing a Six-Column Work Sheet	140
	Summary of Key Points	141
	Review and Applications	142
	Focus on Computers: Planning for Disasters	147
8	Preparing Financial Statements for a Sole Proprietorship	148
	The Seventh Step of the Accounting Cycle	149
	The Income Statement	150
	The Statement of Changes in Owner's Equity	155
	The Balance Sheet	157
	Preparing Financial Statements on the Computer	160
	Summary of Key Points	161
	Review and Applications	162
	Focus on Computers: Invisible Computers	167
9	Completing the Accounting Cycle for a Sole Proprietorship	168
	The Eighth and Ninth Steps in the Accounting Cycle	169
	The Closing Process	169
	The Income Summary Account	170
	Journalizing the Closing Entries	171
	Posting the Closing Entries to the General Ledger	176
	Preparing a Post-Closing Trial Balance	178
	The Computer and Closing Entries	179
	Summary of Key Points	179
	Review and Applications	181

Focus on Computers: Computers in Sports: New Angles on the
Winning Performance 186

10 Cash Control and Banking Activities 187
    Protecting Cash 188
    Opening a Checking Account 189
    Making Deposits to a Checking Account 191
    Writing Checks 192
    Proving Cash 195
    The Bank Statement 195
    Recording Bank Service Charges 199
    Special Banking Procedures 199
    Electronic Funds Transfer System 200
    Summary of Key Points 201
    Review and Applications 202
    Focus on Accounting Careers: Today's CPA 206

Application Activity 2: Completing the Accounting Cycle
for a Sole Proprietorship 207

*AquaClean Pool Service, An Accounting Simulation Using a
General Journal* 210

Unit 3

Accounting for a Payroll System 211

11 Payroll Accounting 212
    The Importance of Payroll Records 213
    Calculating Gross Earnings 213
    Determining Deductions From Gross Earnings 216
    Completing the Payroll Register 222
    Preparing Payroll Checks 223
    The Employee's Earnings Record 224
    A Computerized Payroll System 226
    Summary of Key Points 226
    Review and Applications 227
    Focus on Computers: Computers in Government 232

12 Payroll and Tax Records 233
    Journalizing and Posting the Payroll 234
    Computing the Employer's Payroll Taxes 238
    Paying the Payroll Tax Liabilities 242
    Filing the Employer's Quarterly Federal Tax Return 246
    Filing the Employer's Annual Tax Reports 246
    Summary of Key Points 249
    Review and Applications 250
    Focus on Computers: Data Access vs. Privacy: A Delicate Balance 254

Application Activity 3: Payroll Accounting 255

Appendix Supplementary Problems 259
Answers to "Check Your Learning" Activities 267
Glossary 271
Credits 277
Index 279

Preface

"The more things change, the more they stay the same." The world of accounting is a good application of this maxim. The computer has revolutionized the generation and processing of financial records. Transactions that were formerly recorded, posted, compiled, sorted, and summarized laboriously by hand are now processed by the computer in the twinkling of an eye. Earlier critical procedures such as balancing and ruling of accounts and time-worn books of original entry such as the combination journal have been discarded or relegated to less important positions by automation. Even the language of accounting has been enlarged to include such terms as *batching, spreadsheets,* and *printouts.*

Yet, in spite of all the changes wrought by the computer, one thing remains the same — the traditional insistence on learning the "why" as well as the "how" of accounting. To gain career success in accounting today without a sound knowledge of computer technology and familiarization with basic computerized accounting procedures would be difficult. But to gain success without a clear, conceptual knowledge of accounting — the "why" and the "how"— would be impossible.

Accounting: Basic Principles and Applications emphasizes the proven method of learning essential concepts and procedures through manual accounting, reinforced liberally with realistic applications. The sound methodology, proven practices, and solid applications of yesterday have been combined with the new approaches, contemporary procedures, and forward-looking computer technology of today to truly prepare students for tomorrow. *Accounting: Basic Principles and Applications* is a comprehensive instructional program thoughtfully designed to help students succeed by meeting and even anticipating the demands of the modern world of accounting.

Course Objectives

Accounting: Basic Principles and Applications is intended for use in an introductory financial accounting course. The primary thrust of the textbook is on learning the rules and procedures of accounting for profit-motivated businesses. Learning the "how" and "why" of accounting will not only enable one to keep the accurate financial records required to produce useful business information, but will give one the capacity to *use* that financial information to make wise business decisions.

After studying this textbook and successfully completing activities in the textbook and the related working papers, students will be able to:

1. Understand the basic accounting principles and procedures that are applied to accounting records kept for businesses that operate in the private enterprise economy of the United States.
2. Explain and appreciate the importance of profit in helping to ensure continued business operations.
3. Describe the three major types of business organization in a private enterprise economy and explain how accounting procedures differ for the three.
4. Gain an awareness of the role of the computer and develop basic proficiency in its use in maintaining accounting records.
5. Understand the types of on-the-job activities that are required of entry-level accounting workers.

Organization of the Textbook

Accounting: Basic Principles and Applications is organized in 3 units of 12 chapters. The first unit of the textbook begins with a presentation in Chapter 1 of the role of accounting in our private enterprise economy and an explanation of several important accounting assumptions. Chapter 2 introduces students to the basic accounting equation. This introduction provides students with a solid foundation on which to build their understanding of accounting theory and procedures.

The second unit of the textbook, "The Basic Accounting Cycle," takes students through a complete accounting cycle for a service business organized as a sole proprietorship. In this unit, students first learn the rules of debit and credit using T accounts and the basic accounting equation. Chapters 3 and 4 present the rules of debit and credit for the permanent accounts and for the temporary capital accounts. In Chapter 5, students learn to use a general journal to record business transactions. The general journal is preferred to other types of journals as a first learning experience because it requires students to think through the effects of transactions rather than memorizing how types of transactions are recorded. The remaining chapters in the unit complete the accounting cycle: posting to the general ledger, preparing a six-column work sheet, generating financial statements, journalizing and posting closing entries, and developing a post-closing trial balance.

In Unit 3, students will learn how to keep payroll records, including those maintained for employees and for the employer's payroll liabilities.

The Appendix contains supplementary problems that can be used for extra and remedial practice.

Special Features

Accounting: Basic Principles and Applications is designed to promote student interest, involvement, and success through a variety of learning features.

Accounting cycle approach. The textbook utilizes a traditional accounting cycle approach to introduce students to new concepts and procedures. This step-by-step development gives students the guidance they look for and clearly demonstrates the continuity and interrelationships of the accounting process.

Chapter objectives. Clearly defined and stated objectives are provided at the beginning of each chapter to help students know exactly what they are expected to learn. The mastery of these objectives is evaluated through end-of-chapter activities, applications, and examinations.

Vocabulary emphasis. The new accounting terms defined in each chapter are listed on the first page of the chapter. This list should be used to "preview" the meaning of each term for students. Research has shown that such vocabulary "previews" help students achieve greater understanding and retention of the material in the chapter. End-of-chapter vocabulary reviews reinforce understanding of key terms. A complete glossary of accounting terms serves as a useful reference tool for students.

Clear, conversational narrative. The textbook is written in an appropriate style, with simple analogies to make concepts meaningful. Abundant illustrations and numerous examples guide students through the preparation of accounting records.

Early emphasis on transaction analysis. A solid foundation in the rules of debit and credit is provided early in the textbook. Understanding the "why" of transaction analysis ensures that the "how" comes naturally.

Guided examples. These frequently used learning aids walk students through sample transactions, step by numbered step, making the "why" behind each procedure very clear.

Frequent learning reinforcement. "Check Your Learning" reinforcement activities follow major sections in every chapter to help students assume the responsibility for their own learning. "Remember" notes summarize key points and help cement important facts in students' minds. "Accounting Tips" at appropriate intervals remind students of essential practices and procedures. "Accounting Notes" inform students of interesting facts about business and the practice of accounting.

Solid end-of-chapter activities. Vocabulary reviews reinforce key accounting terms. Review questions help students expand their understanding of accounting concepts. Short activities encourage students to improve their skills in such important areas as decision making, communications, analysis, math, and human relations. A variety of exercises and problems, ranging from easy to challenging, gives students of all abilities the chance to gain practical accounting experience and to enjoy success.

Three comprehensive application activities. These "mini-simulations," at appropriate points in the textbook, require students to integrate new knowledge with learned procedures and to apply their cumulative skills. The applications may be completed manually, with the computer, or both manually and with the computer.

Computer orientation. Information about computerized accounting systems is integrated into the narrative, providing computer awareness for all students. Short vignettes, called "Focus on Computers," introduce specific aspects of computer technology. A broad range of computer activities is available on optional software: end-of-chapter problems and application activities; simulations; and a microcomputer program for review, remediation, and reinforcement of key accounting principles. All such activities are completely optional. While the computer orientation is provided, the use of a computer is *not required* for successful completion of the course.

Career orientation. Three "Focus on Accounting Careers" vignettes provide students with a look at interesting jobs in the accounting world.

Acknowledgments

We wish to thank those individuals and companies that provided advice and assistance in the development of this program. We owe a debt of gratitude to thousands of teachers and students who offered encouragement, suggestions, and advice in making a good accounting program even better.

We especially thank the Accounting Advisory Committee, composed of ten accounting teachers from across the country—DeVon Allmaras, Gail Blair, Jackie Dean, Gloria Farris, Ruth Hennessy, David McDonald, John Nigro, Nate Rosenberg, Michael Sailes, and Emma Jo Spiegelberg—who provided excellent guidance and advice in the development and review of this program.

Finally, we wish to thank our families, colleagues, and friends who offered constant encouragement and support as we worked on this program.

Donald J. Guerrieri
F. Barry Haber
William B. Hoyt
Robert E. Turner

UNIT
1

INTRODUCTION TO ACCOUNTING

In this first unit on accounting, you will study the role that accounting plays in the private enterprise economy of the United States. In our private enterprise economy, businesses must earn a profit if they are to continue to operate. Keeping accounting records is an important part of operating a business. Accounting records help businesses operate efficiently—and profitably—by keeping track of how much is earned and how much is spent.

Accounting is so much a part of our business lives that much of its terminology has become a part of our everyday language. Throughout this textbook, you will learn why accounting has been called the "language of business."

Accounting in a Private Enterprise Economy

Every business is somewhat like a stage production. For a play to be a success, everyone from the star to the electrician is held responsible for a task that must be performed a certain way. A stage production must run repeatedly for a certain length of time in order to make a profit. In our private enterprise economy, businesses are no different. Each business has many players, many tasks, and the need to perform successfully within certain time periods.

This textbook will describe how businesses operate in our private enterprise economy and the role accounting plays in business operations. Chapter 1 sets the stage for you to see the role accounting plays in our private enterprise economy.

LEARNING OBJECTIVES

After studying this chapter, you should be able to

1. Describe the three types of businesses operated to earn a profit in our private enterprise economy.
2. Discuss the three major forms of business organizations in our private enterprise economy.
3. Describe the role of accounting in our private enterprise economy.
4. Describe the variety of jobs available in accounting.
5. Recognize the major organizations that influence accounting practices.
6. Define the accounting terms introduced in this chapter.

NEW Terms

profit • loss • capital • service business • merchandising business • manufacturing business • sole proprietorship • partnership • corporation • charter • accounting system • business entity • going concern • fiscal period • accounting clerk • general bookkeeper • accountant • certified public accountant

The United States Private Enterprise Economy

All societies have ways of providing their members with goods and services. These ways range from very simple to very complex. The simple end of the scale is a pure barter economy: "I'll give you two bushels of corn if you give me ten chickens." In a slightly more advanced economy, the corn might be exchanged for money. The amount of money exchanged for the corn would depend on the value the owner placed on the corn and on whether the buyer could buy corn from someone else for less.

The most complex type of economy is represented by the electronic exchange of money through an electronic funds transfer system, or EFTS. With EFTS, money can be speedily transferred from one account to another, from bank account to account holder, or from one country to another. A sophisticated, computerized banking system keeps records of the amount of money transferred and to whom.

The economy of the United States is an example of a highly developed, complex economy. The United States economy is referred to as a *private enterprise economy*. In such an economy, people are free to produce the goods and services they choose. Individual buyers are free to use their money as they wish. They may choose to spend it, save it, or invest it. Since the amount of money available is limited, however, businesses must compete to attract the dollars of buyers. One measure of success in attracting dollars is the amount of profit a business earns. The amount of money earned over and above the amount spent to keep the business operating is called **profit.** Businesses that have more operating costs than earnings operate at a **loss.** In a private enterprise economy, only the businesses that consistently earn a profit will have the economic resources to continue to operate.

Businesses Operated for Profit

Groups of people get together in our economy for many different reasons, but each group is organized for some common purpose and with some common goal in mind. Some organizations are service-oriented and do not operate to earn a profit. Examples of such *not-for-profit organizations* include churches, private colleges, professional or social clubs, charitable organizations such as the United Way, and federal, state, and local governments. Other groups are business-oriented and operate to earn a profit. Both types of groups need financial information if they are to operate efficiently. In this textbook, however, you will learn about business organizations operated to earn a profit.

There are three types of businesses in our private enterprise economy that operate for profit: service businesses, merchandising businesses, and manufacturing businesses. Each type of business needs money to get started and to maintain its operations. Money is needed to buy or to make products. Money is also needed for such operating costs as rent, telephone service, and employee wages. Some of this money can be borrowed, but most of it is supplied by one or more owners of the business. The money so invested in a business by an owner is called **capital.**

Service, merchandising, and manufacturing businesses are alike in many ways, as shown in Figure 1-1 on page 4. Each business combines capital with

	Service Business	Merchandising Business	Manufacturing Business
USES:	Capital and labor	Capital and labor	Capital, labor, and materials
HAS:	Operating costs	Operating costs	Operating costs
TO:	Provide services at a fee	Buy and sell finished products	Make and sell finished products
FOR:	Profit	Profit	Profit

Figure 1-1   Types of Businesses Operated for Profit

labor, has operating costs, and hopes to make a profit. They differ from one another, however, in some basic ways. A **service business** operates to provide a needed service for a fee. Service businesses include travel agencies, beauty salons, movers, repair shops, real estate offices, and medical centers. A **merchandising business** buys finished products and resells them to individuals or other businesses. Clothing stores, new and used car dealers, supermarkets, florists, and hobby shops are all examples of merchandising businesses. A **manufacturing business,** on the other hand, buys raw materials, such as wood or iron ore, and transforms them into finished products through the use of labor and machinery. It then sells the finished products to individuals or other businesses. Manufacturing businesses range from steel makers to the corner bakery.

In the United States, businesses come in all varieties and sizes. Yet all of these businesses need to keep accounting records to help them operate both efficiently and profitably.

Each type of business uses an accounting system to help guide the business's operations. In this accounting course, you will learn about the accounting systems used by service businesses.

Forms of Business Organization

To start a business, an owner must have a sufficient amount of money (capital) and must choose an appropriate form of business organization. With few exceptions, businesses in the United States are organized in one of three ways: as a sole proprietorship, a partnership, or a corporation.

▲ **The Sole Proprietorship** "Sole" means "single" or "one." "Proprietor" means "owner." A **sole proprietorship** then is a business owned by one person. It is the oldest and most common form of business organization. It is also the simplest and easiest form of business to start. Usually, only one person invests capital in a sole proprietorship. The business may be started with little or no legal paperwork (forms and documents required by law). The success or failure of the business depends heavily on the efforts and talent of its owner. Some examples of common sole proprietorships are small neighborhood grocery stores, gift shops, and repair shops.

▲ **The Partnership** A **partnership** is a business owned by two or more persons (called "partners") who agree to operate the business as co-owners. Business partners usually enter into a written, legal agreement. This agreement specifies the amount of money to be invested by each partner, the responsibilities of each partner, and how profits and losses are to be divided. Partnerships are often formed when the need for capital is greater than the amount of money one person can invest. Law firms, real estate offices, and "Mom and Pop" stores are frequently organized as partnerships.

▲ **The Corporation** A **corporation** is a business organization that is recognized by law to have a life of its own. In contrast to a sole proprietorship and a partnership, a corporation must get permission to operate from the state. This legal permission is called a **charter** and gives a corporation certain rights and privileges. The charter spells out the rules under which the corporation is to operate.

Many people think that only large businesses like IBM or McDonald's are corporations. This is not always the case. Some corporations are owned and operated by a few people or by one family. Corporations often start out as sole proprietorships or partnerships. The owner(s) of a business may choose to "incorporate" to acquire the money needed to expand the business's operations. To raise this money, shares of stock are sold to hundreds or even thousands of people. These shares represent investments in the corporation. Shareholders, who are also called stockholders, are therefore the legal owners of a corporation.

Whatever their form of organization, all businesses share common financial characteristics and methods of recording and reporting the transactions that occur during the operation of the business.

The Role of Accounting

Accounting plays a very important role in our private enterprise system because its function is to process financial information and to report on profits and losses. An **accounting system** is the process of recording and reporting financial events, or transactions. The steps involved in an accounting system are illustrated in Figure 1-2.

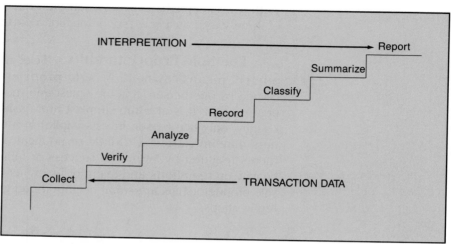

Figure 1-2 Steps in an Accounting System

As you can see, the first step in the process is to collect and verify the financial information for transactions. Each event or transaction having a financial impact on the business must be analyzed and recorded. The recorded information is then classified to make it more useful. After the information has been recorded and classified, it is summarized and presented in the form of accounting reports or statements. Examples of financial reports commonly prepared by accountants are presented in Figure 1-3. Accountants interpret the reports by looking for relationships and trends to help make the information more meaningful to the reader. Accounting is often called the "language of business" because it is a standard means of communicating financial information in a form that is clearly understood by all those interested in the operations and financial condition of a business.

The information in accounting reports has a wide audience. The owner of a business uses financial information to make decisions that affect day-to-day operations. People or institutions who loan money to a business use financial information to determine whether the business will be able to repay loans. Local, state, and federal governments may want to see financial records to determine whether a business is paying the proper amount of taxes. Finally, people who are thinking of investing money in a business want to know whether they can expect a return on their investments.

The Basis of an Accounting System

Accounting consists of many rules and procedures. These rules (or principles) and procedures guide the setting up and maintaining of financial records. Each business sets up its accounting system according to its specific needs, but all businesses follow the same basic rules and procedures.

Eastgate Furniture Corporation
Income Statement for Year Ended December 31, 19--

Revenue from sales:		
Gross sales		$650,000
Less: Sales returns and allowances	$ 1,500	
Sales discounts	4,500	6,000
Net sales		$644,000
Cost of goods sold:		
Merchandise inventory, Jan. 1, 19--		
Purchases		
Less: Purchases returns and allowances		
Purchases discounts		
Net purchases		
Add freight in		
Cost of goods purchased		
Goods available for sale		
Merchandise inventory, Dec. 31, 19--		
Cost of goods sold		
Gross profit from sales		
Operating expenses:		
Selling expenses:		
Sales salaries expense		
Rent expense, selling space		
Advertising expense		
Store supplies expense		
Depreciation expense, store equipment		
Total selling expenses		
General and administrative expenses:		
Office salaries expense		
Rent expense, office space		
Insurance expense		
Office supplies expense		
Depreciation expense, office equipment		
Total general and admin. expenses		
Total operating expenses		
Income from operations		
Less income taxes expense		
Net income		

Eastgate Furniture Corporation
Balance Sheet, December 31, 19--

Assets			
Current assets:			
Cash		$38,900	
Accounts receivable		9,900	
Merchandise inventory		23,000	
Prepaid expenses		4,400	
Total current assets			$ 76,200
Plant and equipment:			
Office equipment	$14,000		
Less accumulated depreciation	1,050	$12,950	
Store equipment	$27,550		
Less accumulated depreciation	4,600	22,950	
Total plant and equipment			35,900
Total assets			$112,100
Liabilities			
Current liabilities:			
Accounts payable		$ 4,000	
Income taxes payable		2,100	
Total current liabilities			$ 6,100
Stockholders' Equity			
Common stock, $5 par value, 4,000 shares authorized and outstanding		$20,000	
Retained earnings		86,000	
Total stockholders' equity			106,000
Total liab. and stockholders' equity			$112,100

Figure 1-3 Accounting Reports

An assumption is something taken for granted as true. When we go to a play, we assume that the show will be as advertised, that the actors can be heard by the audience, and that they are all speaking a language we understand. If our assumptions are wrong, the play will be disappointing or make no sense. Business "audiences" also must be able to make assumptions.

Accounting is based on four assumptions about business operations. These assumptions underlie all reports and are summarized by the terms "business entity," "going concern," "unit of measure," and "time period."

Business Entity A **business entity** is an organization that exists independently of its owner's personal holdings. This means that accounting records contain only the financial information related to the business. The business owner's personal financial activities or other investments are not included in the reports of the business. For example, the personal residence of a business owner, valued at $75,000, is not reported in the accounting records of the business. However, buildings owned by the business are included in its financial records and reports.

Going Concern In accounting, it is assumed that a business will continue to operate in the future. In other words, a business is said to be a **going concern.** Financial reports are prepared on the assumption that the business will operate long enough to carry out its operations and meet future obligations. That assumption is why a business might report that its long-term debts of $100,000 must be paid in the year 2010.

▲ **Unit of Measure**   The effects of business transactions are measured in money amounts. In the United States, the monetary unit of measure is the dollar. For accounting records, the dollar is assumed to have a fixed buying power. In other words, the effects of inflation or deflation are not reflected in the financial records of a business. Everything is recorded at cost. For example, a business purchased an office building for $150,000. The office building might now cost $180,000 to replace due to inflation. In the accounting records, however, the building would be listed at its original cost of $150,000.

▲ **Time Period**   Accounting reports are prepared for a specific period of time. A period of time covered by an accounting report is referred to as a **fiscal period.** The fiscal period can cover any period of time—such as one month or three months—but the most common period is one year.

Accounting and the Computer

Before the invention of calculators and computers, all business transactions were recorded by hand. Now the computer performs routine record-keeping tasks and prepares reports that sometimes took accounting workers months to summarize manually. The computer is ideally suited to accounting work, and accountants were among the earliest users to recognize its practical applications. Found only in large businesses at first, computers are now commonplace. Microcomputers give even one-person businesses the option of using a computerized accounting system.

In today's business world, it is becoming increasingly important for accounting workers to be familiar with computerized accounting.

Regardless of how or whether a business uses computers, the nature of accounting remains the same. Information may be recorded in a manual accounting system and a computerized accounting system in different ways, but the same financial reports will result. The rules and principles that you learn from this textbook will apply to both manual and computerized accounting systems.

Career Opportunities in Accounting

According to the *Occupational Outlook Handbook,* the number of jobs for bookkeeping and accounting workers is expected to increase substantially during the 1990s. Although the jobs will require varying amounts of education and experience, most of the jobs will fall into the categories of accounting clerk, general bookkeeper, or accountant. Let's take a look at the requirements of these jobs and their roles in business.

Accounting Clerk

Most entry-level jobs in accounting are clerical. The people who hold these jobs are generally called **accounting clerks.** According to the *Dictionary of Occupational Titles,* an accounting clerk does "routine computing, calculating, and posting of financial, statistical, and other numerical data, manually or by machine, to maintain accounting records and to record details of business transactions."

The job of an accounting clerk varies with the size of the company. In a small business, the clerk might handle most of the business's recordkeeping tasks. In a large company, clerks might specialize in one part of the accounting system. Minimum requirements for most accounting clerk positions are graduation from high school and one or two years of accounting courses. More and more employers want workers who can handle computerized accounting tasks. Some of the entry-level clerical jobs that you see in want ads call for accounting clerks in these categories: payroll, accounts receivable, accounts payable, general ledger, cash, inventory, and purchasing.

General Bookkeeper

Many small- or medium-sized businesses employ only one person to keep their accounting records. This person is usually called a **general bookkeeper.** In addition to processing and recording all the information from a company's transactions, a general bookkeeper often calculates wages and prepares checks for the payment of those wages. In companies with several accounting clerks, a general bookkeeper will often also be a supervisor.

Education requirements vary with the size of the company and the complexity of its accounting system. A general bookkeeper may or may not be required to have a four-year college degree in accounting. Experience or an associate's degree in accounting is sometimes enough to fulfill the job's requirements.

Accountant

The term **accountant** describes a fairly broad range of jobs. In general, an accountant is expected to make choices and decisions about the design of accounting systems and to prepare and explain financial reports. An accountant may also supervise the work of accounting clerks who perform routine recordkeeping functions.

Many accountants enter the field with either a bachelor's or a master's degree in accounting. However, it is not unusual for accountants to have started at entry-level positions and studied for their degrees while on the job. Although accountants work in every kind of business, their work can be divided into four major categories: public accounting, managerial accounting, not-for-profit accounting, and teaching.

▲ **Public Accounting**   Public accountants provide services to clients on a fee basis. Like medicine and law, public accounting requires a license, or certification by the state. To become a **certified public accountant,** or CPA, an accountant must pass a rigorous examination on accounting theory, accounting practices, auditing, and business law. CPAs provide a variety of services to their clients. They often prepare income tax returns and give financial advice about the operation of a business.

▲ **Managerial Accounting**   Unlike public accounting, *managerial accounting* takes place only inside a business firm. A managerial accountant may determine the cost of products, prepare budgets and tax returns, and provide financial information to the business's managers. By passing an examination similar to the CPA's, a managerial accountant may receive a Certificate in Management Accounting (CMA). A CMA, however, is not a license to practice and does not allow the accountant to perform services for the general public.

▲ **Not-for-Profit Accounting**   Groups that provide services to the general public and do not operate to make money are called not-for-profit organizations. Not-for-profit organizations include universities, churches, government agencies, and most hospitals. Although these organizations do not have profit as their main goal, they still require accounting services. They are concerned with the efficient use of the resources available to them. Not-for-profit accountants specialize in accounting for these organizations.

▲ **Teaching Accounting**   The field of education offers many opportunities for people with degrees and experience in accounting. High schools, colleges, and universities offer a wide variety of accounting courses that require qualified instructors.

Organizations that Influence Accounting Practice

In the United States, four groups have had a major impact on accounting practice. The four groups are the American Institute of Certified Public Accountants, the Financial Accounting Standards Board, the Securities and Exchange Commission, and the Internal Revenue Service.

The American Institute of Certified Public Accountants

The American Institute of Certified Public Accountants (AICPA) fessional association. Its members are certified public accountants in practice, business and industry, education, and government. The Insti main concern has been the development of standards of professional p. tice for its members. Although the AICPA no longer issues official statemen. on accounting standards, it still has a strong influence.

Financial Accounting Standards Board

The Financial Accounting Standards Board (FASB) was established in 1973 to develop financial accounting standards for businesses and not-for-profit organizations. The FASB is authorized to issue two publications: *Statements of Financial Accounting Standards* and *Interpretations*. The *Statements* and *Interpretations* help in preparing and auditing financial reports.

Securities and Exchange Commission

The Securities and Exchange Commission (SEC) was established by Congress in 1934 to regulate the sale of stock certificates to the general public. The SEC was also given broad authority to regulate and control accounting and other information distributed by corporations. However, the SEC has generally relied on the accounting profession to perform these functions. In only a few cases has the SEC exerted its legal power by disagreeing with a position taken by the AICPA or the FASB.

Internal Revenue Service

The Internal Revenue Service (IRS) has a widespread impact on many aspects of our economy. The IRS is charged with the collection of federal taxes, the enforcement of tax regulations, and the interpretation of tax laws relating to particular businesses or situations. Through these functions, the IRS has a direct effect on tax-related aspects of accounting.

Other Influences

Several other organizations continue to influence accounting practices and standards. The National Council on Governmental Accounting (NCGA) develops and interprets principles of accounting and financial reporting for state and local governments. The American Accounting Association (AAA), an organization of accounting professors and certified public accountants, is concerned with developing accounting standards. The Institute of Management Accountants is concerned with accounting for management purposes.

SUMMARY OF KEY POINTS

1. In the United States private enterprise economy, businesses are concerned with earning a profit. Businesses that do not earn a profit over a period of time will not be able to continue operating.

2. The three types of businesses organized to earn a profit are service businesses, merchandising businesses, and manufacturing businesses.
3. The three major forms of business organization found in the United States are the sole proprietorship, the partnership, and the corporation.
4. Accounting is a systematic process of recording and reporting the financial information resulting from business transactions.
5. Accounting information is used by a wide variety of people to make decisions about how well or how poorly a business is operating.
6. Computers have affected the speed with which accounting is performed, but their use has not altered the basic accounting system.
7. There is a wide variety of jobs available in bookkeeping and accounting. The number of job openings in this area is expected to increase in the next decade.
8. Accounting practices are influenced and regulated by such groups as the AICPA, FASB, SEC, and IRS.

REVIEW AND APPLICATIONS

Building Your Accounting Vocabulary

In your own words, write the definitions of each of the following accounting terms. Use complete sentences for your definitions.

accountant
accounting clerk
accounting system
business entity
capital
certified public
   accountant
charter

corporation
fiscal period
general bookkeeper
going concern
loss
manufacturing
   business

merchandising
   business
partnership
profit
service business
sole proprietorship

Reviewing Your Accounting Knowledge

1. The United States economy is referred to as a private enterprise economy. What is the major characteristic of our private enterprise economy?
2. What is one measure of business success?
3. What is the major difference between a merchandising business and a manufacturing business?
4. List the main difference between a partnership and a corporation.
5. What is the basic function of an accounting system?
6. Who are the users of accounting information?
7. List and briefly explain the four assumptions about business operations on which accounting is based.
8. What are some of the duties of an accounting clerk?
9. What are the four possible career areas in the field of accounting?
10. What organizations influence accounting as it is practiced in the United States?

Improving Your Decision-Making Skills

One way to make a decision is to follow a step-by-step pattern that is called the decision-making process. The steps in this process are:

1. Face the problem (recognize the need for a decision).
2. Get information about the problem.
3. List alternative ways of dealing with the problem.
4. Evaluate the alternatives.
5. Reach a decision.
6. Act on the decision.

Suppose you are trying to decide whether a career in accounting is right for you. Using the steps in the decision-making process, describe the actions you would take at each step. Be specific about information you would need and where you would get it.

Applying Accounting Procedures

Exercise 1-1   Understanding Business and Accounting Terms

Instructions: Number a sheet of paper from 1 to 10. Write the word or words from the list below that best matches each numbered statement.

accounting reports
dollar
electronic funds transfer system
managerial accounting
not-for-profit organization

organization
partners
private enterprise economy
shareholders
stock

1. An economy in which people are free to produce the goods or services they choose
2. An organization that is service-oriented and that does not operate to earn a profit
3. The legal owners of a corporation
4. The end results of an accounting system
5. The unit of measure for financial information in the United States
6. Co-owners of a business
7. Shares of ownership in a corporation
8. A system that provides financial information to interested persons within an organization
9. A computerized system for transferring funds
10. A group of people who come together with a common goal in mind

Exercise 1-2   Using Financial Information

Instructions: Give one or more reasons why each of the following would be interested in the financial reports of the Pacific Company, a fishing fleet.

1. James Taylor is looking for an investment in which he can make a profit, even if a little risk is involved.
2. Rita Hays, the local union agent, is preparing the bargaining position for employee wage increases.
3. Diane Hauser, a buyer for a fish market, is seeking a new supplier from which to buy fresh fish.
4. Mark Siebert, a credit manager, has been asked to approve a loan for the Pacific Company.
5. Jill Mercer, a retired widow, is looking for an investment that will provide a steady income for her retirement years.

Exercise 1-3   Exploring Accounting Careers

Instructions: Read the following paragraph and assume that you are Lee Harms. On a sheet of paper, write what you think Lee's response would be.

A CAREER DAY MEETING

Two accounting students, Richard Cummings and Nancy Purcell, were discussing whether they should become accountants. They met Lee Harms, a CPA, at a career day meeting and asked her what types of employment opportunities they might find in accounting.

Exercise 1-4   Describing Types of Businesses

Instructions: On a sheet of paper, indicate whether each of the followi businesses is a service business, a merchandising business, or a manufa turing business.

1. International Business Machines (IBM)
2. J. C. Penney Co., Inc.
3. Glendale Medical Center
4. Avis Rent-a-Car
5. Ford Motor Company
6. The Chase Manhattan Bank
7. Ace Hardware Stores
8. Michigan City Animal Hospital
9. Apple Computer, Inc.
10. K Mart Discount Department Store
11. Prudential Insurance Company of America
12. Bethelehem Steel Corporation

Computers

Buying or sending gifts over long distances is easy today with the help of computers.

Automation: A Business's Life Support System

In today's business world, time and money are precious resources. Wise decision making can help control spending and productivity. And to this end, one of the wisest decisions management can make is to automate.

Small businesses have discovered that computers can help them in a big way. Consider these cases.

The estimator in a family-owned metal fabricating shop in the Midwest wrote his own computer program to help him prepare price estimates. He keys in the quantity and size of material, and the program prepares the estimate. By hand, estimates take 15 to 20 *minutes;* the electronic estimates take 15 to 20 *seconds.* Not only are the computer estimates faster — they're also more accurate.

A property management company oversees 65 properties, some of which are shopping centers. The work is done with just 4 bookkeepers, 8 property managers, and a network of computers. Without automation, the company president estimates they'd need 20 bookkeepers instead of 4 and 24 property managers instead of 8. The company saves over $400,000 a year in payroll costs alone. The company president says that savings is the difference between profit and bankruptcy.

Big businesses can save even more. Commercial banks move about $300 billion every day in international electronic funds transfers. The cost of a single international transfer is $10-$12 if done on paper. Done electronically, the cost drops to about $2 per transfer.

Government agencies save time and money through automation, too. The U.S. Forest Service says that, since it automated, its environmental impact statements take 39% less time to prepare. Timber sales contracts take 27% less time. A study revealed that automation saved the Forestry Service $125 million in 1985.

To business owners, the question is not, "*Should* I automate?" Rather the question is, "How long will I survive without it?"

CHAPTER

2

Business Transactions and the Basic Accounting Equation

In Chapter 1 you learned that accounting has been called the "language of business." Accounting provides financial information that is essential for the success of any business. Accounting provides that financial information to a wide variety of users: owners, managers, employees, investors, and so on.

In this chapter you will begin to learn some of the language of accounting. You'll learn about the basic accounting equation—the foundation of accounting. This equation expresses the relationship between property and the rights or claims to that property.

Business transactions are the raw materials of an accounting system. In this chapter, you will learn about various types of business transactions and the effects those transactions have on the accounting equation.

 LEARNING OBJECTIVES

When you have completed this chapter, you should be able to

1. Describe the relationship between property and property rights.
2. Explain the meaning of "equity" as it is used in accounting.
3. List the parts of the basic accounting equation and define each part.
4. Show how various business transactions affect the basic accounting equation.
5. Check the balance of the basic accounting equation after a business transaction has been analyzed and recorded.
6. Define the accounting terms introduced in this chapter.

NEW Terms

property • property rights • credit • creditor • assets • equity • owner's equity • liabilities • basic accounting equation • business transaction • account • accounts receivable • accounts payable • capital • on account • revenue • expense • withdrawal

Property and Property Rights

The right to own property is basic to our private enterprise system. **Property** is anything of value that is owned or controlled. When you own an item of property, you have a legal right to that item. When you have control over an item, you have the right only to the use of the item. For example, you own a pair of skis you have bought. If you had rented the skis for a weekend instead of buying them, you would have control of the skis. You would have the right to use the skis for the weekend, but you would not own them. As you can see from this example, you can have certain rights, or claims, to the items that you either own or control.

When you purchase property, you acquire certain rights, or financial claims to that property.

Businesses also own and control property. One of the purposes of accounting is to provide financial information about property and a business's rights to that property. In accounting, property and property rights are measured in dollar amounts. Dollar amounts measure both the cost of the property and the **property rights,** or financial claims, to the property. For example, if you had paid $100 cash to buy the skis mentioned above, you would have a property right or financial claim of $100 to those skis. This relationship between property and property rights is shown in the equation that follows.

PROPERTY (COST)	=	PROPERTY RIGHTS (FINANCIAL CLAIMS)
Skis	=	Your Claim to Skis
$100	=	$100

When you buy property with cash, you acquire all of the property rights (financial claims) to that property at the time of purchase. What happens, however, when you buy property on credit? What happens to the financial claim when you don't pay for the property right away?

When you buy property and agree to pay for it later, you are buying on **credit.** The business or person selling you the property on credit is called a **creditor.** A creditor can be any person or business to which you owe money. When you buy property on credit, you do not have the only financial claim to the property. You share the financial claim to that property with your creditor. For example, suppose you want to buy a pair of ski boots that costs $150, but you have only $75. A store agrees to sell you the boots on credit. You pay the store $75 and sign an agreement to pay the remaining $75 over the next three months. Since you owe the store (the creditor) $75, you share the financial claim to the boots with the creditor. The creditor's financial claim to the ski boots is $75 and your claim is $75. The combined claims equal the cost of the property (the boots). Your purchase of the ski boots can be expressed in terms of the equation PROPERTY = PROPERTY RIGHTS.

PROPERTY =	PROPERTY RIGHTS		
Ski Boots	= Creditor's Financial Claim	+	Owner's Financial Claim
$150	= $75	+	$75

As you can see, two (or more) people can have financial claims to the same property. The total financial claims always equal the total cost of the property. Before you read any further, answer the following questions to check your understanding of the relationship between property and property rights.

Check Your Learning

The equation below shows the relationship between property and its corresponding financial claims. Use the equation to answer the questions that follow. (Use notebook paper if you want to write your answer.)

Property = Creditor's Financial Claim + Owner's Financial Claim

1. What are the missing dollar amounts in each equation?
   a. Property (?) = Creditor's Claim ($1,000) + Owner's Claim ($6,000)
   b. Property ($2,000) = Creditor's Claim ($500) + Owner's Claim (?)
   c. Property ($30,000) = Creditor's Claim (?) + Owner's Claim ($22,000)
2. What is the amount of a creditor's claim to a radio if the radio cost $75 and the owner has paid $35 on it?
3. What is the amount of the owner's claim to a baseball glove if the glove cost $32 and the amount still owed is $12?
4. What was the cost of an automobile if the owner has a $3,000 claim and a creditor has an $11,000 claim?

The answers to these questions can be found in the answers section at the back of this book. Compare your answers to the answers for this activity. If you missed the answer to a question, find out why. Go back to the appropriate section of the chapter and study the material related to the answer you may have missed.

Financial Claims in Accounting

As you learned in Chapter 1, every business is considered a separate entity. In other words, the property of a business is separate from the personal property of its owner(s). Thus, the accounting records of a business are kept only for transactions affecting the business itself. The owner's personal financial transactions are not a part of the business's records. For example, if the owner buys a car for her or his personal use, that car would not be recorded as property of the business.

In accounting, the property or items of value owned by a business are referred to as **assets.** Some examples of assets are cash, office equipment, manufacturing equipment, buildings, and land. There is also an accounting term for the financial claims to these assets. The total financial claims to the assets, or property, of a business are referred to as **equity.** If you have a financial claim to property, you are said to have equity in that property. Let's explore the meaning of this term.

Suppose Book Ends, a small book store, has just bought a new building for its operations. The building cost $45,000 and Book Ends made a cash down payment of $15,000 to the seller of the building. A local bank loaned the store the remaining $30,000. Both the book store and the bank now have financial claims to the building. As creditor, the bank has equity in the building equal to its investment of $30,000. Book Ends has equity equal to its down payment of $15,000. Over the years, as Book Ends repays the loan, its equity will increase. As less money is owed, the equity of the creditor (the bank) will decrease. When the loan is completely repaid, the creditor's financial claim will be canceled. In other words, the owner's equity will then equal the cost of the building. Book Ends will both own and control the property and will therefore have full property rights to it.

As you can see from this example, equity is simply the claims — of both creditor(s) and owner(s) — to the assets of a business. In accounting, there are separate terms for owner's claims and creditor's claims. The owner's claims to the assets of the business are called **owner's equity.** Owner's equity is measured by the dollar amount of the owner's claims to the total assets of the business.

The creditor's claims to the assets of the business are called **liabilities.** Liabilities are the debts of a business. They are measured by the amount of money owed by a business to its creditors. The relationship between assets and total equities — liabilities plus owner's equity — can be shown in the **basic accounting equation,** which is

$$\text{ASSETS} = \text{LIABILITIES} + \text{OWNER'S EQUITY}$$

Figure 2-1 shows the basic accounting equation applied to the example of Book Ends and the bank that gave it a loan. Notice that assets equal the combined claims to those assets.

R E M E M B E R

Total equities includes both the creditor's claims and the owner's claims.

ASSETS	=		EQUITIES

$45,000 Building

$30,000 Loan

$15,000 Investment

Property	=	Creditor's Claim	+	Owner's Claim
$45,000		$30,000		$15,000
ASSETS	=	LIABILITIES	+	OWNER'S EQUITY

Figure 2-1 The Basic Accounting Equation

Before you go on to learn about business transactions, do the Check Your Learning activity that follows to check your understanding of the basic accounting equation.

Check Your Learning

Use the basic accounting equation to answer the following questions. (If you want to write your answers, use notebook paper.)

1. If a business has invested $50,000 in an asset that cost $75,000, what is the amount of its liability?
2. In accounting, there are two kinds of equity: ___?___ and owner's equity.
3. If a business has liabilities of $60,000 and assets of $218,000, what is the amount of owner's equity?

Compare your answers to those in the answers section. Re-read the preceding part of the chapter to find the correct answers to any questions that you may have missed.

Business Transactions

A **business transaction** is an economic event that causes a change in assets, liabilities, or owner's equity. Business transactions involve the buying, selling, or exchange of goods and services. Some businesses have hundreds, or even thousands, of business transactions every day. When a business transaction occurs, the financial position of the business changes. The change is reflected in the accounting system of the business as an increase or decrease in assets, liabilities, or owner's equity. Let's look at an example.

If a business buys a typewriter and pays cash for it, the amount of cash the business has is decreased. At the same time, the business has increased its equipment. In an accounting system, the increases and decreases caused by business transactions are recorded in specific accounts. An **account,** then, is a record of the increases or decreases in and the balance for a specific item such as cash or equipment.

Accounts represent things in the real world, such as money invested in a business, office furniture, or money owed to a creditor. For example, an account for office furniture represents the dollar cost of all the office furniture bought by the business.

Each business sets up its accounts and its accounting system according to its needs. There is no standard number of accounts a business should use. Some businesses have only a few accounts, while others have hundreds. Regardless of the number of accounts a business has, all its accounts may be classified as either assets, liabilities, or owner's equity. The following account titles are but a few examples of the types of accounts a business can have.

ASSETS	=	LIABILITIES	+	OWNER'S EQUITY
Cash in Bank		Accounts Payable		Paul Howard, Capital
Accounts Receivable				
Office Furniture				
Equipment				

Some of these account titles need more explanation. The second asset account listed is Accounts Receivable. **Accounts receivable** is the total amount of money to be received in the future for goods or services sold on credit. Accounts receivable is an asset because it represents something owned: a business's claim to the assets of another person or another business. It represents a future value that eventually will bring cash into the business. When the business eventually receives payment in cash, the claim will be canceled.

The liability account listed is Accounts Payable. **Accounts payable** is the amount of money owed, or payable, to a business's creditors. It is a future obligation requiring the payment of cash or services to another person or business. Finally, note that the owner's equity account in a business is identified by the owner's name followed by a comma and the word "Capital." **Capital** refers to the dollar amount of the owner's investment in the business.

ACCOUNTING Notes....

The word *capital* has its roots in the Latin word *capitalis,* meaning "property." *Capital* first meant "main." Later the term came to stand for a person's wealth, which was the main source of a person's importance.

Effects of Business Transactions on the Basic Accounting Equation

When a business transaction occurs, an accounting clerk analyzes the transaction to see how it affects each part of the basic accounting equation. As an accounting clerk, you must select the information in a transaction that indicates any change in assets, liabilities, or owner's equity. You will find it easy to analyze the effects of a transaction if you follow the steps that are listed below.

1. Identify the accounts affected.
2. Classify the accounts affected (asset, liability, or owner's equity).
3. Determine the amount of increase or decrease for each account affected.
4. Make sure the basic accounting equation remains in balance.

The business transactions that follow are examples of transactions that occur often in most businesses. To help you learn about various kinds of transactions, these examples are categorized as follows: (1) investments by the owner, (2) cash transactions, (3) credit transactions, (4) revenue and expense transactions, and (5) withdrawals by the owner.

Investments by the Owner

Paul Howard has decided to start a word processing service business. He plans to call the business WordService.

Business Transactions 1 and 2 concern investments made in the business by the owner. Transaction 1 is a cash investment; Transaction 2 is an investment of equipment.

Business Transaction 1: *The owner of WordService, Paul Howard, deposited $20,000 in a bank checking account under the name of WordService.*

Analysis:

1. Identify the accounts affected.

   Every transaction will affect at least two accounts. You can determine the accounts affected by analyzing the transaction to see which accounts are being changed. Here are the accounts used by WordService.

ASSETS	=	LIABILITIES	+	OWNER'S EQUITY
Cash in Bank		Accounts Payable		Paul Howard, Capital
Accounts Receivable				
Office Furniture				
Equipment				

   Now look at Transaction 1 again. The business has received cash. Cash transactions are summarized in the account entitled Cash in Bank. Paul Howard is investing his personal funds in the business. An owner's investments in the business are summarized in the account called Paul Howard, Capital.

2. Classify the accounts affected.

   Cash in Bank is an asset account. Paul Howard, Capital is an owner's equity account.

3. Determine the amount of increase or decrease for each account affected.

   Cash in Bank is increased by $20,000. Paul Howard, Capital is increased by $20,000.

4. Make sure the basic accounting equation remains in balance.

	ASSETS	=	LIABILITIES	+	OWNER'S EQUITY
	Cash in Bank				Paul Howard, Capital
Trans. 1	+$20,000				+$20,000
Balance	$20,000	=	0	+	$20,000

   The asset account Cash in Bank totals $20,000. Liabilities plus owner's equity also total $20,000. The basic accounting equation remains in balance.

R — E — M — E — M — B — E — R

Each transaction affects at least two accounts.

Business Transaction 2: *The owner, Paul Howard, invested an electric typewriter worth $300 in the business.*

Analysis:
1. Identify the accounts affected.

   The business has received an electric typewriter. Since a typewriter is equipment, the account Equipment is affected. Paul Howard has invested a personal asset in the business, so the account Paul Howard, Capital is also affected.
2. Classify the accounts affected.

   Equipment is an asset account and Paul Howard, Capital is an owner's equity account.
3. Determine the amount of increase or decrease for each account affected.

   Equipment is increased by $300. Paul Howard, Capital is increased by $300.
4. Make sure the basic accounting equation remains in balance.

	ASSETS		= LIABILITIES	+ OWNER'S EQUITY
	Cash in Bank	Equipment		Paul Howard, Capital
Prev. Bal.	$20,000	0	0	$20,000
Trans. 2		+$300		+ 300
Balance	$20,000 +	$300	= 0 +	$20,300

The asset accounts Cash in Bank and Equipment total $20,300. Liabilities and owner's equity total $20,300, so the basic accounting equation is in balance.

Cash Payment Transactions

Transaction 3 is an example of a transaction in which an asset is purchased for cash. Any asset that is purchased for cash will be recorded as in this transaction. In similar transactions, the account title will change, depending upon the asset bought.

Business Transaction 3: *WordService issued a $4,000 check for the purchase of a microcomputer.*

Analysis:
1. Identify the accounts affected.

   The business has purchased a microcomputer. The Equipment account is used to summarize transactions involving any type of equipment. Since the business has paid out cash for the microcomputer, the account Cash in Bank is affected. (Payments made by check are always treated as cash payments and are summarized in the Cash in Bank account.)
2. Classify the accounts affected.

   Equipment and Cash in Bank are both asset accounts.
3. Determine the amount of increase or decrease for each account affected.

   Equipment is increased by $4,000. The account Cash in Bank is decreased by $4,000.
4. Make sure the basic accounting equation remains in balance.

	ASSETS		= LIABILITIES	+ OWNER'S EQUITY
	Cash in Bank	Equipment		Paul Howard, Capital
Prev. Bal.	$20,000	$ 300	0	$20,300
Trans. 3	− 4,000	+ 4,000		
Balance	$16,000 +	$4,300	= 0	+ $20,300

Transaction 3 affected only the assets side of the equation. WordService exchanged one asset (cash) for another asset (equipment). The total assets remain at $20,300. Liabilities plus owner's equity total $20,300, so the equation remains in balance.

Credit Transactions

Now that you have learned about cash transactions, let's look at how the use of credit affects the basic accounting equation. When a business buys on credit, it is often said to be buying **on account.** In the next three transactions, you will learn about a purchase on account, a payment on account, and a sale on account.

Business Transaction 4: WordService bought office furniture on account from Office Interiors for $3,000.

Analysis:
1. Identify the accounts affected.
   WordService has received additional property (office furniture), so the account Office Furniture is affected. The business has promised to pay for the office furniture at a later time. This promise to pay is a liability of WordService, therefore, the Accounts Payable account is affected.
2. Classify the accounts affected.
   Office Furniture is an asset account and Accounts Payable is a liability account.
3. Determine the amount of increase or decrease for each account affected.
   Office Furniture is increased by $3,000. Accounts Payable is also increased by $3,000.
4. Make sure the basic accounting equation remains in balance.

	ASSETS			= LIABILITIES	+ OWNER'S EQUITY
	Cash in Bank	Office Furniture	Equipment	Accounts Payable	Paul Howard, Capital
Prev. Bal.	$16,000	0	$4,300	0	$20,300
Trans. 4		+$3,000		+$3,000	
Balance	$16,000 +	$3,000 +	$4,300	= $3,000	+ $20,300

Assets now total $23,300. Liabilities plus owner's equity also total $23,300, so the equation remains in balance.

Business Transaction 5: WordService issued a check for $1,000 in partial payment of the amount owed to its creditor, Office Interiors.

Analysis:
1. Identify the accounts affected.
   The payment decreased the total amount owed to the creditor, so Accounts Payable is affected. A check was given in payment, so the account Cash in Bank is affected.
2. Classify the accounts affected.
   Accounts Payable is a liability account, while Cash in Bank is an asset account.
3. Determine the amount of increase or decrease for each account affected.
   Accounts Payable is decreased by $1,000. Cash in Bank is also decreased by $1,000.
4. Make sure the basic accounting equation remains in balance.

	ASSETS			= LIABILITIES +	OWNER'S EQUITY
	Cash in Bank	Office Furniture	Equipment	Accounts Payable	Paul Howard, Capital
Prev. Bal.	$16,000	$3,000	$4,300	$3,000	$20,300
Trans. 5	− 1,000			− 1,000	
Balance	$15,000 +	$3,000	+ $4,300	= $2,000	+ $20,300

The asset accounts total $22,300, and liabilities plus owner's equity total $22,300, so the equation is in balance.

Business Transaction 6: *WordService sold the electric typewriter for $300 on account.*

Analysis:
1. Identify the accounts affected.
   Since WordService has agreed to receive payment for the typewriter at a later time, the Accounts Receivable account is affected. The business sold equipment, so the account Equipment is also affected.
2. Classify the accounts affected.
   Accounts Receivable is an asset account, as is Equipment.
3. Determine the amount of increase or decrease for each account affected.
   Accounts Receivable is increased by $300. Equipment is decreased by $300.
4. Make sure the basic accounting equation remains in balance.

	ASSETS				= LIABILITIES +	OWNER'S EQUITY
	Cash in Bank	Accounts Receivable	Office Furniture	Equipment	Accounts Payable	Paul Howard, Capital
Prev. Bal.	$15,000	0	$3,000	$4,300	$2,000	$20,300
Trans. 6		+$300		− 300		
Balance	$15,000 +	$300	+ $3,000	+ $4,000	= $2,000	+ $20,300

The four asset accounts total $22,300. Liabilities plus owner's equity total $22,300, so the equation is in balance.

Before you go on to the next transaction, do the following activity to check your understanding of the transactions you have studied so far.

Check Your Learning

Revenue and Expense Transactions

Most businesses have to earn profits to survive. In addition, business owners expect a return on their investment in a business. The most common way for a business to provide a return for its owner(s) is by selling goods and services. Income earned from the sale of goods and services is called **revenue.** Examples of revenue are fees earned for services performed and income earned from the sale of merchandise. Revenue increases owner's equity because it increases the business's assets.

In order to operate, most businesses must also buy goods and services. These goods and services are routine needs of the business (much as we need food, clothing, and shelter to keep ourselves operating). An **expense** is any price paid for goods and services used to operate a business. Examples of business expenses are rent, utility bills, and newspaper advertising. Expenses decrease owner's equity because they decrease the business's assets or increase liabilities.

Business Transaction 7: *WordService wrote a check for $500 to pay the rent for the month.*

Analysis:
1. Identify the accounts affected.
   WordService is receiving the use of a building it rents. Since rent is an expense, and expenses decrease owner's equity, the account Paul Howard, Capital is affected. The business is paying out cash for the use of the building, so Cash in Bank is affected.
2. Classify the accounts affected.
   Paul Howard, Capital is an owner's equity account. Cash in Bank is an asset account.
3. Determine the amount of increase or decrease for each account affected.
   Paul Howard, Capital is decreased by $500. Cash in Bank is decreased by $500.
4. Make sure the basic accounting equation remains in balance.

	ASSETS				= LIABILITIES +	OWNER'S EQUITY
	Cash in Bank	Accounts Receivable	Office Furniture	Equipment	Accounts Payable	Paul Howard, Capital
Prev. Bal.	$15,000	$300	$3,000	$4,000	$2,000	$20,300
Trans. 7	− 500					− 500
Balance	$14,500 +	$300	+ $3,000	+ $4,000	= $2,000	+ $19,800

The assets total $21,800. Liabilities and owner's equity total $21,800, so the equation remains in balance.

Business Transaction 8: *WordService received a check for $1,200 from a customer for preparing a report.*

Analysis:
1. Identify the accounts affected.
   WordService has received cash, so Cash in Bank is affected. The payment is revenue to WordService. Revenue increases owner's equity, so Paul Howard, Capital is also affected.
2. Classify the accounts affected.
   Cash in Bank is an asset account; Paul Howard, Capital is an owner's equity account.
3. Determine the amount of increase or decrease for each account affected.
   Cash in Bank is increased by $1,200. Paul Howard, Capital is also increased by $1,200.
4. Make sure the basic accounting equation remains in balance.

	ASSETS				= LIABILITIES +	OWNER'S EQUITY
	Cash in Bank	Accounts Receivable	Office Furniture	Equipment	Accounts Payable	Paul Howard, Capital
Prev. Bal.	$14,500	$300	$3,000	$4,000	$2,000	$19,800
Trans. 8	+ 1,200					+ 1,200
Balance	$15,700 +	$300	+ $3,000	+ $4,000	= $2,000	+ $21,000

The total assets equal the total of liabilities plus owner's equity: $23,000. The equation remains in balance.

Business owners and accounting workers today can quickly and easily determine account balances when business transaction data is stored in computer memory.

Withdrawals by the Owner

Generally, if a business earns revenue, the owner will take cash or other assets from the business for personal use. This transaction is called a **withdrawal.** Withdrawals are often made in anticipation of future profits. Many new small-business owners get into financial trouble because they "withdraw" without realizing that they must have more profits than withdrawals if they are to keep their businesses operating.

When business assets are decreased because of a withdrawal by the owner, the owner's financial claim to the business's assets is also decreased. Thus, a withdrawal decreases both assets and owner's equity. Look at Transaction 9 to see how a withdrawal affects the basic accounting equation.

Business Transaction 9: *Paul Howard withdrew $400 from the business for his personal use.*

Analysis:
1. Identify the accounts affected.
    A withdrawal decreases the owner's claim to the business's assets, so Paul Howard, Capital is affected. Cash has been paid out, so the Cash in Bank account is affected.
2. Classify the accounts affected.
    Paul Howard, Capital is an owner's equity account. Cash in Bank is an asset account.
3. Determine the amount of increase or decrease for each account affected.
    Paul Howard, Capital is decreased by $400. Cash in Bank is decreased by $400.

4. Make sure the basic accounting equation remains in balance.

	ASSETS				= LIABILITIES +	OWNER'S EQUITY
	Cash in Bank	Accounts Receivable	Office Furniture	Equipment	Accounts Payable	Paul Howard, Capital
Prev. Bal.	$15,700	$300	$3,000	$4,000	$2,000	$21,000
Trans. 9	− 400					− 400
Balance	$15,300 +	$300	+ $3,000	+ $4,000	= $2,000	+ $20,600

The total assets equal $22,600. Liabilities plus owner's equity are $22,600, so the equation remains in balance.

Before you go on to the end-of-chapter activities, do the following activity to check your understanding of the analysis of business transactions.

Check Your Learning

Use the accounts of Swift Delivery Service to analyze the business transactions that follow. The previous balance for each is shown following the account title.

ASSETS	= LIABILITIES	+ OWNER'S EQUITY
Cash in Bank, $18,000	Accounts Payable	Jan Swift, Capital
Accounts Receivable, $700	$3,000	$30,700
Office Furniture, $5,000		
Delivery Equipment, $10,000		

Identify the accounts affected by each transaction and the amount of the increase or decrease for each acccount. Make sure the basic accounting equation is in balance after each transaction.

1. Paid $50 for advertising in the local newspaper.
2. Received $1,000 as payment for delivery services.
3. Wrote a $600 check for the month's rent.
4. Jan Swift withdrew $800 for her personal use.
5. Received $200 on account from the person who had purchased the old office furniture.

Compare your answers to those in the answers section. Re-read the preceding part of the chapter to find the correct answers to any questions you may have missed.

Using a Computer in Accounting

As you have just learned, each business transaction changes one or more parts of the basic accounting equation. The changes in the equation were summarized as increases or decreases in accounts. A simple worksheet was used to illustrate the various changes in the accounts. This worksheet, called a *spreadsheet,* is used in accounting to perform financial calculations and to record transactions.

An electronic spreadsheet can be used by an accounting clerk to record the same changes. The accounting clerk can use a computer to show the effects of business transactions on the basic accounting equation quickly and accurately. If the computer is programmed properly, all the accounting clerk must do is determine (1) the accounts affected, (2) the amounts involved, and (3) whether the accounts are being increased or decreased. Once that data is entered, the computer will automatically calculate the new account balances and determine whether the equation is in balance. Figure 2-2 illustrates how the transactions you just studied would be prepared on a computer spreadsheet.

	A	B	C	D	E	F	G	H	I	J	K	L
1		Cash		Accts.		Off.				Accts.		P. Howard,
2		in Bank	+	Rec.	+	Furn.	+	Equip.	=	Pay.	+	Capital
3												
4	1	20000										20000
5	Balance	20000	+	0	+	0	+	0	=	0	+	20000
6	2							300				300
7	Balance	20000	+	0	+	0	+	300	=	0	+	20300
8	3	-4000						4000				
9	Balance	16000	+	0	+	0	+	4300	=	0	+	20300
10	4					3000				3000		
11	Balance	16000	+	0	+	3000	+	4300	=	3000	+	20300
12	5	-1000								-1000		
13	Balance	15000	+	0	+	3000	+	4300	=	2000	+	20300
14	6			300				-300				
15	Balance	15000	+	300	+	3000	+	4000	=	2000	+	20300
16	7	-500										-500
17	Balance	14500	+	300	+	3000	+	4000	=	2000	+	19800
18	8	1200										1200
19	Balance	15700	+	300	+	3000	+	4000	=	2000	+	21000
20	9	-400										-400
21	Balance	15300	+	300	+	3000	+	4000	=	2000	+	20600
22												
23												
24												
25												

Figure 2-2 A Computerized Spreadsheet

SUMMARY OF KEY POINTS

1. The right to own property is basic to our private enterprise system. For all property that is owned or controlled, there are corresponding financial claims equal to the cost of the property.
2. The accounting term for a financial claim to a business's assets is *equity*. In accounting, total assets are always equal to total equities.

3. The relationship between total assets and total equities is shown in the basic accounting equation: Assets = Liabilities + Owner's Equity. Assets are items owned by a business. Liabilities are the debts of the business. Owner's equity is the owner's claim to the assets of the business.

4. Each business transaction changes one or more parts of the basic accounting equation. Businesses use accounts to summarize the changes caused by business transactions.

5. When a business buys on account, the amounts owed to creditors are called accounts payable. When a business sells on account, the total amounts owed to the business by the customers are called accounts receivable.

6. Businesses must earn revenue to provide a return on the owner's investment and to allow the business to continue its operations. Revenue increases the owner's equity in the business.

7. The costs of items used in the operation of a business are called expenses. Expenses decrease the owner's equity in the business.

8. Withdrawals decrease the owner's financial claim.

REVIEW AND APPLICATIONS

Building Your Accounting Vocabulary

In your own words, write a definition for each of the following accounting terms. Use complete sentences.

account
accounts payable
accounts receivable
assets
basic accounting
  equation
business transaction

capital
credit
creditor
equity
expense
liabilities
on account

owner's equity
property
property rights
revenue
withdrawal

Reviewing Your Accounting Knowledge

1. What is the relationship between property and property rights?
2. Why are a business's assets separate from the owner's personal assets?
3. List five examples of business assets. Explain why they are business assets rather than personal assets.
4. Name two types of equity in a business, and explain what each type represents. Give an example of each.
5. Why are accounts used in an accounting system?
6. Explain the difference between accounts receivable and accounts payable.
7. Why are at least two accounts affected by each business transaction?
8. What steps should you follow in analyzing a business transaction?
9. How can you determine if the basic accounting equation is in balance?
10. Why is it important for a business to earn revenue?
11. Explain the difference between revenue and expenses.
12. Why does the withdrawal of cash by the owner for personal use decrease owner's equity?

Improving Your Decision-Making Skills

Liberty Fashions, a manufacturing company, was started by Helen Baker as a sole proprietorship. The company needs to expand its plant facilities at an estimated cost of $125,000. Helen does not have the money needed herself. What should she do now? Remember to follow the decision-making process you used in Chapter 1.

Applying Accounting Procedures

Exercise 2-1   Balancing the Accounting Equation

Determine the missing dollar amounts in each equation at the top of the next page. Use either the form in your workbook or plain paper and write in the missing amounts for each question mark.

	ASSETS	=	LIABILITIES	+	OWNER'S EQUITY
1.	$17,000	=	$7,000	+	?
2.	$10,000	=	?	+	$ 7,000
3.	?	=	$9,000	+	$17,000
4.	$ 8,000	=	$2,000	+	?
5.	?	=	$6,000	+	$20,000

Exercise 2-2 Classifying Accounts

All accounts belong in one of the following classifications: Asset, Liability, Owner's Equity.

Instructions: For each of the following accounts, indicate the classification in which it belongs.

1. John Jones, Capital
2. Cash in Bank
3. Accounts Receivable
4. Accounts Payable
5. Computer Equipment
6. Calculator
7. Delivery Trucks
8. Building
9. Land
10. Typewriter

Exercise 2-3 Completing the Accounting Equation

The following accounts are used in a business owned and operated by Mike Murray.

Instructions: Look at the following list of accounts and determine the missing amount for each of the question marks.

ASSETS		=	LIABILITIES	+	OWNER'S EQUITY
Cash in Bank	$4,500	=	Accounts Payable ?	+	Mike Murray, Capital $9,250
Accounts Receivable	1,350				
Office Equipment	5,000				
	?				

Problem 2-1 Classifying Accounts within the Accounting Equation

Listed below, in alphabetical order, are the account titles and account balances for a business owned by Larry Hicks.

Accounts Payable	$7,000	Equipment	$12,000
Accounts Receivable	$2,000	Larry Hicks, Capital	$15,000
Cash in Bank	$5,000	Office Equipment	$ 3,000

Instructions: Using these account titles and balances,
(1) List and total the assets of the business.
(2) Determine the amount owed by the business.
(3) Give the amount of the owner's equity in the business.
(4) Determine whether the basic accounting equation is in balance for this business.

Problem 2-2 Determining Increases and Decreases in Accounts

Listed at the top of the next page are the account titles used by A-1 Carpet Cleaners.

	ASSETS	=	LIABILITIES	+	OWNER'S EQUITY
	Cash in Bank		Accounts Payable		Kay Gentry, Capital
	Accounts Receivable				
	Cleaning Equipment				
	Office Equipment				

Instructions: Use a form similar to the one that follows. For each transaction that follows,

(1) Identify the accounts affected.
(2) Classify the accounts.
(3) Determine the amount of the increase (+) or decrease (−) for each account affected.

The first transaction is completed as an example.

Trans.	Accounts Affected	Classification	Amount of Increase (+) or Decrease (−)
1	Cash in Bank	Asset	+$25,000
	Kay Gentry, Capital	Owner's Equity	+$25,000

Transactions:

1. Kay Gentry, the owner, invested $25,000 cash in the business.
2. Bought cleaning equipment with cash, $12,000.
3. Purchased $2,500 worth of office equipment on account.
4. Wrote a check for the monthly rent, $800.
5. Received cash for services performed, $1,000.
6. The owner withdrew $600 cash from the business for personal use.

Problem 2-3 Determining the Effects of Transactions on the Accounting Equation

After becoming a CPA, Tony LaBato decided to start an accounting business.

Instructions: Use a form similar to the one that follows. For each of the following transactions,

(1) Identify the accounts affected, using the account titles on the form.
(2) Determine the amount of the increase or decrease for each account.
(3) Write the amount of the increase (+) or decrease (−) in the space under each account affected.
(4) On the following line, write the new balance for each account.

	ASSETS				=	LIABILITIES	+	OWNER'S EQUITY
Trans.	Cash in Bank	Accts. Rec.	Office Equip.	Acctg. Supplies	=	Accounts Payable	+	Tony LaBato, Capital
1	+$10,000							+$10,000

Transactions:

1. Tony LaBato began the business by depositing $10,000 in a checking account at the Lakeside National Bank in the name of the business, Tony LaBato, CPA.

Transactions:

2. Bought accounting supplies for cash, $250.
3. Issued a check for $900 for the monthly rent on the office.
4. Bought $6,000 worth of new office equipment on account for use in the business.
5. Received $700 cash for accounting services performed for a customer.
6. Issued a $2,000 check to the creditor as partial payment for the office equipment purchased on account.
7. Performed accounting services and agreed to be paid for them later, $500.

Problem 2-4   Determining the Effects of Business Transactions on the Accounting Equation

Andrea Hunt has decided to go into business for herself as a professional photographer.

Instructions: Use a form similar to the one below. For each of the following transactions,

(1) Identify the accounts affected.
(2) Write the amount of the increase (+) or decrease (−) in the space provided on the form.
(3) Determine the new balance for each account.

			ASSETS			=	LIABILITIES	+	OWNER'S EQUITY
Trans.	Cash in Bank	Accts. Rec.	Camera Equip.	Photo Supplies	Office Equip.	=	Accounts Payable	+	Andrea Hunt, Capital

Transactions:

1. Ms. Hunt, the owner, opened a checking account for the business by depositing $60,000 of her personal funds.
2. Paid the monthly rent of $3,000.
3. Bought supplies for developing photographs by writing a check for $300.
4. Bought $24,000 worth of camera equipment for cash.
5. Purchased office equipment on account for $4,000.
6. Received payment for photography services, $2,500.
7. Andrea Hunt invested an electric typewriter, which was valued at $450, in the business.
8. Withdrew $3,000 cash from the business for personal use.
9. Wrote a check to a creditor as partial payment on account, $2,000.
10. Took wedding photographs and agreed to accept payment later, $1,200.

Problem 2-5   Describing Business Transactions

The transactions for Oglesby Electrical Repair Service that follow are shown as they would appear in the basic accounting equation. In your own words, describe what has happened in each transaction. Transaction 1 is completed as an example.

Example:

1. The owner invested $30,000 in the business.

Trans.	ASSETS				=	LIABILITIES	+	OWNER'S EQUITY
	Cash in Bank	Accts. Rec.	Office Equip.	Repair Tools	=	Accounts Payable	+	Jane Oglesby, Capital
1	+$30,000							+$30,000
2	−$ 2,000		+$2,000					
3				+$8,000		+$8,000		
4	+$ 700							+$ 700
5		+$500						+$ 500
6				+$ 200				+$ 200
7	−$ 3,000					−$3,000		
8		+$200		−$ 200				
9	+$ 500	−$500						
10	−$ 1,000							−$ 1,000

Problem 2-6   Completing the Accounting Equation

Look at the following account titles and balances for a business owned by Fran Henry. Determine the missing amount for each of the question marks. Use the form in your workbook or plain paper and write in the missing amounts.

	ASSETS			=	LIABILITIES	+	OWNER'S EQUITY
	Cash in Bank	Accounts Receivable	Business Equipment	=	Accounts Payable	+	Fran Henry, Capital
1.	?	$ 2,000	$ 1,000		$ 500		$ 7,500
2.	$ 3,000	$ 9,000	?		$2,000		$16,000
3.	$ 8,000	$ 1,000	$10,000		?		$15,000
4.	$ 4,000	?	$ 4,000		$1,000		$17,000
5.	$ 9,000	$ 7,000	$ 6,000		$5,000		?
6.	$10,000	$14,000	?		$6,000		$32,000
7.	$ 6,000	$ 4,000	$10,000		?		$15,000
8.	?	$ 5,000	$ 9,000		$1,000		?

In #8, total assets are $18,000.

Careers

Accounting: A Mobile Profession

Accountants have been around for a long time. As early as 3600 B.C., priests in Babylonia kept accounts on clay tablets. In today's economic era, there are well over a million accountants in the United States. In spite of this, there simply are not enough accountants and accounting workers to go around.

A bachelor's degree with a major in accounting can lead to a variety of career choices. Today's accounting positions offer attractive salaries and are more challenging than ever before.

Public accountants offer professional services to the public for a fee. These services include tax preparation, auditing, management, consulting, and general accounting. To become a certified public accountant (CPA), you must pass a rigorous, state-administered examination in accounting theory and practice, auditing, and business law. Many public accountants leave the field to take high-level positions with clients.

Managerial accountants perform accounting functions for businesses. They might specialize in corporate taxes, operations, budgeting, investing, or internal auditing. Managerial accountants provide critical information for corporate executives and take active roles in long-range planning. Like the CPA, the managerial accountant can take an examination to become a certified management accountant (CMA). Managerial accountants are in a good position to learn about all aspects of a business's operations. As a result, many work their way into top management positions.

Not-for-profit accountants work for hospitals, school districts, colleges, or government agencies. They can be general accountants, auditors, controllers, bank examiners, or even IRS or FBI agents. Like accountants who work for profit-making businesses, these accountants offer consulting and other services to ensure the successful financial operation of the organization. Not-for-profit accounting, particularly in government, offers high job security, an important consideration for many people.

Today, accounting is more than simply balancing debits and credits. It may even be a steppingstone to that corner office.

THE BASIC ACCOUNTING CYCLE

All businesses keep financial records. In Unit 2 you will learn how business transactions affect the financial records of a business. Learning to analyze business transactions correctly is the first step toward learning accounting. You will then learn how to record those transactions in the business's accounting records. The business used in the examples in this unit is a sole proprietorship. The business, called Global Travel Agency, provides travel services to its customers. After studying the chapters in this unit, you will have learned how to keep accounting records through a complete accounting cycle.

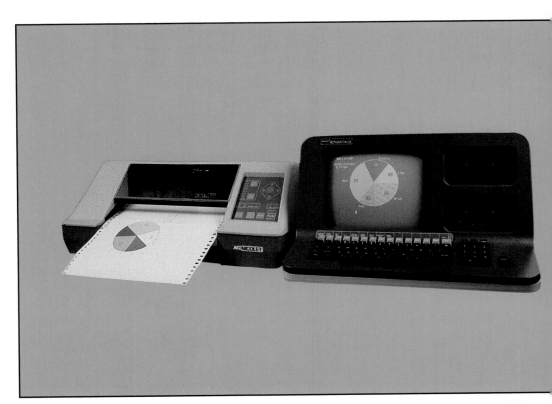

GLOBAL TRAVEL AGENCY
Chart of Accounts

	101	Cash in Bank
ASSETS	105	Accounts Receivable — Burton Co.
	110	Accounts Receivable — Greer's Market
	120	Computer Equipment
	130	Office Equipment

| LIABILITIES | 201 | Accounts Payable — City News |
| | 205 | Accounts Payable — Modern Office Suppliers |

OWNER'S EQUITY	301	Jan Harter, Capital
	305	Jan Harter, Withdrawals
	310	Income Summary

| REVENUE | 401 | Fees |

EXPENSES	501	Advertising Expense
	510	Maintenance Expense
	520	Rent Expense
	530	Utilities Expense

Analyzing Transactions Affecting Assets, Liabilities, and Owner's Equity

In Chapter 2, you learned that there is a relationship between property and the financial claims to that property. In accounting, this relationship is expressed by the basic accounting equation. You also learned that each business transaction causes a change in the basic accounting equation. This change is reflected as an increase or a decrease in assets, liabilities, or owner's equity. Even though a change does occur, the basic accounting equation remains in balance.

In this chapter, you will learn the rules of debit and credit for asset, liability, and owner's equity accounts. These rules state how increases and decreases are to be recorded. You will then learn to apply these rules as you analyze typical business transactions.

As you study Chapter 3, always keep in mind the basic accounting equation: ASSETS = LIABILITIES + OWNER'S EQUITY.

LEARNING OBJECTIVES

When you have completed Chapter 3, you should be able to

1. List and apply the rules of debit and credit for asset, liability, and owner's equity accounts.
2. Use T accounts to analyze a business transaction into its debit and credit parts.
3. Determine the balances of the accounts affected by a business transaction.
4. Define the accounting terms new to this chapter.

NEW Terms

double-entry accounting • T account • debit • credit • balance side

The Basis of an Accounting System

You learned in Chapter 2 that every business transaction affects at least two accounts. When you recorded the dollar amount of a transaction in one account, you recorded that same amount in another account. You did this to keep the sides of the basic accounting equation equal, or in balance. In entering the transaction amount twice, you were using a "double-entry" system of recordkeeping.

In accounting, the financial recordkeeping system in which each business transaction affects at least two accounts is called **double-entry accounting.** Double-entry accounting forms the basis for the accounting concepts and procedures that you will study in this textbook. Although you will mainly study manual accounting systems, the rules of double-entry accounting apply as well to computerized accounting systems. In other words, whether you are keeping accounting records by writing information on accounting stationery or by entering information into a computer, the resulting reports are the same.

The T Account

In Chapter 2, you used the basic accounting equation to analyze business transactions. This method works well when a business has only a few accounts. However, it becomes awkward when a business has several accounts and many transactions to analyze. A more efficient and convenient tool is the T account. The **T account,** so called because of its T shape, is used to show the increase or decrease in an account caused by a transaction. Accountants use T accounts to analyze the parts of a transaction.

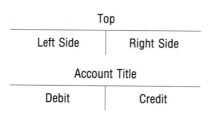

Top	
Left Side	Right Side

Account Title	
Debit	Credit

As you can see from the illustration, a T account has a top, a left side, and a right side. On the top of the T is the title of an account. The left side of the T is always used for debit amounts. A **debit** then is an amount entered on the *left* side of the T account. The right side of the T account is always used for credit amounts. A **credit** is an amount entered on the *right* side of the T account. The words "debit" and "credit" are simply the accountant's terms for "left" and "right." Remember, *debit = left side* and *credit = right side.*

The Rules of Debit and Credit

Debits and credits are used to record the increases and decreases in each account affected by a business transaction. Under the double-entry system, for each debit entry made in one account, a credit of an equal amount must be made in another account. The rules of debit and credit vary according to whether an account is classified as an asset, a liability, or an owner's equity account. Let's look first at the rules of debit and credit for accounts classified as assets.

Rules for Asset Accounts

There are three rules of debit and credit for asset accounts.

1. An asset account is increased (+) on the debit side.
2. An asset account is decreased (−) on the credit side.
3. The normal balance for an asset account is a debit balance.

We can illustrate these rules using T accounts and the basic accounting equation. Look at the left-hand side of the equation below.

ASSETS = LIABILITIES + OWNER'S EQUITY

Asset Accounts	
Debit	Credit
+	−
Increase Side	Decrease Side
Balance Side	

For asset accounts, the *increase* side is the debit (left) side of the T account. The *decrease* side is the credit (right) side of the T account. Notice the + and − signs. These signs are used to indicate the increase and decrease sides of the account. They do not mean the same thing as "debit" and "credit."

Each classification of account also has a specific side that is its normal balance side. This **balance side** is always the same as the side used to record increases to the account. Since the increase side of an asset account is always the debit side, asset accounts have a normal debit balance. The word "normal" used here means "usual." For example, in the normal course of business, total increases to assets are larger than total decreases. You would expect an asset account, then, to have a normal debit balance.

We can summarize the rules of debit and credit for asset accounts by using a T account.

Asset Accounts	
Debit	Credit
+	−
1 Increase Side	2 Decrease Side
3 Balance Side	

Rule 1: Asset accounts are increased by debits.
Rule 2: Asset accounts are decreased by credits.
Rule 3: The normal balance for asset accounts is a debit balance.

Let's apply these rules now to an actual asset account. Look at the entries in the T account below for Cash in Bank.

Cash in Bank	
Debit	Credit
+	−
$200	$ 70
150	40
$350	$110
Balance, $240	

The increases in the account are recorded on the left, or debit, side. The decreases in the account are recorded on the right, or credit, side. Total debits equal $350 ($200 + $150). Total credits equal $110 ($70 + $40). To find the balance, subtract total credits from total debits ($350 − $110). The debit balance is $240.

R — E — M — E — M — B — E — R

The normal balance side of any account is the same as the side used to increase that account.

Before you go any further, do the activity below to see if you understand the rules of debit and credit for asset accounts.

Check Your Learning

Answer the following questions using the rules of debit and credit for asset accounts.

1. Asset accounts are increased on the left, or ____?____ , side.
2. Asset accounts are decreased on the right, or ____?____ , side.
3. The normal balance for asset accounts is a ____?____ balance.
4. On notebook paper, draw a T account for the asset account Office Equipment. Enter debits of $2,000 and $1,500. Enter a credit of $500. What is the balance, and on what side of the T account is it shown?

Compare your answers to those in the answers section. Re-read the preceding part of the chapter to find the correct answers to any questions you may have missed.

Rules for Liability and Owner's Equity Accounts

The rules for liability accounts and owner's equity accounts—specifically, the owner's capital account—are listed below.

1. The liability and capital accounts are increased (+) on the credit side.
2. The liability and capital accounts are decreased (−) on the debit side.
3. The normal balance for the liability and capital accounts is a credit balance.

Let's look again at the T accounts within the basic accounting equation, particularly those on the right-hand side. How do the T accounts for the liability and capital accounts differ from the T account for assets?

ASSETS		=	LIABILITIES		+	OWNER'S EQUITY	
Asset Accounts		=	Liability Accounts		+	Capital Account	
Debit	Credit		Debit	Credit		Debit	Credit
+	−		−	+		−	+
Increase Side	Decrease Side		Decrease Side	Increase Side		Decrease Side	Increase Side
Balance Side				Balance Side			Balance Side

The debit side of all three accounts is still on the left side of the T account, and the credit side of all three types of accounts remains on the right. Notice, however, that the increase (+) and decrease (−) sides of the liability and capital accounts are the opposite of those for assets. This is because accounts classified as liabilities and owner's equity are on the opposite side of the equation from accounts classified as assets. As a result, debit and credit rules on one side of the equation—and the T accounts within it—are mirror images of those on the other side.

We can summarize the rules of debit and credit for liability accounts and the owner's capital account by using a T account.

Liabilities and Capital	
Debit	Credit
–	+
2 Decrease Side	1 Increase Side
	3 Balance Side

Rule 1: Liability and capital accounts are increased by credits.
Rule 2: Liability and capital accounts are decreased by debits.
Rule 3: The normal balance for liability and capital accounts is a credit balance.

Assets appear on the *left* side of the basic accounting equation. The *left* (debit) side of an asset account is the side used to increase that account and its normal balance side.

Liabilities and the owner's capital account appear on the *right* side of the basic accounting equation. The *right* (credit) side of liability and capital accounts is the side used to increase those accounts. It is also the balance side.

Let's apply these rules now to actual accounts. First, look at the entries in the T account below for the liability account Accounts Payable.

Accounts Payable	
Debit	Credit
–	+
$100	$200
75	175
$175	$375
	Balance, $200

The increases in the account are recorded on the right, or credit, side. The decreases in the account are recorded on the left, or debit, side. Total credits equal $375 ($200 + $175); total debits equal $175 ($100 + $75). To find the balance, subtract the total debits from the total credits ($375 − $175). The credit balance is $200.

Now look at the entries in the T account below for the owner's equity account Jan Harter, Capital. Remember, the rules of debit and credit for the capital account are the same as for a liability account.

Jan Harter, Capital	
Debit	Credit
–	+
$350	$1,500
200	2,500
$550	$4,000
	Balance, $3,450

Increases to capital are recorded on the right, or credit, side of the account. Decreases are recorded on the left, or debit, side. The capital account has a normal credit balance. If you subtract the total debits from the total credits ($4,000 − $550), you have a credit balance of $3,450.

Summary of the Rules of Debit and Credit

Let's summarize the rules of debit and credit in terms of the basic accounting equation and T accounts.

ASSETS		=	LIABILITIES		+	OWNER'S EQUITY	
Asset Accounts		=	Liability Accounts		+	Capital Account	
Debit	Credit		Debit	Credit		Debit	Credit
+	–		–	+		–	+
Increase Side	Decrease Side		Decrease Side	Increase Side		Decrease Side	Increase Side
Balance Side				Balance Side			Balance Side

Asset accounts are increased on the debit side and decreased on the credit side. The normal balance for an asset account is a debit. Liability and capital accounts are increased on the credit side and decreased on the debit side. The normal balance for liability and capital accounts is a credit.

Before you read any further, complete the following activity to see if you understand the rules of debit and credit for liability and capital accounts.

Check Your Learning

Answer the following questions using the rules of debit and credit for liabilities and capital.

1. Liability and capital accounts are increased on the ___?___ side.
2. Liability and capital accounts are decreased on the ___?___ side.
3. The normal balance side for liability and capital accounts is the ___?___ .
4. On notebook paper, draw a T account for the liability account Accounts Payable. Enter debits of $600, $200, and $400. Enter credits of $700, $500, and $300. What is the amount of the balance, and on what side of the T account is it shown?
5. Draw a T account for the account Patrick Vance, Capital. Enter debits of $1,500 and $700. Enter credits of $9,000, $3,000, and $1,500. What is the amount of the balance, and on what side of the T account is it shown?

Compare your answers to those in the answers section. Re-read the preceding part of the chapter to find the correct answers to any questions you may have missed.

Applying the Rules of Debit and Credit

Now that you are familiar with the rules of debit and credit for asset, liability, and capital accounts, the next step is to apply those rules to the analysis of business transactions. When analyzing business transactions, you should ask yourself these six questions.

1. Which accounts are affected?
2. What is the classification of each account?
3. Is each account increased or decreased?
4. Which account is debited, and for what amount?
5. Which account is credited, and for what amount?
6. What is the complete entry?

R — E — M — E — M — B — E — R

Debits are used to:	Credits are used to:
1. Increase (+) assets.	1. Decrease (−) assets.
2. Decrease (−) liabilities.	2. Increase (+) liabilities.
3. Decrease (−) owner's capital.	3. Increase (+) owner's capital.

The business transactions that follow are for Global Travel Agency. Global Travel Agency is a small business that provides travel services to individuals and businesses. Global Travel is owned and operated as a sole proprietorship by Jan Harter. Jan has set up her accounting system to include the following asset, liability, and owner's equity accounts.

ASSETS	LIABILITIES	OWNER'S EQUITY
Cash in Bank Accounts Receivable Computer Equipment Office Equipment	Accounts Payable	Jan Harter, Capital

These accounts will be used to analyze several business transactions.

Business Transaction 1: *On October 1, Jan Harter took $25,000 from personal savings and deposited that amount to open a business checking account in the name of Global Travel Agency.*

1. Which accounts are affected?
   The accounts affected are Cash in Bank and Jan Harter, Capital.
2. What is the classification of each account?
   Cash in Bank is an asset account, and Jan Harter, Capital is an owner's equity account.
3. Is each account increased or decreased?
   Cash in Bank is increased because the owner, Jan Harter, has deposited cash in the business checking account. Jan Harter, Capital is also increased because the owner's financial claim to the assets of the business has increased.
4. Which account is debited, and for what amount?

Cash in Bank	
Debit	Credit
+	−
$25,000	
Balance, $25,000	

Cash in Bank is an asset account. Increases in assets are recorded as debits. Cash in Bank is therefore debited for $25,000. Since this is an asset account, the normal balance is a debit balance.

5. Which account is credited, and for what amount?

Jan Harter, Capital	
Debit	Credit
−	+
	$25,000
	Balance, $25,000

Jan Harter, Capital is an owner's equity account. Increases in the owner's capital account are recorded as credits. Jan Harter, Capital is therefore credited for $25,000. The normal balance for the owner's capital account is a credit balance.

6. What is the complete entry?
   Remember that in the double-entry system, each transaction affects at least two accounts. Cash in Bank is debited for $25,000 and Jan Harter, Capital is credited for $25,000. You can see from the T accounts on page 48 that the amount of the debit equals the amount of the credit.

Jan Harter must analyze each business transaction carefully to determine the accounts affected.

Cash in Bank			Jan Harter, Capital	
Debit	Credit		Debit	Credit
+	−		−	+
$25,000				$25,000

Business Transaction 2: *On October 2, Global Travel Agency issued Check 101 for $8,000 to buy a microcomputer system from Info-Systems, Inc.*

1. Which accounts are affected?
   Computer Equipment and Cash in Bank are affected.
2. What is the classification of each account?
   Computer Equipment and Cash in Bank are both asset accounts.
3. Is each account increased or decreased?
   Computer Equipment is increased because the purchase of the microcomputer increased the assets of the business. Cash in Bank is decreased because the business paid out cash.
4. Which account is debited and for what amount?

Computer Equipment	
Debit	Credit
+	−
$8,000	
Balance, $8,000	

Computer Equipment is an asset account. Increases in assets are recorded as debits. Computer Equipment is therefore debited for $8,000.

5. Which account is credited, and for what amount?

Cash in Bank	
Debit	Credit
+	−
$25,000	$8,000
Balance, $17,000	

$25,000
− 8,000
$17,000

Cash in Bank is also an asset account. Since decreases in asset accounts are recorded as credits, Cash in Bank is credited for $8,000.

6. What is the complete entry?
   Computer Equipment is debited for $8,000 and Cash in Bank is credited for $8,000. The debit entry is equal to the credit entry.

Computer Equipment			Cash in Bank	
Debit	Credit		Debit	Credit
+	−		+	−
$8,000				$8,000

Business Transaction 3: *On October 4, Jan Harter took a $200 electric typewriter from home and invested it in the business as office equipment.*

1. Which accounts are affected?
   Office Equipment and Jan Harter, Capital are affected.
2. What is the classification of each account?
   Office Equipment is an asset account. Jan Harter, Capital is an owner's equity account.
3. Is each account increased or decreased?
   The investment of the typewriter increased the assets owned by the business. Office Equipment is thus increased. Since the typewriter is an investment by the owner of personal property, Jan Harter, Capital is also increased.
4. Which account is debited, and for what amount?

Office Equipment	
Debit	Credit
+	−
$200	
Balance, $200	

Office Equipment is an asset account. Since increases in assets are recorded as debits, Office Equipment is debited for $200.

5. Which account is credited and for what amount?

Jan Harter, Capital	
Debit	Credit
−	+
	$25,000
	200
	Balance, $25,200

$25,000
+ 200
$25,200

Jan Harter, Capital is an owner's equity account. Increases in owner's equity are recorded as credits. Jan Harter, Capital is credited for $200.

6. What is the complete entry?
   Office Equipment is debited for $200 and Jan Harter, Capital is credited for the same amount. These amounts are shown in the T accounts below. The amount of the debit equals the amount of the credit.

Office Equipment			Jan Harter, Capital	
Debit	Credit		Debit	Credit
+	−		−	+
$200				$200

Business Transaction 4: *On October 9, Global Travel bought a new electronic typewriter on account for $1,500 from Modern Office Suppliers.*

1. Which accounts are affected?
   Office Equipment and Accounts Payable are affected. Remember, an item bought on account (on credit) is to be paid for in the future. The amount owed for the purchase is recorded in Accounts Payable until actual payment is made.

Many different types of items are purchased for use in a business's operations, such as a microcomputer or even a car.

2. What is the classification of each account?

Office Equipment is an asset account and Accounts Payable is a liability account.

3. Is each account increased or decreased?

Each account is increased. Office Equipment is increased because property is being acquired. Accounts Payable is increased because the business owes money on account.

4. Which account is debited, and for what amount?

Office Equipment	
Debit	Credit
+	−

$ 200	$ 200
+1,500	1,500
$1,700	Balance, $1,700

Office Equipment is debited for $1,500. Office Equipment is an asset account, and increases in assets are recorded as debits.

5. Which account is credited, and for what amount?

Accounts Payable	
Debit	Credit
−	+
	$1,500
	Balance, $1,500

Accounts Payable is a liability account. Increases in liability accounts are recorded as credits. The amount of the credit is $1,500.

6. What is the complete entry?

Office Equipment is debited for $1,500 and Accounts Payable is credited for $1,500. The changes caused by this transaction are summarized in the T accounts on the next page.

Office Equipment			Accounts Payable	
Debit	Credit		Debit	Credit
+	−		−	+
$1,500				$1,500

Business Transaction 5: *On October 11, Global Travel sold the electric typewriter on account to Greer's Market for $200.*

1. Which accounts are affected?
   Accounts Receivable and Office Equipment are affected.
2. What is the classification of each account?
   Both Accounts Receivable and Office Equipment are asset accounts.
3. Is each account increased or decreased?
   Money that is to be received in the future increases Accounts Receivable. The sale of the typewriter decreases Office Equipment.
4. Which account is debited, and for what amount?

Accounts Receivable	
Debit	Credit
+	−
$200	
Balance, $200	

Increases in assets are recorded as debits. Accounts Receivable is an asset account, so it is debited for $200.

5. Which account is credited, and for what amount?

	Office Equipment	
	Debit	Credit
	+	−
$ 200	$ 200	$200
+1,500	1,500	
− 200		
$1,500	Balance, $1,500	

Decreases in assets are recorded as credits. Office Equipment is an asset account, so it is credited for $200.

6. What is the complete entry?
   Accounts Receivable is debited for $200 and Office Equipment is credited for the same amount. The debit amount equals the credit amount.

Accounts Receivable			Office Equipment	
Debit	Credit		Debit	Credit
+	−		+	−
$200				$200

Business Transaction 6: *On October 14, Global Travel mailed Check 102 for $750 as a partial payment to Modern Office Suppliers (for the $1,500 electronic typewriter bought in Transaction 4).*

1. Which accounts are affected?
   The accounts affected are Accounts Payable and Cash in Bank.

2. What is the classification of each account?
Accounts Payable is a liability account and Cash in Bank is an asset account.

3. Is each account increased or decreased?
The partial payment of a debt reduces the business's liability. Therefore, there is a decrease in Accounts Payable. Making a payment by check decreases the balance in Cash in Bank.

4. Which account is debited, and for what amount?

	Accounts Payable	
	Debit	Credit
	−	+
	$750	$1,500
		Balance, $750

$1,500
− 750
$ 750

Decreases in liabilities are recorded as debits. Since Accounts Payable is a liability account, it is decreased. The amount of the decrease is the amount of the partial payment, $750.

5. Which account is credited, and for what amount?

	Cash in Bank	
	Debit	Credit
	+	−
	$25,000	$8,000
		750
	Balance, $16,250	

$25,000
− 8,000
− 750
$16,250

Decreases in assets are recorded as credits. Since Cash in Bank is an asset account, it is credited for $750, the amount of the check.

6. What is the complete entry?
Accounts Payable is debited for $750 and Cash in Bank is credited for the same amount. As you can see, the amount of the debit equals the amount of the credit.

	Accounts Payable			Cash in Bank	
	Debit	Credit		Debit	Credit
	−	+		+	−
	$750				$750

Business Transaction 7: *On October 26, Global Travel received and deposited a check for $200 from Greer's Market. This is full payment for the electric typewriter that was sold on account on October 9.*

1. Which accounts are affected?
Cash in Bank and Accounts Receivable are affected.

2. What is the classification of each account?
Cash in Bank and Accounts Receivable are both asset accounts.

3. Is each account increased or decreased?
Cash in Bank is increased by the receipt and deposit of the check. Accounts Receivable is decreased because the money Global Travel was to receive is now being paid.

4. Which account is debited, and for what amount?

Cash in Bank is debited for $200.

	Cash in Bank	
	Debit	Credit
$25,000	+	−
− 8,000	$25,000	$8,000
− 750	200	750
+ 200	Balance, $16,450	
$16,450		

5. Which account is credited, and for what amount?

Accounts Receivable is decreased, so it is credited for $200.

	Accounts Receivable	
	Debit	Credit
$200	+	−
−200	$200	$200
$ 0	Balance, $0	

6. What is the complete entry?
Cash in Bank is debited for $200 and Accounts Receivable is credited for $200. The amount of the debit equals the amount of the credit.

Cash in Bank		Accounts Receivable	
Debit	Credit	Debit	Credit
+	−	+	−
$200			$200

SUMMARY OF KEY POINTS

1. Double-entry accounting is a system of recordkeeping in which each business transaction affects at least two accounts.
2. The T account is a tool for analyzing the debit and credit parts of a business transaction.
3. The top of the T is used for the account title; debits are entered on the left side of the T; credits, on the right.
4. Every account has an increase side and a decrease side.
5. For asset accounts, the increase side is the debit side and the decrease side is the credit side.
6. The normal balance for an asset account is a debit balance.
7. For liability accounts and the owner's capital account, the increase side is the credit side and the decrease side is the debit side.
8. The normal balance for both liability and capital accounts is a credit balance.
9. In double-entry accounting, the amount of the debit must equal the amount of the credit.

REVIEW AND APPLICATIONS

Building Your Accounting Vocabulary

Using your own words, write a definition of each of the following accounting terms. Use complete sentences for your definitions.

balance side   double-entry
credit   accounting
debit   T account

Reviewing Your Accounting Knowledge

1. Why is a transaction amount entered in at least two accounts?
2. Would double-entry accounting be used in a computerized accounting system? Why or why not?
3. Why do accountants use T accounts?
4. Name the three basic parts of a T account.
5. What is the left side of a T account called? the right side?
6. State briefly the rules of debit and credit for increasing and decreasing: (a) asset accounts, (b) liability accounts, (c) owner's capital account.
7. What is the normal balance side of asset accounts? liability accounts? the owner's capital account?
8. Classify the following accounts.
   a. Office Equipment
   b. Delivery Truck
   c. Accounts Receivable
   d. Store Supplies
   e. Cash in Bank
   f. Lee Jones, Capital
   g. Office Supplies
   h. Accounts Payable
9. Explain briefly what is meant by each of the following phrases.
   a. A debit of $100 to Cash in Bank.
   b. A credit balance.
   c. A credit of $500 to Accounts Payable.
   d. A debit balance.
10. What are the six questions that should be answered whenever a business transaction is analyzed?

Improving Your Math Skills

Calculators and computers do a lot of number crunching for us today, but it is still important to know your numbers if you plan to work in accounting. Complete the exercises that follow to check your skills.

1. Identify each place value in this number: 1,495.885.
2. Round the following numbers to the nearest hundredth.
   (a) 0.578   (c) 1.9001   (e) 10.38601
   (b) 4.89182   (d) 70.475   (f) 583.70121
3. Write the following amounts in words.
   (a) $2.00   (c) $31.56   (e) $1,492.61
   (b) $0.50   (d) $387.81   (f) $21.65

Applying Accounting Procedures

Exercise 3-1 Applying the Rules of Debit and Credit

Shultz's Speedy Delivery uses the following accounts.

Cash in Bank	Office Equipment	Accounts Payable
Accounts Receivable	Delivery Van	A. Schultz, Capital

Instructions: Use a form similar to the one below. For each account,
(1) Classify the account as an asset, liability, or owner's equity account.
(2) Indicate whether the increase side is a debit or a credit.
(3) Indicate whether the decrease side is a debit or a credit.
(4) Indicate whether the account has a normal debit or credit balance.

Account Title	Account Classification	Increase Side	Decrease Side	Normal Balance
Cash in Bank	Asset	Debit	Credit	Debit

Exercise 3-2 Identifying Accounts Affected by Transactions

Shirley Adams uses the following accounts in her business.

Cash in Bank	Office Furniture	Accounts Payable
Accounts Receivable	Office Supplies	Shirley Adams, Capital
Office Equipment		

Instructions: For each of the following transactions,
(1) Indicate the two accounts affected.
(2) Indicate whether each account is debited or credited.

Transactions:
1. Sold an unneeded office typewriter to Jay's Department Store on account.
2. Purchased a computer on credit, promising to pay for it within 60 days.
3. Shirley Adams brought a filing cabinet from home and invested it in the business (office furniture).
4. Bought office supplies for cash.

Exercise 3-3 Identifying Increases and Decreases in Accounts

Alice Roberts uses the following accounts in her business.

Cash in Bank	Office Equipment	Accounts Payable
Accounts Receivable	Office Furniture	Alice Roberts, Capital

Instructions: Analyze each of the following transactions using the format shown below. Explain the debit, then the credit.

Example:
On June 2, Alice Roberts invested $5,000 of her own money into a business called Roberts Employment Agency.

a. The asset Cash in Bank is increased. Increases in assets are recorded as debits.
b. The owner's equity account Alice Roberts, Capital is increased. Increases in the capital account are recorded as credits.

Transactions:
1. Sold an unneeded office desk (office furniture) for $750 cash.
2. Bought a used computer from Computer, Inc., on account for $2,500.
3. Paid $750 on account to Computer, Inc.

Problem 3-1   Using T Accounts to Analyze Transactions

Norman Rocky decided to start his own business. He plans to use the following accounts.

Cash in Bank	Fishing Equipment	Accounts Payable
Accounts Receivable	Boat	Norman Rocky, Capital

Instructions: For each transaction,
(1) Determine which two accounts are affected.
(2) Prepare two T accounts for the accounts identified in Instruction #1.
(3) Enter the debit and credit amounts in the T accounts.

Transactions:
1. Norman Rocky invested $40,000 cash in a business called Rocky's Charter Service.
2. Bought a fishing boat on account for $27,000 from Charter Boats, Inc.
3. Norman Rocky invested his personal fishing equipment, valued at $3,750.
4. Rocky's purchased new fishing equipment for $7,500 cash.
5. Rocky's Charter Service sold some of the old fishing equipment on account to Fish & Bait Charters for $1,200.

Problem 3-2   Analyzing Transactions into Debit and Credit Parts

Abraham Schultz completed the following transactions soon after opening Schultz's Speedy Delivery.

Instructions:
(1) Prepare a T account for each account listed in Exercise 3-1.
(2) Analyze and record each of the business transactions using the appropriate T accounts. Identify each transaction by number.
(3) After recording all transactions, write the word "Balance" on the normal balance side of each T account. Then compute and record the balance for each account.

Transactions:
1. Mr. Schultz invested $45,000 cash in his business.
2. Bought a van on account for $8,500 to use for deliveries.
3. Purchased an office lamp for $85, Check 100.
4. Mr. Schultz invested a typewriter worth $200 in the business.
5. Made a $3,000 payment on the van bought on account, Check 101.
6. Sold the old typewriter on account for $200.
7. Bought a new typewriter for $1,500, Check 102.
8. Received a $100 payment for the typewriter sold on account.

Problem 3-3   Analyzing Transactions into Debit and Credit Parts

Helen Marquez owns a dog grooming business. The accounts she uses to record and report business transactions are listed on page 57.

Cash in Bank   Grooming Equipment   Accounts Payable
Accounts Receivable   Store Equipment   Helen Marquez, Capital
Grooming Supplies

Instructions:

(1) Prepare a T account for each account listed above.
(2) Analyze and record each business transaction in the appropriate T accounts. Identify each transaction by number.
(3) After recording all transactions, compute and record the account balance on the normal balance side of each T account.
(4) Add the balances of those accounts with normal debit balances.
(5) Add the balances of those accounts with normal credit balances.
(6) Compare the two totals. Are they the same?

Transactions:

1. Helen Marquez invested $53,250 from savings into the business.
2. Bought grooming supplies for $550, Check 1000.
3. Bought grooming equipment on account from Dogs & Cats, Inc., for $2,675.
4. Ms. Marquez invested a dog drying lamp, value $150, in the business.
5. Bought a cash register for the store on account from Able Store Equipment for $1,250.
6. Sold the drying lamp on credit for $150.
7. Paid $500 on account to Able Store Equipment, Check 1001.
8. Purchased display shelves for the store for $650, Check 1002.
9. Paid $1,250 on account to Dogs & Cats, Inc., Check 1003.
10. Bought grooming supplies for $175, Check 1004.

Problem 3-4   Analyzing Transactions

Bob Hamilton completed the following transactions soon after opening his business, Your Cleaning Shop.

Cash in Bank   Office Equipment   Accounts Payable
Accounts Receivable   Cleaning Equipment   Bob Hamilton, Capital
Cleaning Supplies

Instructions:

(1) Prepare a T account for each account used by Your Cleaning Shop.
(2) Analyze and enter each transaction in the appropriate T accounts.
(3) After recording all transactions, compute and record each balance.
(4) Make a list of the asset accounts and their balances.
(5) Add the asset account balances.
(6) Make a list of the liability and owner's equity accounts and balances.
(7) Add the liability and owner's equity account balances.
(8) Compare the totals. Are the totals the same?

Transactions:

1. Mr. Hamilton invested $10,000 of his personal savings in the business.
2. Bought cleaning supplies on account for $750 from Jack's Cleaning.
3. Bought an office desk for $175, Check 1001.
4. Mr. Hamilton invested his $100 calculator in the business.
5. Purchased a new carpet cleaning machine on account for $1,000 from Acme Industrial Equipment.

6. Bought a used typewriter for $195, Check 1002.
7. Made a $350 payment to Jack's Cleaning for the supplies purchased earlier, Check 1003.
8. Sold the old calculator on account for $100.
9. Paid Acme Industrial Equipment $500 on account, Check 1004.
10. Bought carpet spray for $35, Check 1005.

 Problem 3-5   Analyzing Transactions Recorded in T Accounts
   Mary McColly owns and operates a word processing service. The T accounts that follow summarize several business transactions that occurred during May.

Instructions: Use a form similar to the one below. For each transaction,
   (1) Identify the account debited and record the account title in the appropriate column.
   (2) Indicate whether the account debited is being increased or decreased.
   (3) Identify the account credited and write the account title in the appropriate column.
   (4) Indicate whether the account credited is being increased or decreased.
   (5) Write a short description of the transaction.

Trans. No.	Account Debited	Increase (I) or Decrease (D)	Account Credited	Increase (I) or Decrease (D)	Description
1	Cash in Bank	I	Mary McColly, Capital	I	Mary McColly invested $15,000 in the business

Cash in Bank

Debit		Credit	
+		−	
(1) $15,000		(4) $1,225	
(9) 225		(6) 900	
		(7) 95	
		(8) 2,000	

Accounts Receivable

Debit		Credit	
+		−	
(5) $225		(9) $225	

Office Equipment

Debit		Credit	
+		−	
(2) $ 225		(5) $225	
(3) 8,000			
(4) 1,225			

Office Furniture

Debit		Credit	
+		−	
(6) $900			
(10) 145			

Office Supplies

Debit		Credit	
+		−	
(7) $95			

Accounts Payable

Debit		Credit	
−		+	
(8) $2,000		(3) $8,000	
		(10) 145	

Mary McColly, Capital

Debit		Credit	
−		+	
		(1) $15,000	
		(2) 225	

Computers help the U.S. Forestry Service manage the nation's forests.

U.S. Forestry Service Fights Fires with *Computers?*

We've all heard that "only you can prevent a forest fire." When a fire does start, however, it takes the U.S. Forestry Service to put it out. Around 1980, fire management specialists in the Forestry Service were determined to roll back soaring fire-fighting costs. To help them, they enlisted a brigade of computers. "Models" were developed to predict how fires spread and how different fire-fighting methods worked. These models were then entered into hand-held computers that fire fighters could carry with them.

By entering information about weather, wind speed, and terrain, fire fighters can determine how a particular fire will spread.

The presence of a river or strong winds make a big difference in how fast a fire spreads. When fire fighters know how a fire will spread, they can then use computers to select the best tactics to control it. They'll also have a good idea how many fire fighters and how much equipment will be needed to get the job done. Getting the jump on a fire means controlling it faster, and controlling the costs of fire management.

How well do the computers perform? Experts predict that, in 1985 alone, the new technology saved the Forestry Service $10 million. In that year, one major fire in Idaho cost less than $400,000 to put out. Without the aid of computers, experts say, the cost could have exceeded $3 million. One technology consultant estimates that the Forestry Service will see a 4900% return on its investment in computer technology over a five-year period.

Computers aren't as cuddly as Smokey the Bear. But if they can help save our tax dollars and preserve our forests, Smokey may have to share the limelight.

Analyzing Transactions Affecting Revenue, Expenses, and Withdrawals

In Chapter 3, you learned the rules of debit and credit for accounts classified as assets, liabilities, and owner's equity. As you applied these rules of debit and credit, you saw that accounting is based upon a double-entry system: For every debit, there is an equal credit. You also learned that the T account is a tool used by accountants to analyze the effects of each business transaction on specific accounts. In other words, you saw how a debit in one account was always offset by an equal credit in another account.

In Chapter 4, you will learn about the temporary capital accounts for revenue, expenses, and withdrawals. You will then learn about the rules of debit and credit for revenue, expense, and withdrawals accounts. You will also learn how to apply these rules to analyze the effects of business transactions involving these accounts.

LEARNING OBJECTIVES

When you have completed Chapter 4, you should be able to

1. Explain the difference between permanent accounts and temporary capital accounts.
2. List and apply the rules of debit and credit for revenue, expense, and withdrawals accounts.
3. Use the six-step method to analyze business transactions affecting revenue, expense, and withdrawals accounts.
4. Test a series of transactions for equality of debits and credits.
5. Define the accounting terms new to this chapter.

NEW Terms

temporary capital accounts • permanent accounts • revenue principle

The Need for Specific Accounting Information

No pilot would take off in a plane equipped with only a speedometer and a gas gauge. These two instruments, although necessary, do not give all the kinds of information needed to keep such a complex machine on course and operating smoothly. Operating a business is a bit like operating a plane. Certain information is needed to keep the business on course. In this chapter, we will take a close look at three types of accounts that provide information about how well the business is doing. These accounts are the revenue, expense, and withdrawals accounts.

The Relationship of Revenue, Expenses, and Withdrawals to Owner's Capital

You learned earlier that the owner's capital account shows the amount of the owner's investment, or equity, in a business. Owner's capital can be increased or decreased, however, by transactions other than owner's investments. For example, the revenue, or income, earned by the business increases owner's capital. Expenses and withdrawals decrease owner's capital.

Revenue, expenses, and withdrawals could be recorded as increases or decreases in the capital account. This method, however, makes finding specific information about these items difficult. A more efficient way to record information about revenue, expenses, and withdrawals is to set up separate accounts for each of these items. By looking at the amounts recorded in the revenue and expense accounts, the owner can tell at a glance whether revenue and expenses are increasing or decreasing. Such information helps the business owner decide, for example, whether some expenses need to be cut to save money.

Temporary Capital Accounts

The revenue, expense, and withdrawals accounts are called **temporary capital accounts.** Temporary capital accounts start each new accounting period with zero balances. That is, the amounts in these accounts are not carried forward from one accounting period to another. Temporary accounts are not temporary in the sense that they are used for a short time and then discarded. They continue to be used in the accounting system, but the amounts recorded in them accumulate for only *one* accounting period. At the end of that period, the balances in the temporary accounts are transferred to the owner's capital account. (The procedure for moving these amounts to the capital account is discussed in Chapter 9.)

Let's use the temporary account Utilities Expense as an example. During an accounting period, utility costs for such items as electricity and telephones are recorded in Utilities Expense. By using this separate account, the owner can see at a glance how much money is being spent on this type of expense. The amounts accumulate in the account during the accounting period. At the end of the period, the total is transferred to the owner's capital account and subtracted from the balance of that account. (As you recall, expenses decrease owner's capital.) Utilities Expense, then, starts the next accounting period with a zero balance—ready to accumulate that period's costs.

Maintenance expense might include the costs of repairing equipment, painting, or taking care of the grounds around the office.

Permanent Accounts

In contrast to the temporary accounts, the owner's capital account is a permanent account. Assets and liabilities are also permanent accounts. **Permanent accounts** are continuous from one accounting period to the next. That is, at the end of an accounting period, the balances in these accounts are carried forward to the next period.

The permanent accounts report balances on hand or amounts owed on a regular basis. They show the day-to-day changes in assets, liabilities, and owner's capital. For example, during an accounting period many increases and decreases are recorded in the Cash in Bank account. The balance in this account reports the amount of cash on hand (in the bank) at any given time. At the end of the accounting period, the ending balance in this account becomes the beginning balance for the next accounting period. In other words, this account—and all other permanent accounts—continues from one accounting period to the next.

The Rules of Debit and Credit for Temporary Capital Accounts

In Chapter 3, you learned the rules of debit and credit for the asset, liability, and owner's capital accounts. In this chapter, we will continue the rules of debit and credit, this time for revenue, expense, and withdrawals accounts. Before looking at these rules, let's review quickly the basic accounting equation with T accounts showing the rules of debit and credit for assets, liabilities, and owner's capital.

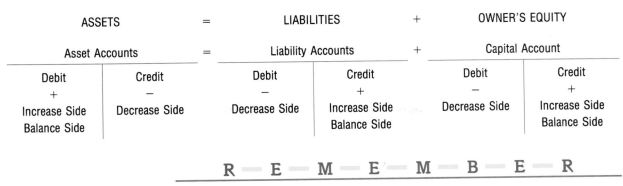

ASSETS	=	LIABILITIES	+	OWNER'S EQUITY

Asset Accounts	=	Liability Accounts	+	Capital Account

Debit	Credit	Debit	Credit	Debit	Credit
+	−	−	+	−	+
Increase Side	Decrease Side	Decrease Side	Increase Side	Decrease Side	Increase Side
Balance Side			Balance Side		Balance Side

R — E — M — E — M — B — E — R

The normal balance for assets is a debit balance. The normal balance for liabilities and owner's capital is a credit balance.

Now let's look at the rules of debit and credit for accounts classified as revenue.

Rules for Revenue Accounts

Accounts set up to record business income are classified as revenue accounts. The following rules of debit and credit apply to revenue accounts.

1. A revenue account is increased (+) on the credit side.
2. A revenue account is decreased (−) on the debit side.
3. The normal balance for a revenue account is a credit balance.

Revenue earned from selling goods or services increases owner's capital. The relationship of the revenue account to the owner's capital account is shown by the T accounts in Figure 4-1. Can you explain why the T account for revenue is used to represent the credit (right) side of the capital account?

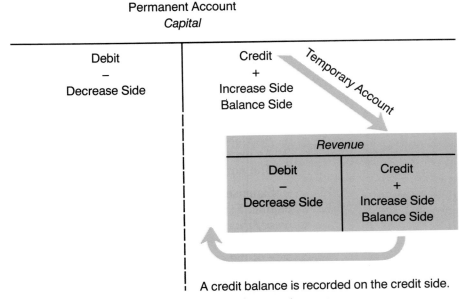

Figure 4-1 Rules of Debit and Credit for Revenue Accounts

The credit side of the capital account is used to increase that account. Since revenue increases capital, the revenue account is used to represent the credit side of the capital account.

We can summarize the rules of debit and credit for revenue accounts with a T account.

Revenue Accounts	
Debit	Credit
−	+
2 Decrease Side	1 Increase Side
	3 Balance Side

Rule 1: Revenue accounts are increased by credits.
Rule 2: Revenue accounts are decreased by debits.
Rule 3: The normal balance for revenue accounts is a credit balance.

Let's apply these rules of debit and credit to an actual revenue account. Look at the entries in the following T account for the revenue account called Fees.

Fees	
Debit	Credit
−	+
$200	$ 500
	1,000
	2,000
	Balance, $3,300

The increases to revenue are recorded on the right, or credit, side of the T account. The decreases to revenue are recorded on the left, or debit, side. To find the balance, subtract total debits ($200) from total credits ($500 + $1,000 + $2,000 = $3,500). You get a balance of $3,300 on the credit side, the normal balance side for a revenue account.

R — E — M — E — M — B — E — R

The normal balance side of any account is the same as the side used to increase that account.

Rules for Expense Accounts

Accounts that are set up to record the costs of goods and services used by the business are classified as expense accounts. Within an expense account itself, the following rules of debit and credit apply.

1. An expense account is increased (+) on the debit side.
2. An expense account is decreased (−) on the credit side.
3. The normal balance for an expense account is a debit balance.

Expenses are the costs of doing business. Expenses decrease owner's capital. Expenses therefore have the opposite effect from revenue on the owner's capital account. Look at the T accounts in Figure 4-2. Can you explain why the T account for expenses is used to represent the debit (left) side of the capital account?

Decreases in capital are shown on the debit side of that account. Since expenses decrease capital, expense accounts are used to represent the debit side of the owner's capital account.

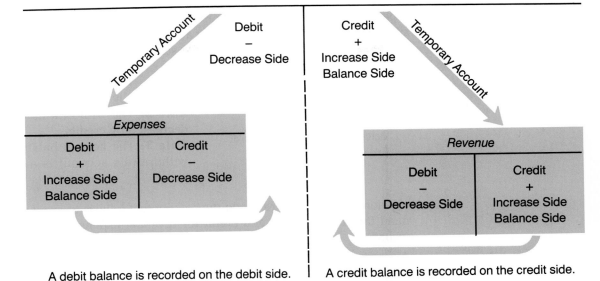

Permanent Account
Capital

A debit balance is recorded on the debit side. | A credit balance is recorded on the credit side.

Figure 4-2   Rules of Debit and Credit for Expense Accounts

Let's use a T account to summarize the rules of debit and credit for expense accounts.

Expense Accounts	
Debit	Credit
+	−
1 Increase Side	2 Decrease Side
3 Balance Side	

Rule 1: Expense accounts are increased by debits.
Rule 2: Expense accounts are decreased by credits.
Rule 3: The normal balance for expense accounts is a debit balance.

Now look at the entries recorded in the following T account for the expense account entitled Advertising Expense.

Advertising Expense	
Debit	Credit
+	−
$400	$125
200	
Balance, $475	

The increases to the expense account are recorded on the left, or debit, side of the T account. The decreases to the account are recorded on the right, or credit, side of the T account. When total credits ($125) are subtracted from total debits ($600), there is a balance of $475 on the debit side, which is the normal balance side for expense accounts.

R — E — M — E — M — B — E — R

The normal balance of a revenue account is a credit. The normal balance for an expense account is a debit.

Rules for the Withdrawals Account

A withdrawal is an amount of money or an asset taken out of the business by the owner. Since withdrawals do not occur as frequently as expenses, no separate classification is used for the withdrawals account. Rather, it is classified as a temporary owner's equity account. Withdrawals decrease capital, so the rules of debit and credit are the same as for expense accounts.

Withdrawals Account	
Debit	Credit
+	−
1 Increase Side	2 Decrease Side
3 Balance Side	

Rule 1: The withdrawals account is increased by debits.

Rule 2: The withdrawals account is decreased by credits.

Rule 3: The normal balance for the withdrawals account is a debit balance.

Before you go any further, do the activity that follows to see if you understand the rules of debit and credit for revenue, expense, and withdrawals accounts.

Check Your Learning

Answer the following questions about revenue, expense, and withdrawals accounts.

1. What is the normal balance side of any account?
2. What effect does a debit have on an expense account?
3. What is the normal balance for a revenue account?
4. What effect does a credit have on a revenue account?
5. What is the normal balance for an expense account?
6. What effect does a credit have on a withdrawals account?
7. What is the normal balance for a withdrawals account?

Compare your answers to those in the answers section. Re-read the preceding part of the chapter to find the correct answers to any questions you may have missed.

Summarizing the Rules of Debit and Credit

Revenue represents the increase side of the capital account. As a result, revenue accounts are increased on the credit side and decreased on the debit side. The normal balance for revenue accounts is a credit balance. The rules of debit and credit for expense and withdrawals accounts are opposite the rules for revenue accounts. Expenses and withdrawals represent the decrease side of the capital account. Expense and withdrawals accounts then are increased on the debit side and decreased on the credit side. The normal balance for expense and withdrawals accounts is a debit balance. These basic accounting relationships are shown in the T accounts in Figure 4-3.

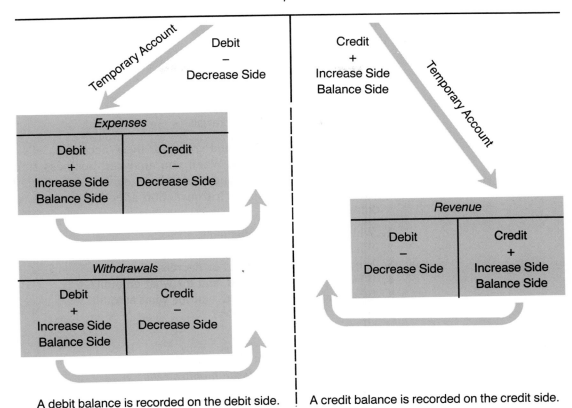

Figure 4-3 Rules of Debit and Credit for Temporary Capital Accounts

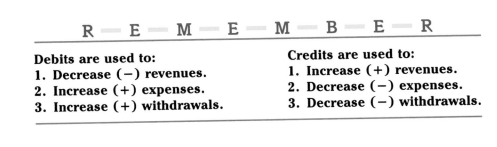

Debits are used to:
1. Decrease (−) revenues.
2. Increase (+) expenses.
3. Increase (+) withdrawals.

Credits are used to:
1. Increase (+) revenues.
2. Decrease (−) expenses.
3. Decrease (−) withdrawals.

Analyzing Transactions Involving Revenue, Expenses, and Withdrawals

The Global Travel Agency transactions in Chapter 3 dealt with asset and liability accounts and with the owner's equity account Jan Harter, Capital. To keep track of revenue, expenses, and withdrawals, Jan Harter has expanded the number of accounts used by the business. The following list shows all the account titles used by Global Travel. As you can see, the accounts have been classified as assets, liabilities, owner's equity, revenue, and expenses. The accounts have also been numbered so that they can be easily and quickly located.

ASSETS
101   Cash in Bank
105   Accounts Receivable
120   Computer Equipment
130   Office Equipment

LIABILITIES
201   Accounts Payable

OWNER'S EQUITY
301   Jan Harter, Capital
305   Jan Harter, Withdrawals

REVENUE
401   Fees

EXPENSES
501   Advertising Expense
505   Maintenance Expense
510   Rent Expense
515   Utilities Expense

Using the rules of debit and credit for these accounts, let's analyze several business transactions. When you analyzed business transactions in Chapter 3, you asked six questions about each transaction. These same questions also apply to each transaction affecting revenue, expenses, or withdrawals.

1. Which accounts are affected?
2. What is the classification of each account?
3. Is each account increased or decreased?
4. Which account is debited, and for what amount?
5. Which account is credited, and for what amount?
6. What is the complete entry?

Business Transaction 8: *On October 15, Global Travel Agency mailed Check 103 for $550 to pay the month's rent.*

1. Which accounts are affected?
   The accounts affected are Rent Expense and Cash in Bank.
2. What is the classification of each account?
   Rent Expense is an expense account. Cash in Bank is an asset account.
3. Is each account increased or decreased?
   The payment of rent increases the business's costs, so Rent Expense is increased. The writing of a check reduces cash, so Cash in Bank is decreased.
4. Which account is debited, and for what amount?

Rent Expense	
Debit	Credit
+	−
$550	
Balance, $550	

Increases in expense accounts are recorded as debits. Rent Expense, therefore, is debited for $550.

5. Which account is credited, and for what amount?

Cash in Bank	
Debit	Credit
+	−
$16,450	$550
Balance, $15,900	

Decreases in assets are recorded as credits. Cash in Bank is therefore credited for $550.

6. What is the complete entry?

Rent Expense is debited for $550 and Cash in Bank is credited for $550. Remember, in the double-entry system, the debit amount of a transaction must equal the credit amount.

Rent Expense		Cash in Bank	
Debit	Credit	Debit	Credit
+	−	+	−
$550			$550

R — E — M — E — M — B — E — R

Expenses decrease owner's capital. As a result, increases to expenses are recorded as debits and the normal balance of an expense account is a debit balance.

Business Transaction 9: On October 16, Jan Harter bought a $75 advertisement on account from City News.

1. Which accounts are affected?

Advertising Expense and Accounts Payable are affected.

2. What is the classification of each account?

Advertising Expense is an expense account; Accounts Payable is a liability account.

3. Is each account increased or decreased?

Buying advertising adds to expenses, so Advertising Expense is increased. Accounts Payable is increased because the amount the business owes is increased.

4. Which account is debited, and for what amount?

Advertising Expense	
Debit	Credit
+	−
$75	
Balance, $75	

Increases in expenses are recorded as debits. Advertising Expense is being increased by $75 and is therefore debited for that amount.

5. Which account is credited, and for what amount?

Accounts Payable	
Debit	Credit
−	+
	$750
	75
	Balance, $825

Increases in liabilities are recorded as credits. Accounts Payable is a liability and is therefore credited for the amount of the increase, $75.

6. What is the complete entry?
Advertising Expense is debited for $75 and Accounts Payable is credited for $75.

Advertising Expense			Accounts Payable	
Debit	Credit		Debit	Credit
+	−		−	+
$75				$75

Business Transaction 10: *On October 18, Jan Harter completed travel plans requested by the Sims Corporation. She received $1,200 as payment for her services.*

1. Which accounts are affected?
Cash in Bank and Fees are affected.
2. What is the classification of each account?
Cash in Bank is an asset account and Fees is a revenue account.
3. Is each account increased or decreased?
Money received increases Cash in Bank. Fees received for services completed add to revenue, so the revenue account Fees is increased.
4. Which account is debited and for what amount?

Cash in Bank	
Debit	Credit
+	−
$16,450	$550
1,200	
Balance, $17,100	

Increases in assets are recorded as debits. The asset account Cash in Bank is debited for $1,200.

5. Which account is credited, and for what amount?

Fees	
Debit	Credit
−	+
	$1,200
	Balance, $1,200

Increases in revenue are recorded as credits. The revenue account Fees is credited for $1,200.

6. What is the complete entry?
Cash in Bank is debited for $1,200 and Fees is credited for the same amount.

Cash in Bank			Fees	
Debit	Credit		Debit	Credit
+	−		−	+
$1,200				$1,200

Global Travel Agency earns revenue by providing travel services to various customers.

Business Transaction 11: *On October 20, Jan Harter completed travel plans for a customer. She billed the customer $450 for the work.*

1. Which accounts are affected?
   The customer has not yet paid for the job, so Accounts Receivable is affected. Fees is also affected.
2. What is the classification of each account?
   Accounts Receivable is classified as an asset account. Fees is a revenue account.
3. Is each account increased or decreased?
   Money to be received in the future increases Accounts Receivable. Accounts Receivable is therefore increased. Money to be received for a job is revenue, so Fees is increased. For accounting purposes, revenue is recognized and recorded on the date it is earned even if cash has not been received on that date. This is known as the **revenue principle.**
4. Which account is debited, and for what amount?

Accounts Receivable	
Debit	Credit
+	−
$450	
Balance, $450	

Increases in assets are recorded as debits. The asset account Accounts Receivable is debited for $450.

5. Which account is credited, and for what amount?

Fees	
Debit	Credit
−	+
	$1,200
	450
	Balance, $1,650

Increases in revenue are recorded as credits. The revenue account Fees is credited for $450.

6. What is the complete entry?
Accounts Receivable is debited for $450 and Fees is credited for $450.

Accounts Receivable			Fees	
Debit	Credit		Debit	Credit
+	−		−	+
$450				$450

Business Transaction 12: *On October 28, Global Travel Agency paid a $125 telephone bill with Check 104.*

1. Which accounts are affected?
The cost of telephone service used by the business is an expense. The account Utilities Expense is affected. ("Utilities" are electricity, gas, heat, telephone service, and water.) Cash in Bank is also affected.

2. What is the classification of each account?
Utilities Expense is an expense account. Cash in Bank is an asset account.

3. Is each account increased or decreased?
The payment of a telephone bill increases expenses, so Utilities Expense is increased. The writing of a check reduces the amount of cash in the bank, so Cash in Bank is decreased.

4. Which account is debited, and for what amount?

Utilities Expense	
Debit	Credit
+	−
$125	
Balance, $125	

Increases in expenses are recorded as debits. Utilities Expense is debited for $125.

5. Which account is credited, and for what amount?

Cash in Bank	
Debit	Credit
+	−
$16,450	$550
1,200	125
Balance, $16,975	

Decreases in assets are recorded as credits. Cash in Bank is credited for $125.

6. What is the complete entry?
Utilities Expense is debited for $125 and Cash in Bank is credited for the same amount.

Utilities Expense			Cash in Bank	
Debit	Credit		Debit	Credit
+	−		+	−
$125				$125

ACCOUNTING
Tips

Revenue represents the *right* side of the capital account. The *right* (credit) side of the revenue account is therefore the side used to increase that account. Expenses and withdrawals represent the *left* side of the capital account. The *left* (debit) side of these accounts is then the side used to increase the accounts.

Business Transaction 13: *On October 29, Jan Harter wrote Check 105 for $450 to have the office repainted.*

1. Which accounts are affected?
Repainting is a cost of maintaining the office, so the Maintenance Expense account is affected. Cash in Bank is also affected since cash is being paid out.

2. What is the classification of each account?
Maintenance Expense is an expense account. Cash in Bank is an asset account.

3. Is each account increased or decreased?
Maintenance Expense is increased and Cash in Bank is decreased.

4. Which account is debited, and for what amount?

Maintenance Expense	
Debit	Credit
+	−
$450	
Balance, $450	

Increases in expenses are recorded as debits. Maintenance Expense is therefore debited for $450.

5. Which account is credited, and for what amount?

Cash in Bank	
Debit	Credit
+	−
$16,450	$550
1,200	125
	450
Balance, $16,525	

Decreases in assets are recorded as credits. Cash in Bank is therefore credited for $450.

6. What is the complete entry?
Maintenance Expense is debited for $450 and Cash in Bank is credited for $450.

Maintenance Expense		Cash in Bank	
Debit	Credit	Debit	Credit
+	−	+	−
$450			$450

Business Transaction 14: *On October 31, Jan Harter withdrew $400 cash for personal use by writing Check 106.*

1. Which accounts are affected?
Money taken out of the business by the owner is recorded in the withdrawals account. Therefore the accounts affected are Jan Harter, Withdrawals and Cash in Bank.

2. What is the classification of each account?

Jan Harter, Withdrawals is classified as a temporary owner's equity account. Cash in Bank is an asset account.

3. Is each account increased or decreased?

Jan Harter, Withdrawals is used to accumulate amounts taken out of the business by the owner. The amount of money withdrawn by the owner increases the account, so Jan Harter, Withdrawals is increased. The writing of a check decreases Cash in Bank.

4. Which account is debited, and for what amount?

Jan Harter, Withdrawals	
Debit	Credit
+	−
$400	
Balance, $400	

Increases in withdrawals are recorded as debits. Jan Harter, Withdrawals is therefore debited for $400.

5. Which account is credited, and for what amount?

Cash in Bank	
Debit	Credit
+	−
$16,450	$550
1,200	125
	450
	400
Balance, $16,125	

Decreases in assets are recorded as credits. Cash in Bank is therefore credited for $400.

6. What is the complete entry?

Jan Harter, Withdrawals is debited for $400 and Cash in Bank is credited for $400.

Jan Harter, Withdrawals		Cash in Bank	
Debit	Credit	Debit	Credit
+	−	+	−
$400			$400

R = E = M = E = M = B = E = R

Amounts taken out of the business decrease owner's capital. Therefore, increases in the withdrawals account are recorded as debits.

Before continuing, complete the following activity to check your understanding of how to analyze transactions involving revenue, expenses, and withdrawals.

Check Your Learning

Analyze the following transaction using the six-step method you used in this chapter.

On March 1, J & L Enterprises mailed Check 107 for $2,000 to pay the month's rent.

1. Which accounts are affected?
2. What is the classification of each account?
3. Is each account increased or decreased?
4. Which account is debited, and for what amount?
5. Which account is credited, and for what amount?
6. What is the complete entry? Show in T account form.

Compare your answers to those in the answers section. Re-read the preceding part of the chapter to find the correct answers to any questions that you may have missed.

Summary of the Rules of Debit and Credit

The rules of debit and credit for the permanent accounts — assets, liabilities, and the owner's capital account — are summarized below using T accounts and the basic accounting equation.

ASSETS	=	LIABILITIES	+	OWNER'S EQUITY

Asset Accounts		=	Liability Accounts		+	Capital Account	
Debit	Credit		Debit	Credit		Debit	Credit
+	−		−	+		−	+
Increase Side	Decrease Side		Decrease Side	Increase Side		Decrease Side	Increase Side
Balance Side				Balance Side			Balance Side

⎿———— Assets have ————⎿
DEBIT BALANCES.

⎿———— Equities (liabilities and capital) have ————⎿
CREDIT BALANCES.

The rules of debit and credit for the temporary capital accounts — expenses, revenue, and the owner's withdrawals account — can also be summarized using T accounts.

TEMPORARY CAPITAL ACCOUNTS

Withdrawals			Expenses			Revenue	
Debit	Credit		Debit	Credit		Debit	Credit
+	−		+	−		−	+
Increase Side	Decrease Side		Increase Side	Decrease Side		Decrease Side	Increase Side
Balance Side			Balance Side				Balance Side

Testing for the Equality of Debits and Credits

In a double-entry accounting system, correct analysis and recording of business transactions should result in total debits being equal to total credits. Testing for the equality of total debits and credits is one way of finding out whether you have made any errors in recording transaction amounts. To test for the equality of total debits and credits, follow these steps:

1. Make a list of the account titles used by the business.
2. Opposite each account title, list the final or current balance of the account. Use two columns, one for debit balances and one for credit.
3. Add each amount column.

If you have recorded all the amounts correctly, the total of the debit column will equal the total of the credit column. The test for equality of debits and credits for the transactions in Chapters 3 and 4 shows that total debits are equal to total credits, so the accounting system is in balance.

ACCOUNT TITLE	DEBIT BALANCES	CREDIT BALANCES
Cash in Bank	$16,125	
Accounts Receivable	450	
Computer Equipment	8,000	
Office Equipment	1,500	
Accounts Payable		$ 825
Jan Harter, Capital		25,200
Jan Harter, Withdrawals	400	
Fees		1,650
Advertising Expense	75	
Maintenance Expense	450	
Rent Expense	550	
Utilities Expense	125	
Totals	$27,675	$27,675

SUMMARY OF KEY POINTS

1. The accounts used by a business can be separated into permanent accounts and temporary capital accounts. Permanent accounts have balances that carry over from one accounting period to the next. Temporary capital accounts start each new accounting period with a zero balance.
2. Revenue, expense, and withdrawals accounts are temporary capital accounts; they are extensions of the owner's capital account.
3. Revenue accounts temporarily substitute for the credit side of the owner's capital account.
4. For revenue accounts, the increase side is the credit side and the decrease side is the debit side. The normal balance is a credit balance.
5. Expense and withdrawals accounts temporarily substitute for the debit side of the owner's capital account.
6. For expense and withdrawals accounts, the increase side is the debit side and the decrease side is the credit side. The normal balance for expense and withdrawals accounts is a debit balance.

REVIEW AND APPLICATIONS

Building Your Accounting Vocabulary

In your own words, write the definition of each of the following accounting terms. Use complete sentences for your definitions.

permanent accounts   temporary capital
revenue principle   accounts

Reviewing Your Accounting Knowledge

1. Why are temporary capital accounts used?
2. What is the difference between a temporary capital account and a permanent account? Give three examples of each type of account.
3. State briefly the rules of debit and credit for increasing and decreasing: (a) revenue accounts, (b) expense accounts, (c) withdrawals account.
4. List the normal balance side of: (a) revenue accounts, (b) expense accounts, (c) withdrawals account, (d) asset accounts, (e) liability accounts, (f) the owner's capital account.
5. Why does a revenue account serve as a temporary substitute for the credit side of the owner's capital account?
6. What effect does a revenue transaction have on owner's capital?
7. Explain why the expense accounts serve as a temporary substitute for the debit side of the owner's capital account.
8. What effect does an expense transaction have on owner's capital?
9. How is a withdrawal different from an expense? How are they the same?
10. How would you test for the equality of debits and credits?

Improving Your Analysis Skills

The basic accounting equation is a simple mathematical equation: $A = L + OE$. The equation can be expanded to include revenue and expenses: $A = L + OE + R - E$. As with any equation, the parts can be rearranged to solve for different amounts. For example, to determine the amount of liabilities when assets and owner's equity are known, the equation becomes $L = A - OE$. Use the basic or expanded equation to find the amounts below.

1. Assets = $22,420; liabilities = $6,408
2. Liabilities = $9,470; revenue = $14,100; expenses = $7,000; owner's equity = $15,000
3. Assets = $18,400; liabilities = $4,900; revenue = $8,500; expenses = $2,300
4. Assets = $19,840; owner's equity = $12,400
5. Revenue = $22,500; liabilities = $12,880; expenses = $8,750; owner's equity = $15,000

Applying Accounting Procedures

Exercise 4-1   Applying the Rules of Debit and Credit

Edward Palmer uses the following accounts in his flying service business.

Cash in Bank
Accounts Receivable
Airplanes
Accounts Payable

Edward Palmer,
   Capital
Edward Palmer,
   Withdrawals
Flying Fees

Advertising Expense
Food Expense
Fuel and Oil Expense
Repairs Expense

Instructions: Use a form similar to the one that follows. For each account,
(1) Classify the account as an asset, liability, owner's equity, revenue, or
   expense account.
(2) Indicate whether the increase side is a debit or a credit.
(3) Indicate whether the decrease side is a debit or a credit.
(4) Indicate whether the account has a normal debit balance or a normal
   credit balance.
   The first account is completed as an example.

Account Title	Account Classification	Increase Side	Decrease Side	Normal Balance
Cash in Bank	Asset	Debit	Credit	Debit

Exercise 4-2   Identifying Accounts Affected by Transactions

John Albers uses the following accounts in his business.

Cash in Bank
Accounts Receivable
Office Equipment
Accounts Payable

John Albers, Capital
John Albers,
   Withdrawals
Service Fees

Advertising Expense
Rent Expense
Utilities Expense

Instructions: For each of the following transactions,
(1) Identify the two accounts affected.
(2) Indicate whether each account is debited or credited.

Transactions:
1. Paid the electric bill for the month of July.
2. Billed a customer for services provided on account.
3. John Albers took cash from the business for his personal use.
4. Issued Check 567 to pay for a recent advertisement.

Exercise 4-3   Identifying Increases and Decreases in Accounts

The following accounts are used by Roy Jenny in his business, the Easy
Rider Driving School.

Cash in Bank
Accounts Receivable
Office Equipment
Cars

Accounts Payable
Roy Jenny, Capital
Roy Jenny, Withdrawals
Instruction Fees

Advertising Expense
Gas and Oil Expense
Maintenance Expense
Utilities Expense

Instructions: Analyze each of the following transactions using the format shown below. Explain the debit, then the credit.

Example:

On June 11, Roy Jenny paid the office cleaning bill of $100.

a. The expense account Maintenance Expense is increased. Increases in expenses are recorded as debits.

b. The asset account Cash in Bank is decreased. Decreases in assets are recorded as credits.

Transactions:

1. On April 3, Roy Jenny withdrew $500 from his business for his own use, Check 768.
2. On April 8, the business received $1,200 cash in instruction fees from various customers.
3. On April 12, the telephone bill of $85 was paid by issuing Check 769.

Problem 4-1   Using T Accounts To Analyze Transactions

Esther Wills plans to open her own law office. She will use the following accounts.

Cash in Bank	Esther Wills, Capital	Rent Expense
Accounts Receivable	Esther Wills,	Repairs Expense
Office Equipment	Withdrawals	Utilities Expense
Accounts Payable	Legal Fees	

Instructions: For each transaction,

(1) Determine which two accounts are affected.
(2) Prepare two T accounts for the accounts identified in Instruction #1.
(3) Enter the amount of the debit and the amount of the credit in the T accounts.

Transactions:

1. On May 7, Esther Wills received a check for $1,675 for professional legal services.
2. On May 12, Esther Wills paid the monthly rent of $450 by writing Check 100.
3. On May 15, Esther Wills withdrew $250 for her personal use, Check 101.
4. On May 29, Esther Wills had the business's computer repaired at a cost of $245 and was given until next month to pay.

Problem 4-2   Analyzing Transactions into Debit and Credit Parts

Edward Palmer completed the transactions that follow soon after opening the Palmer Flying Service.

Instructions:

(1) Prepare a T account for each account listed in Exercise 4-1.
(2) Enter a balance of $15,000 in the Cash in Bank account; also enter a balance of $15,000 in the Edward Palmer, Capital account.
(3) Analyze and record each business transaction, using the appropriate T accounts. Identify each transaction by number.

(4) After all the transactions have been recorded, write the word "Balance" on the normal balance side of each account.

(5) Compute and record the balance for each account.

Transactions:

1. Purchased an airplane for $12,700, Check 1001.
2. Wrote Check 1002 for fuel for the airplane, $125.
3. Received $1,850 cash for charter flight services.
4. Paid $150 (Check 1003) for in-flight lunches.
5. Placed an ad in the newspaper for $75 and agreed to pay for it later.
6. Edward Palmer withdrew $150 for personal use, Check 1004.
7. Provided flight services on account, $775.
8. Paid for plane repairs by writing Check 1005 for $325.
9. Refueled the airplane at a cost of $115, Check 1006.
10. Purchased in-flight lunches for $75, Check 1007.
11. Received $225 on account from a charge customer.

Problem 4-3 Analyzing Transactions into Debit and Credit Parts

Marna Ritter operates Ritter's Cycle Rental Service. She uses the following accounts to record and summarize her business transactions.

Cash in Bank	M. Ritter, Capital	Equipment Repairs
Accounts Receivable	M. Ritter, Withdrawals	Expense
Bike Equipment	Rental Fees	Rent Expense
Accounts Payable		Utilities Expense

Instructions:

(1) Prepare a T account for each account used by the business.

(2) Analyze and record each of the following transactions using the appropriate T accounts. Identify each transaction by number.

(3) After recording all transactions, compute and record the account balance on the normal balance side of each T account.

(4) Test for the equality of debits and credits.

Transactions:

1. Marna Ritter invested $12,000 cash in her new business.
2. Bought five new touring bikes on account for $3,750.
3. Allowed a group to charge bike rental fees in the amount of $750.
4. Had three bikes repaired at a cost of $123, Check 1.
5. Wrote Check 2 to pay the electric bill of $95.
6. Received $225 for bike rental fees.
7. Paid the $225 rent for the month, Check 3.
8. Paid $1,750 toward the touring bikes bought on account, Check 4.
9. Marna Ritter withdrew $250 cash for personal use, Check 5.
10. Received bike rental fees of $250.

Problem 4-4 Analyzing Transactions

Juanita Nash owns the Hi-Style Images beauty salon. She plans to use the following accounts for recording and reporting business transactions.

Cash in Bank	Accounts Payable	Styling Fees
Accounts Receivable	Juanita Nash, Capital	Rent Expense
Salon Supplies	Juanita Nash,	Utilities Expense
Equipment	Withdrawals	Wages Expense

Instructions:

(1) Prepare a T account for each account listed above.

(2) Analyze and record each transaction using the appropriate T accounts. Identify each transaction by number.

(3) After recording all transactions, compute a balance for each account.

(4) Test for the equality of debits and credits.

Transactions:

1. Juanita Nash invested $17,500 cash in Hi-Style Images.

2. Bought equipment on account from Salon Products, Inc., for $2,400.

3. Bought salon supplies from Beauty Aids on account for $75.

4. Paid the rent for the month of $150, Check 1.

5. Wrote Check 2 to pay a part-time hair stylist $65.

6. Sent a bill for $67 to Pines Nursing Home for haircuts and shampoos completed for patients at the home.

7. Deposited the daily receipts from styling services, $233.

8. Paid the gas and electric bill of $125, Check 3.

9. Sent Check 4 for $75 to Beauty Aids as payment on account.

10. Ms. Nash withdrew $150 for her personal use, Check 5.

11. Paid the part-time hair stylist $45, Check 6.

12. Mary Jones, a customer, charged a $25 hair set to her account.

13. Deposited daily receipts of $264 in the bank.

Problem 4-5   Completing the Accounting Equation

With the addition of temporary capital accounts, the basic accounting equation can be expanded as follows:

Assets = Liabilities + Owner's Equity − Withdrawals + Revenue − Expenses

Instructions: Using this formula, determine the missing amounts for each of the question marks below. Use the form in your workbook or plain paper. The first one is completed as an example.

	Assets =	Liabilities +	Owner's Equity	− Withdrawals	+ Revenue	− Expenses
1.	$64,400	$8,200	$56,300	$ 500	$10,000	$ 9,600
2.	$22,150	525	18,800	1,200	12,100	?
3.	17,500	75	21,650	?	4,115	3,250
4.	49,450	?	47,840	1,500	20,300	17,610
5.	21,900	1,150	20,005	950	?	16,570
6.	72,640	2,790	?	10,750	67,908	39,749
7.	?	1,988	41,194	6,196	52,210	42,597
8.	50,780	1,493	64,110	16,050	?	29,986
9.	?	3,840	61,774	?	40,163	21,637

(Expenses plus withdrawals equal $27,749.)

10.	64,070	?	49,102	4,875	53,166	?

(Total owner's equity after adding revenue and subtracting expenses and withdrawals is $50,643.)

Home Is Where the Office Is

The alarm jolts Meg out of a sound sleep at 5:30 A.M. She rolls out of bed, heads for the shower, dresses, gulps down breakfast, races for the car, makes her way to the highway, and then drives 28 miles in bumper-to-bumper traffic to the office. When she finally arrives, there are 12 phone messages stuck to her phone. And the staff meeting is already underway. Back at home, Meg's husband, Jim, is already at work — and he hasn't left the house. He slept until 7:00, jogged three miles, had a hearty breakfast, skimmed *The Wall Street Journal,* and made five phone calls. Then he hooked up a modem to his personal computer and started work.

Advances in technology have enabled millions of Americans to work at home.

Jim is a "telecommuter," one of a new breed of home-based workers. Advances in computer technology have enabled workers to use home computers and modems to receive and deliver information and assignments via telephone lines. Within the last ten years, home offices have grown over 50%. The Department of Labor predicts that half of the American work force will be doing the same in the next 10-15 years.

The likely candidates for telecommuting are people who do not require much space or staff, such as tax and financial consultants and freelance designers, reporters, or writers. Or the at-home worker may be a handicapped person employed by a corporation or a parent who wants to stay home to care for children.

What are the benefits? With fewer meetings and memos, telecommuters experience a lower stress level, greater productivity, and improved creativity. If they are self-employed, overhead and operating costs are usually lower. Telecommuters also have more control over their lives and greater flexibility.

There are also disadvantages. At-home workers often need to "escape" for relaxation and lack peer interaction. If they are self-employed, their insurance costs are higher while their pay may be less.

What's best: an office in the home or outside the home? It depends on the quality of life that a worker strives for and what he or she is willing to sacrifice for it. Waiting for the bus in a Monday morning rainstorm could make working at home sound awfully sweet!

CHAPTER 5

Recording Transactions in a General Journal

In earlier chapters, you learned to use the accounting equation and T accounts to analyze business transactions. You also studied the rules of debit and credit for asset, liability, owner's equity, revenue, and expense accounts. In this chapter, you will learn how to record information about business transactions in a journal.

The accurate recording of business transactions depends on accurate analyses of those transactions. In this chapter, you will follow step-by-step procedures for journalizing the transactions you have analyzed in previous chapters. These procedures are very important in ensuring accurate accounting records because they reduce the chance of error. Since errors do occasionally occur, however, you will be shown a procedure for correcting them.

In this chapter, you will also learn more about the chart of accounts, a formal listing of the accounts used in a business's accounting system.

 LEARNING OBJECTIVES

When you have completed Chapter 5, you should be able to

1. Describe the first three steps in the accounting cycle.
2. Explain why source documents are created and give several examples of source documents.
3. Explain the need for journalizing.
4. Describe the steps followed to make a general journal entry.
5. Make accurate entries for business transactions in a general journal.
6. Correct errors in general journal entries.
7. Explain the purpose and use of a chart of accounts.
8. Define the accounting terms new to this chapter.

NEW Terms

accounting cycle • source document • invoice • receipt • memorandum • check stub • journal • journalizing • manual accounting system • computerized accounting system • general journal • chart of accounts • liquidity

The Accounting Cycle

Accounting records are kept and then summarized for a certain period of time called a *fiscal period.* A fiscal period may be for any length of time, such as a month or even a quarter of a year. However, most businesses use a year as their fiscal period. The year does not have to be a calendar year; that is, from January 1 to December 31. Many businesses start their fiscal periods in months other than January. For example, many department stores have fiscal periods that begin February 1 and end January 31. Other businesses may have fiscal periods that begin July 1 and end June 30 of the following calendar year.

The fiscal period of a business is separated into activities that help the business keep its accounting records in an orderly fashion. These activities are called the **accounting cycle.** The steps in the accounting cycle are:

1. Collect source documents and verify the financial information on them.
2. Analyze business transactions into their debit and credit parts.
3. Record the debit and credit parts of each business transaction in a journal.
4. Post each journal entry to the ledger accounts.
5. Prepare a trial balance.
6. Prepare a work sheet to summarize the financial information for the accounting period.
7. Prepare the financial statements.
8. Record and post the closing entries.
9. Prepare a post-closing trial balance.

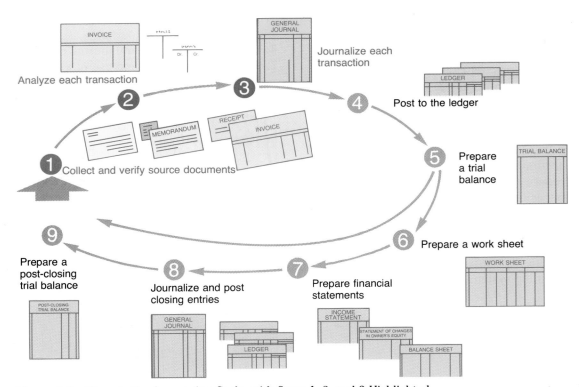

Figure 5-1 Steps in the Accounting Cycle, with Steps 1, 2, and 3 Highlighted

The steps in the accounting cycle are shown in Figure 5-1. In this chapter, you will read about and use Steps 1, 2, and 3. Each of the remaining chapters in this unit will cover at least one more step in the accounting cycle. After studying Chapters 3 through 9, you will have completed the accounting cycle for a service business organized as a sole proprietorship. The business used in these chapters is Global Travel Agency, which you first read about in Chapter 3. Now let's look at the first step in the accounting cycle: collecting source documents and verifying the information on them.

Step 1: Collecting and Verifying Source Documents

Most business transactions take place during the daily operations of a business. When a business transaction occurs, a paper is prepared as evidence of that transaction. This paper is called a **source document.** The source documents for business transactions are sent regularly to the accounting clerk for use in keeping the business's accounting records. The accounting clerk begins the accounting cycle by collecting and verifying the source documents. The accounting clerk checks the accuracy of the documents first. One way is to verify the arithmetic on the source documents.

There are several types of source documents, which may be prepared in different ways. Some source documents are written by hand. Others may be prepared by machine or by computer. The type of source document prepared as a record of a transaction depends upon the nature of the transaction. Some commonly used source documents are (1) invoices, (2) receipts, (3) memorandums, and (4) check stubs.

An **invoice** is a form that lists specific information about a business transaction involving the buying or selling of an item. The invoice includes such information as the date of the transaction and the quantity, description, and cost of each item. For example, if Global Travel buys a new typewriter, the invoice prepared as a record of the transaction would include the information shown on the invoice in Figure 5-2 on page 86.

A **receipt** is a form prepared as a record of cash received by a business. For example, when Global Travel receives payment for a service completed for a client, a receipt is prepared to indicate the date the payment was received, the name of the person or business from whom the payment was received, and the amount of the payment. An example of a receipt is shown in Figure 5-2.

A **memorandum** is a brief message that is usually written to describe a transaction that takes place within a business. A memorandum like that shown in Figure 5-2 may also be prepared if no other source document exists for the business transaction.

A **check stub** is the part remaining in the business's checkbook after a check has been torn out. The check stub lists the same information that appears on a check: the date a check was written, the person or business to whom the check was written, and the amount of the check (see Figure 5-2). The check stub also shows the balance in the checking account before and after each check is written.

A business also receives bills for other items or services such as electricity, water, or telephones. One example is a utility bill, such as the one shown in Figure 5-2. This bill shows the charge for telephone service for the month of October.

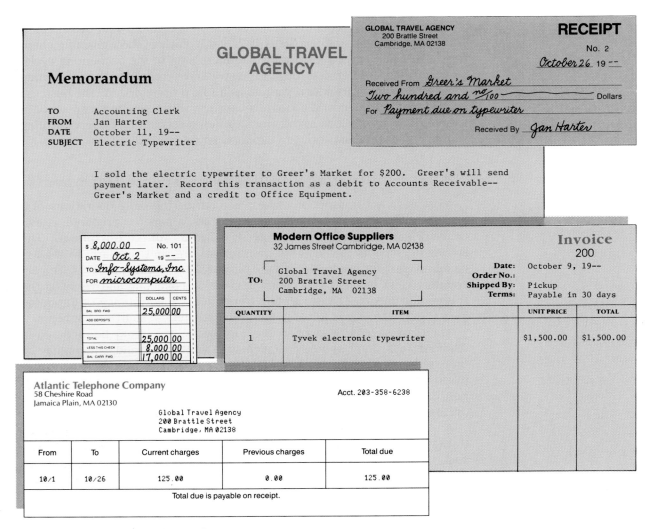

Figure 5-2 Examples of Source Documents

Step 2: Analyzing Business Transactions

After collecting and verifying source documents, the accounting clerk performs the second step in the accounting cycle. This is analyzing the information on the source documents to determine their debit and credit parts.

You have already learned how to analyze business transactions using the rules of debit and credit. When you first learned to analyze transactions, you were given a description of each transaction, such as the one that follows: Global Travel Agency bought a microcomputer for $8,000 and issued Check 101 in payment.

In real life, the accounting clerk must look at a source document to determine what has occurred during a business transaction. There is not enough space in this textbook to show you the source documents for all the transactions that you will study. As a result, you will continue to analyze descriptions of business transactions. However, you should remember that source documents are evidence of business transactions, and they are the basis for the information recorded in the accounting system.

Step 3:
Recording Business Transactions in a Journal

The third step in the accounting cycle is to record the debit and credit parts of each business transaction in a journal. A **journal** is a chronological record of a business's transactions. The process of recording these business transactions in a journal is called **journalizing.** Keeping a journal can be compared to keeping a diary in which all important events are written. The journal contains the most important information relating to a business transaction. It is the only place in which the complete details, including both the debit and credit parts of the transaction, are recorded. For this reason, the journal is often called a *record or "book" of original entry.*

Without accurate financial records, a business cannot keep track of either how well or how poorly it is doing. It cannot operate efficiently or, in the long run, profitably. A company without records, and a system for keeping them, is like a spaceship without an instrument panel and monitoring system. It cannot reach its destination if its operators receive no feedback.

Keeping accurate financial records begins with the recording of information from business transactions. The recording of such information is a part of each business's accounting system. Some businesses use a **manual accounting system** in which information is recorded by hand. Other businesses have a **computerized accounting system** in which information is recorded by entering it into a computer. Although some small businesses still use a manual accounting system, many use a computerized one. Large businesses rely almost entirely on computerized accounting systems because they must process vast amounts of financial information quickly.

Although computerized accounting systems are becoming more and more common for all businesses, understanding manual systems serves as background for understanding computerized systems. A basic procedure in a manual accounting system is the recording of daily business transactions in a journal.

The General Journal

Many kinds of journals are used in business. One of the most common is the general journal. As its name suggests, the **general journal** is an all-purpose journal in which all of a business's transactions may be recorded. The general journal you will be using throughout the accounting cycle for Global Travel, shown in Figure 5-3 on page 88, has two amount columns. The first amount column in the journal is used to record debit amounts. The second amount column is used to record credit amounts.

Each entry made in the general journal includes the following information, entered in this order:

1. the date of the transaction
2. the title of the account debited
3. the amount of the debit
4. the title of the account credited
5. the amount of the credit
6. a brief reference to the source document for the transaction or an explanation of the entry.

The preceding information must be entered for each transaction that you journalize. Look at the general journal shown in Figure 5-3 to find where each kind of information should be entered.

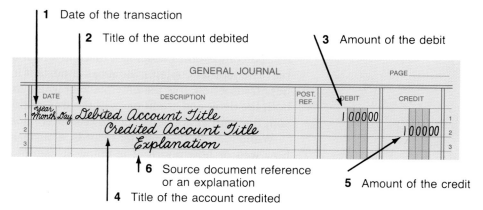

Figure 5-3 Two-Column General Journal

Before reading any further, complete the following activity to check your understanding of the material covering the first three steps of the accounting cycle.

Check Your Learning

Write your answers to the questions below on notebook paper.

1. A period of time into which a business separates its accounting records is called a(n) __?__ .
2. The accounting __?__ includes all the activities that help a business keep its accounting records during its __?__ .
3. Papers prepared as records of business transactions are called __?__ .
4. An all-purpose journal in which all of a business's transactions can be recorded is the __?__ .

Compare your answers to those in the answers section. Re-read the preceding part of the chapter to find the correct answers to any questions you may have missed.

Journalizing Business Transactions

In Chapters 3 and 4, you learned a six-step method for analyzing business transactions. The steps are the answers to these questions.

1. Which accounts are affected?
2. What is the classification of each account?
3. Is each account increased or decreased?
4. Which account is debited, and for what amount?
5. Which account is credited, and for what amount?
6. What is the complete entry?

Continue to use these steps to determine the debit and credit parts of each journal entry. You may also want to use T accounts to help you analyze transactions. After analyzing many transactions, you will find that you need these tools less and less to determine the debit and credit parts of a journal entry.

Business Transaction 1: *On October 1, Jan Harter took $25,000 from personal savings and deposited that amount to open a business checking account in the name of Global Travel Agency, Memorandum 1.*

1. Which accounts are affected? The accounts affected are Cash in Bank and Jan Harter, Capital.
2. What is the classification of each account? Cash in Bank is an asset account, and Jan Harter, Capital is an owner's equity account.
3. Is each account increased or decreased? Both are increased.
4. Which account is debited, and for what amount?

Cash in Bank	
Dr.	Cr.
+	−
$25,000	

Using T accounts to show the effects of this transaction, we can see that Cash in Bank is debited for $25,000 since increases to asset accounts are recorded as debits.

5. Which account is credited, and for what amount?

Jan Harter, Capital	
Dr.	Cr.
−	+
	$25,000

Increases to the capital account are recorded as credits, so Jan Harter, Capital is credited for $25,000.

6. What is the complete entry? The complete entry for this transaction is shown in the general journal illustrated in Figure 5-4 on page 90. Be sure you understand how to journalize this transaction before you go on to Business Transaction 2.

Look again at the journal page shown in Figure 5-4. Notice that in the upper, right-hand corner there is a line for the page number. Journal pages are numbered in consecutive order; that is, 1, 2, 3, and so on. When you fill one page with journal entries, go on to the next page. Be sure to number each new page before you make any more journal entries.

R — E — M — E — M — B — E — R

Six types of information must be entered in the general journal for each transaction: the date, the title of the account to be debited, the amount of the debit, the title of the account to be credited, the amount of the credit, and a reference to the source document or a brief explanation.

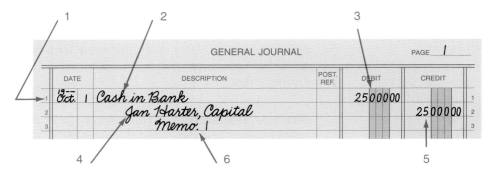

1 Enter the date of the transaction first. Note that the year and the month are written in the left side of the date section. The day is written in the right side. The year is written only once for all the journal entries on a page unless it changes. The day of each transaction is always entered, even when it is the same as the preceding transaction.

2 Write the title of the account to be debited at the extreme left of the Description column.

3 Write the amount of the debit in the Debit column. Do not use commas or decimals when entering amounts in a journal. If the amount is a whole number, enter zeroes in the cents part of the column.

4 Write the title of the account to be credited about 1/2 inch from the left edge of the Description column. Do not skip a line between the title of the account debited and the title of the account credited.

5 Write the amount of the credit in the Credit column.

6 Write the source document reference for the transaction on the line under the title of the account credited. Indent about 1 inch from the left edge of the Description column when writing the source document reference.

Figure 5-4   General Journal Entry for Business Transaction 1

Business Transaction 2: *On October 2, Global Travel Agency issued Check 101 for $8,000 to buy a microcomputer system from Info-Systems, Inc.*

1. Which accounts are affected? The accounts affected are Computer Equipment and Cash in Bank.
2. What is the classification of each account? Both are asset accounts.
3. Is each account increased or decreased? Computer Equipment is increased. Cash in Bank is decreased.
4. Which account is debited, and for what amount?

Computer Equipment	
Dr.	Cr.
+	−
$8,000	

Increases to asset accounts are recorded as debits, so Computer Equipment is debited for $8,000.

5. Which account is credited, and for what amount?

Cash in Bank	
Dr.	Cr.
+	−
	$8,000

Decreases to asset accounts are recorded as credits, so Cash in Bank is credited for $8,000.

6. What is the complete entry? The complete entry is shown in the general journal that follows. Note that there is no blank line between the journal entries.

	GENERAL JOURNAL			PAGE ___1___	

	DATE	DESCRIPTION	POST. REF.	DEBIT	CREDIT	
1	19-- Oct. 1	Cash in Bank		25 00 00		1
2		Jan Harter, Capital			25 00 00	2
3		Memo. 1				3
4	2	Computer Equipment		8 00 00		4
5		Cash in Bank			8 00 00	5
6		Check 101				6

Before going on to the next transaction, complete the activity that follows to check your understanding of how to make an entry in the general journal.

Check Your Learning

Use a sheet of notebook paper to answer the following questions about this transaction.

Today's date is September 14. The accounting clerk for Keeton Storage Co. is journalizing transactions. On September 12, Keeton issued Check 424 to Miami Office Supplies for the cash purchase of letterhead stationery. The amount of the check was $125.

1. Which date should be recorded in the journal entry for this transaction?
2. What is the title of the account to be debited and the amount of the debit?
3. What is the title of the account to be credited and the amount of the credit?
4. What is the source document reference or the explanation?

Compare your answers to those in the answers section. Re-read the preceding part of the chapter to find the correct answers to any questions you may have missed.

After analyzing a number of transactions, the rules of debit and credit will become second nature to you. Remember when you first learned to play a sport? You had to concentrate to remember how to do even simple actions. Learning to analyze business transactions is the same as learning anything else: the more you do it, the easier it gets.

Let's look now at the remaining transactions Global Travel completed during the month of October.

Business Transaction 3: *On October 4, Jan Harter took a $200 electric typewriter from home and invested it in the business as office equipment, Memorandum 2.*

In this transaction, the owner is investing personal property in the business. The two accounts affected are Office Equipment and Jan Harter, Capital. Both accounts are increased by the transaction. The increase in office equipment is recorded as a debit to Office Equipment. The increase in owner's equity is recorded as a credit to Jan Harter, Capital. This transaction is shown in the following journal entry.

	GENERAL JOURNAL			PAGE 1	
DATE	DESCRIPTION	POST. REF.	DEBIT	CREDIT	
7	4 Office Equipment		20000		7
8	Jan Harter, Capital			20000	8
9	Memo. 2				9

Business Transaction 4: *On October 9, Global Travel bought a new electronic typewriter on account for $1,500 from Modern Office Suppliers, Invoice 200.*

With this transaction, Global Travel has increased its office equipment in return for money to be paid later to Modern Office Suppliers. Money owed to a creditor is recorded as an account payable. To keep the amounts owed to different creditors separate, Global Travel uses Accounts Payable followed by the creditor's name as the account title. The title of the account used to record this transaction then is Accounts Payable—Modern Office Suppliers. When making the journal entry, you may have to abbreviate the title to fit it all on one line. An acceptable abbreviation is Accts. Pay.—Modern Off. Supp. or AP—Modern Office Suppliers.

This transaction increases an asset and also increases a liability. As you recall, debits increase asset accounts and credits increase liability accounts. The journal entry for this transaction follows.

	GENERAL JOURNAL			PAGE 1	
DATE	DESCRIPTION	POST. REF.	DEBIT	CREDIT	
10	9 Office Equipment		150000		10
11	Accts Pay.–Modern Off. Supp.			150000	11
12	Invoice 200				12

Business Transaction 5: *On October 11, Global Travel sold the electric typewriter on account to Greer's Market for $200, Memorandum 3.*

With this transaction, Global Travel has increased one asset account and decreased another. Accounts Receivable is increased because Greer's Market now owes Global Travel $200. Increases to assets are recorded as debits, so Accounts Receivable is debited for $200. The title of the account used to record money owed by Greer's Market is Accounts Receivable—Greer's Market. This title may be abbreviated as Accts. Rec.—Greer's Market or as AR—Greer's Market to fit it on one line of the journal. The journal entry for this transaction follows.

		GENERAL JOURNAL			PAGE 1
	DATE	DESCRIPTION	POST. REF.	DEBIT	CREDIT
13	11	Accts. Rec. — Greer's Market		2 0 0 00	
14		Office Equipment			2 0 0 00
15		Memo. 3			

Business Transaction 6: *On October 14, Global Travel mailed Check 102 for $750 as a partial payment to Modern Office Suppliers.*

This partial payment decreases the amount of money owed to Modern Office Suppliers, an account payable. Decreases to the liability account Accounts Payable are recorded as debits. Accounts Payable — Modern Office Suppliers is then debited for $750. The payment also decreases cash, so Cash in Bank is credited for $750. The complete journal entry follows.

		GENERAL JOURNAL			PAGE 1
	DATE	DESCRIPTION	POST. REF.	DEBIT	CREDIT
16	14	Accts. Pay. — Modern Off. Supp.		7 5 0 00	
17		Cash in Bank			7 5 0 00
18		Check 102			

Business Transaction 7: *On October 15, Global Travel mailed Check 103 for $550 to pay the month's rent.*

With this transaction, Global Travel increased its expenses. Increases to an expense account are recorded as debits. The account Rent Expense is debited for $550. The payment of the rent decreased the asset account Cash in Bank. Decreases to assets are recorded as credits. Cash in Bank is therefore credited for $550. The journal entry for this transaction follows.

		GENERAL JOURNAL			PAGE 1
	DATE	DESCRIPTION	POST. REF.	DEBIT	CREDIT
19	15	Rent Expense		5 5 0 00	
20		Cash in Bank			5 5 0 00
21		Check 103			

Business Transaction 8: *On October 16, Jan Harter bought an advertisement on account from City News for $75, Invoice 129.*

The purchase of the ad has increased the expense account Advertising Expense. An increase to an expense account is recorded as a debit. Advertising Expense is debited for $75. Buying the ad on account has also increased Global Travel's liabilities. An increase to a liability account is recorded as a credit. To keep this transaction separate from other accounts payable transactions, the account title Accounts Payable — City News is used. Accounts Payable — City News is therefore credited for $75. The journal entry for this transaction appears at the top of page 94.

GENERAL JOURNAL					PAGE 1
DATE	DESCRIPTION	POST. REF.	DEBIT	CREDIT	
22	16 Advertising Expense		75 00		22
23	Accts Payable - City News			75 00	23
24	Invoice 129				24

Business Transaction 9: *On October 18, Global Travel completed travel plans for the Sims Corporation and received $1,200 as payment, Receipt 1.*

This transaction increases the asset account Cash in Bank. Increases to asset accounts are recorded as debits, so Cash in Bank is debited for $1,200. Fees earned for a service completed for a customer increase the revenue account Fees. Increases to a revenue account are recorded as credits, so Fees is credited for $1,200. The journal entry for this transaction follows.

GENERAL JOURNAL					PAGE 1
DATE	DESCRIPTION	POST. REF.	DEBIT	CREDIT	
25	18 Cash in Bank		1 200 00		25
26	Fees			1 200 00	26
27	Receipt 1				27

Business Transaction 10: *On October 20, Jan Harter completed travel plans for Burton Co. She billed Burton $450 for the work, Invoice 1000.*

In this transaction, Global Travel has provided a service for money to be received in the future. The account Accounts Receivable is thus increased. The asset account Accounts Receivable—Burton Co. is debited for $450. Revenue for Global Travel has also increased, so the revenue account Fees is credited for $450. The journal entry for this transaction follows.

GENERAL JOURNAL					PAGE 1
DATE	DESCRIPTION	POST. REF.	DEBIT	CREDIT	
28	20 Accts. Receivable—Burton Company		450 00		28
29	Fees			450 00	29
30	Invoice 1000				30

Business Transaction 11: *On October 26, Global Travel received and deposited a check for $200 from Greer's Market, Receipt 2.*

The deposit of the check in the business's checking account increases the asset account Cash in Bank. Asset accounts are increased by debits, so Cash in Bank is debited for $200. The receipt of money owed to Global Travel decreases the asset account Accounts Receivable. Accounts Receivable—Greer's Market is therefore credited for $200. The complete journal entry follows.

		GENERAL JOURNAL			PAGE___1___
	DATE	DESCRIPTION	POST. REF.	DEBIT	CREDIT
31	26	Cash in Bank		2000 00	
32		Accts. Rec. – Greer's Market			2000 00
33		Receipt 2			

Business Transaction 12: *On October 28, Global Travel paid a $125 telephone bill with Check 104.*

The payment of the telephone bill increases the expense account Utilities Expense. Expense accounts are increased by debits, so Utilities Expense is debited for $125. This payment decreases Global Travel's cash, so Cash in Bank is decreased by a credit of $125. The complete journal entry follows.

		GENERAL JOURNAL			PAGE___1___
	DATE	DESCRIPTION	POST. REF.	DEBIT	CREDIT
34	28	Utilities Expense		125 00	
35		Cash in Bank			125 00
36		Check 104			

R — E — M — E — M — B — E — R

Every business transaction requires a debit and a credit entry. In a general journal, the debit part of the entry is made first. The credit part of the entry is entered next, and then the source document reference is written.

Business Transaction 13: *On October 29, Jan Harter wrote Check 105 for $450 to have the office repainted.*

The cost of having the office repainted is an expense to Global Travel. The expense account Maintenance Expense is thus increased with a debit of $450. The payment of the expense decreases the amount of cash, so Cash in Bank is credited for $450. The complete journal entry follows.

		GENERAL JOURNAL			PAGE___2___
	DATE	DESCRIPTION	POST. REF.	DEBIT	CREDIT
1	19-- Oct. 29	Maintenance Expense		450 00	
2		Cash in Bank			450 00
3		Check 105			

Business Transaction 14: *On October 31, Jan Harter withdrew $400 cash for her personal use by writing Check 106.*

In this transaction, the owner is taking an asset out of the business (cash) for personal use. The withdrawals account is used to record such amounts.

The withdrawals account is increased by debits, so Jan Harter, Withdrawals is debited for $400. The business's cash is decreased by the withdrawal, so Cash in Bank is credited for $400. The complete journal entry follows.

	GENERAL JOURNAL			PAGE 2	
DATE	DESCRIPTION	POST. REF.	DEBIT	CREDIT	
31	Jan Harter, Withdrawals		4 0 0 00		4
	Cash in Bank			4 0 0 00	5
	Check 106				6

Correcting Errors in Journal Entries

Occasionally, errors in journalizing do occur. When an error is discovered, it must be corrected. Note, however, that *an error should never be erased.* An erasure looks suspicious. It might be seen as an attempt to cover up a mistake or, worse, to cheat or to change the accounting records.

If you find an error in a journal entry shortly after journalizing, the error is easy to correct. Use a ruler to draw a horizontal line through the entire incorrect item and write the correct information above the crossed-out error. A correction for an incorrect amount is shown in the journal below.

	GENERAL JOURNAL			PAGE 1	
DATE	DESCRIPTION	POST. REF.	DEBIT	CREDIT	
19-- Oct. 1	Cash in Bank		~~25000 00~~ 52000 00		1
	Jan Harter, Capital			~~25000 00~~ 52000 00	2
	Memo. 1				3

A correction for an incorrect account title is shown below.

	GENERAL JOURNAL			PAGE 1	
DATE	DESCRIPTION	POST. REF.	DEBIT	CREDIT	
19-- Oct. 1	Cash in Bank ~~Office Equipment~~		2 5 0 0 0 00		1
	Jan Harter, Capital			2 5 0 0 0 00	2
	Memo. 1				3

Recording Transactions in a Computerized Accounting System

Journalizing business transactions is basically the same whether a business uses a manual accounting system or a computerized accounting system. A journal entry recorded in a computer contains the same six types of information: the date, the title of the account debited, the debit amount, the title of the account credited, the credit amount, and the source document reference or explanation of the transaction. Figure 5-5 shows how Global Travel Agency's business transactions would appear in a computerized accounting system.

```
                    GENERAL JOURNAL                    Page  1

         DATE              DESCRIPTION              DEBIT      CREDIT

         19--
         Oct.  1  Cash in Bank                   25000.00
                     Jan Harter, Capital                     25000.00
                        Memo. 1
               2  Computer Equipment              8000.00
                     Cash in Bank                             8000.00
                        Check 101
               4  Office Equipment                 200.00
                     Jan Harter, Capital                       200.00
                        Memo. 2
               9  Office Equipment                1500.00
                     Accts. Pay.--Modern Off. Supp.           1500.00
                        Invoice 200
              11  Accts. Rec.--Greer's Market      200.00
                     Office Equipment                          200.00
                        Memo. 3
              14  Accts. Pay.--Modern Off. Supp.   750.00
                     Cash in Bank                              750.00
                        Check 102
              15  Rent Expense                     550.00
                     Cash in Bank                              550.00
                        Check 103
              16  Advertising Expense               75.00
                     Accts. Pay.--City News                     75.00
                        Invoice 129
              18  Cash in Bank                    1200.00
                     Fees                                     1200.00
                        Receipt 1
              20  Accts. Rec.--Burton Company      450.00
                     Fees                                      450.00
                        Invoice 1000
              26  Cash in Bank                     200.00
                     Accts. Rec.--Greer's Market                200.00
                        Receipt 2
              28  Utilities Expense                125.00
                     Cash in Bank                              125.00
                        Check 104
              29  Maintenance Expense              450.00
                     Cash in Bank                              450.00
                        Check 105
              31  Jan Harter, Withdrawals          400.00
                     Cash in Bank                              400.00
                        Check 106
```

Figure 5-5 General Journal Entries in a Computerized Accounting System

Check Your Learning

Use Figure 5-5 to answer the following questions. Write your answers on a sheet of notebook paper.

1. What account was debited in the October 16 transaction?
2. How many entries affected the Cash in Bank account during October?
3. What was the source document for the October 4 transaction?
4. On what date was a check written to pay the monthly rent?
5. How many entries affected the Fees account during October?
6. Describe the transaction recorded on October 20.

Compare your answers to those in the answers section.

At the touch of a button, an accounting worker can obtain printed copies of journal transactions.

The Chart of Accounts

In Chapter 3, you were shown a list of accounts used by Global Travel Agency. An "official" list of all the accounts used for journalizing a business's transactions is called a **chart of accounts.** Look at the chart of accounts in Figure 5-6. As you can see, each account is listed in the chart of accounts first by classification and then by account number.

You will also see in the chart of accounts an account you have not yet used, the Income Summary account. This account is used only at the end of the fiscal period when the balances in the temporary capital accounts are transferred to the owner's capital account. This process will be explained in detail in Chapter 9.

The Order of Accounts

In accounting, it is traditional to list accounts in the chart of accounts according to certain rules. Asset accounts are listed according to their liquidity. **Liquidity** refers to the ease with which an asset can be converted to cash. The accounts that can be most easily converted to cash are listed first. In the chart of accounts, Cash in Bank is the most "liquid" asset, so it is listed first. Since it is assumed that money owed to the business — accounts receivable — will soon be paid, Accounts Receivable accounts are listed next. The other asset accounts are then listed according to the next easiest to convert to cash, and so on. The accounts within each of the remaining classifications are listed in alphabetical order.

The Numbering of Accounts

An account number identifies an account much as a Dewey Decimal number identifies the location of a library book or a ZIP Code identifies the location of an address. Account numbers may have two, three, four, or more

Global Travel Agency
Chart of Accounts

ASSETS (100-199)
101 Cash in Bank
105 Accounts Receivable—Burton Co.
110 Accounts Receivable—Greer's Market
120 Computer Equipment
130 Office Equipment

LIABILITIES (200-299)
201 Accounts Payable—City News
205 Accounts Payable—Modern Office Suppliers

OWNER'S EQUITY (300-399)
301 Jan Harter, Capital
305 Jan Harter, Withdrawals
310 Income Summary

REVENUE (400-499)
401 Fees

EXPENSES (500-599)
501 Advertising Expense
510 Maintenance Expense
520 Rent Expense
530 Utilities Expense

Figure 5-6   Global Travel Agency's Chart of Accounts

digits. The number of digits used varies with the needs of the business. In this textbook, we will use three-digit numbers for accounts.

Think of each account number as a code. Each digit in the code has a special meaning. The first digit in an account number tells you the classification of an account. Asset accounts begin with the number 1; liability accounts, 2; owner's equity accounts, 3; revenue accounts, 4; and expense accounts, 5. The accounts are "filed" according to their classification. That is, the asset accounts appear first, the liability accounts appear second, and so on.

The second and third digits in the account number tell you the position of an account within its classification. For example, in Global Travel's chart of accounts, Cash in Bank has the number 101. The "01" tells you that the Cash in Bank account is the first asset account.

In an accounting system using three-digit account numbers, there can be up to ninety-nine accounts within each classification.

Assets	100-199
Liabilities	200-299
Owner's Equity	300-399
Revenue	400-499
Expenses	500-599

Look again at the account numbers in the chart of accounts for Global Travel (Figure 5-6). The account numbers are not consecutive. The "gap" between numbers allows a business to add other accounts as needed and still keep all the accounts properly ordered. Now that you know how accounts are numbered and organized, do the following activity.

Check Your Learning

Write your answers to each of the following questions on notebook paper.

1. What is the classification of each of the following accounts?
   a. Accounts Receivable—Martinez Company
   b. Cash in Bank
   c. B. Watson, Capital
   d. Miscellaneous Expense
   e. Membership Fees
   f. Accounts Payable—Podaski Co.
   g. Maintenance Expense
2. List the above accounts in the order in which they would be listed on a chart of accounts.
3. For each of the accounts in #1, list the first digit in the account number.

Compare your answers to those in the answers section. Re-read the preceding part of the chapter to find the correct answers to any questions you may have missed.

SUMMARY OF KEY POINTS

1. Each business keeps its accounting records for a certain period of time called a fiscal period. A fiscal period can be any length of time, but most businesses use a year as their fiscal period.
2. The activities involved in keeping accounting records during a fiscal period make up the accounting cycle for a business.
3. The first step in the accounting cycle is to collect and verify source documents. Source documents are business papers prepared as evidence of business transactions.
4. The second step in the accounting cycle is to analyze the business transactions into their debit and credit parts.
5. Entering information from a business transaction in a journal is the third step in the accounting cycle. Each journal entry contains the date of the transaction, the title of the account debited, the amount of the debit, the title of the account credited, the amount of the credit, and a source document reference or brief explanation of the transaction.
6. If an error is made in a journal entry, a correction must be made. An account title or an amount is often the part of the journal entry that is incorrect. To correct either of these errors, use a ruler to draw a line through the incorrect part of the entry. Then write the correct information above the line.
7. Each business has a chart of accounts listing the accounts used in its accounting system by classification, account number, and account title.
8. Asset accounts are listed on the chart of accounts in the order of liquidity. Liquidity is the ease with which an asset can be converted to cash. The accounts in the other classifications are listed in alphabetical order.

REVIEW AND APPLICATIONS

Building Your Accounting Vocabulary

In your own words, write the definition of each of the following accounting terms. Use complete sentences for your definitions.

accounting cycle
chart of accounts
check stub
computerized
   accounting system

general journal
invoice
journal
journalizing
liquidity

manual accounting
   system
memorandum
receipt
source document

Reviewing Your Accounting Knowledge

1. What is meant by the term "fiscal period"?
2. List the nine steps of the accounting cycle.
3. What is the purpose of a source document?
4. List four source documents and explain when each is used.
5. Why is a journal often called a record or book of original entry?
6. Why is it important for businesses to keep accurate financial records?
7. How are the two amount columns of the general journal used to record dollar amounts?
8. What information is included in each general journal entry?
9. What procedure is used for correcting an error in a journal entry?
10. What two rules are followed in listing accounts in the chart of accounts?
11. What is the meaning of each digit in an account number?

Improving Your Decision-Making Skills

Miguel Ortega is planning to start his own bicycle repair shop, using the garage of his home as his place of business. Miguel has saved $7,000 to buy tools and equipment and get his business started. He also knows that he should have an accounting system for his new business. He has asked for your help in planning the accounting system. Can you suggest some titles for the accounts that Miguel will need in his accounting system?

Applying Accounting Procedures

Exercise 5-1 Analyzing Business Transactions

Patti Fair recently started a day care center. She uses the following accounts to record business transactions.

Cash in Bank
Accounts Receivable — Tiny Tots Nursery
Office Furniture
Delivery Van
Accounts Payable — Acme Truck Service
Patti Fair, Capital

Patti Fair, Withdrawals
Day Care Fees
Rent Expense
Utilities Expense
Van Expense

Instructions: Use a form similar to the one that follows. For each transaction,

(1) Determine which accounts are affected.
(2) Classify each account.
(3) Determine whether the accounts are being increased or decreased.
(4) Indicate which account is debited and which account is credited in the general journal entry. The first transaction is completed as an example.

Trans.	Account Title	Account Classification	Account Increase	Account Decrease	General Journal Debit	General Journal Credit
1	Delivery Van	Asset	✔		✔	
	Cash in Bank	Asset		✔		✔

Transactions:

1. Bought a delivery van for cash.
2. Paid the telephone bill for the month.
3. Received cash from customers for day care services.
4. Patti Fair withdrew cash from the business for personal use.
5. Billed Tiny Tots Nursery for services provided.
6. Patti Fair invested a desk and chair in the business.

Exercise 5-2   Correcting Errors in Journal Entries

After journalizing several business transactions, the accounting clerk for Blake's discovered that errors had been made.

Instructions: Use the following information to correct the general journal transactions illustrated in the working papers accompanying this textbook.

1. On July 2, the debit should have been made to Office Supplies.
2. The amounts of the July 3 transaction should have been $300.

Exercise 5-3   Numbering Accounts

The list that follows describes the location of accounts used by Fit-Right Shoe Repairs.

Instructions: Use a form similar to the one that follows. For each account,
(1) Write the account description.
(2) Indicate an account number that would likely be assigned to the account. The first account is completed as an example.

Location of Account	Account Number
1. The first asset account	101

1. The first asset account
2. The first liability account
3. The owner's capital account
4. The first revenue account
5. The first expense account
6. The owner's withdrawals account

7. The second asset account
8. The second expense account
9. The third asset account
10. The second liability account
11. The third expense account
12. The fourth asset account

Problem 5-1 Preparing a Chart of Accounts

The accountant for the Northwood Insurance Agency recommends the following accounts be used in recording transactions for the company.

210	Accounts Payable—BMI, Inc.	510	Rent Expense
105	Office Supplies	401	Commissions
501	Advertising Expense	110	Office Equipment
305	William Bair, Withdrawals	215	Accounts Payable—Fleming Co.
101	Cash in Bank	505	Office Expense
120	Office Furniture	301	William Bair, Capital
310	Income Summary		

Instructions: Prepare a chart of accounts for the Northwood Insurance Agency. Refer to Figure 5-6 on page 99 as an example.
(1) Write the heading, including the company name and the title "Chart of Accounts."
(2) List the assets including each account number and account title.
(3) List the liabilities including each account number and title.
(4) List the owner's equity accounts including the account number and title.
(5) List the revenue account by account number and title.
(6) List the expenses with each account number and title.

Problem 5-2 Recording General Journal Transactions

Dan Decaro, an architect, owns and operates an architectural firm called Decaro and Co., Architects. The following accounts are needed to journalize the business's transactions.

Cash in Bank	Dan Decaro, Withdrawals
Accounts Receivable—Modern Builders	Professional Fees
Office Furniture	Equipment Rental Expense
Office Equipment	Salary Expense
Accounts Payable—Office Suppliers	Utilities Expense
Dan Decaro, Capital	

Instructions: Record the transactions that follow on page 1 of a general journal. For each transaction,
(1) Enter the date. Use the current year.
(2) Enter the title of the account debited.
(3) Enter the amount of the debit.
(4) Enter the title of the account credited.
(5) Enter the amount of the credit.
(6) Enter a source document reference.

Transactions:

Apr. 1 Wrote Check 410 for the secretary's salary, $270.
   3 Bought a $900 desk on account from Office Suppliers, Invoice 320.
   5 Received $500 for preparing house plans for a client, Receipt 10.

Apr. 7 Wrote Check 411 to pay the electric bill of $110.
      11 Billed a client, Modern Builders, $1,700 for drawing up office plans, Invoice 462.
      12 Dan Decaro withdrew $325 for personal use, Check 412.
      14 Bought a desk calculator from Dante Business Equipment Co. for $300, Check 413.
      16 Wrote Check 414 for $450 to Office Suppliers in partial payment of the amount owed.
      25 Received $850 from Modern Builders on account, Receipt 11.
      30 Paid Office Equipment Leasing Co. $75 for the rental of an electronic typewriter, Check 415.

Problem 5-3   Recording General Journal Transactions

Ellen Day operates Phoenix Computer Center, which provides computer services to small businesses. The following accounts are used to record Phoenix Computer Center's business transactions.

Cash in Bank
Accounts Receivable — Connare Co.
Computer Equipment
Office Equipment
Accounts Payable — Star Systems

Ellen Day, Capital
Ellen Day, Withdrawals
Service Fees
Advertising Expense
Rent Expense

Instructions: Record the transactions that follow on page 1 of a general journal.

June 1 Ellen Day invested $12,000 in the business, Memorandum 1.
       5 Purchased $5,000 worth of computer equipment from Star Systems on account, Invoice 1632.
       8 Received $1,600 for computer services completed for a customer, Receipt 101.
      10 Paid the *Village Bulletin* $75 for running an ad, Check 101.
      13 Ellen Day withdrew $300 for personal use, Check 102.
      17 Billed the Connare Co. $700 for computer services, Invoice 102.
      18 Paid Star Systems $2,500 as part payment on account, Check 103.
      20 Ellen Day invested an electric typewriter valued at $350 in the business, Memorandum 2.
      22 Wrote Check 104 for $600 to Shadyside Realty for the rent.
      24 Paid Star Systems the remaining $2,500 owed, Check 105.
      28 Received a $700 check from Connare Co. in full payment of its account, Receipt 102.

Problem 5-4   Recording General Journal Transactions

Frank Palmer, a certified public accountant, owns and operates a public accounting office called Palmer Associates, CPAs. The following accounts are used to journalize the business's transactions.

101	Cash in Bank
110	Accounts Receivable — Lisa Logan
120	Computer Equipment
130	Office Furniture & Equipment
210	Accounts Payable — Comp Systems, Inc.
220	Accounts Payable — Premier Processors

301	Frank Palmer, Capital
305	Frank Palmer, Withdrawals
401	Fees
505	Maintenance Expense
545	Rent Expense
570	Salaries Expense
580	Utilities Expense

Instructions: Record the following transactions on general journal page 7.

Mar. 2 Received $125 for preparing a client's tax return, Receipt 300.

3 Frank Palmer invested a desk, chair, and lamp, valued at $270, in the business, Memorandum 63.

5 Completed accounting work for Lisa Logan and billed her $1,600, Invoice A12.

9 Wrote Check 711 for $150 for the secretary's salary.

11 Frank Palmer withdrew $380 for personal use, Check 712.

14 Purchased a microcomputer, monitor, and printer for $2,600 from Comp Systems, Inc., on account, Invoice 911.

16 Paid the monthly rent of $400 by issuing Check 713.

18 Wrote Check 714 to Leone & Sons for painting the office, $290.

21 Received $3,600 for completing an audit for a client, Receipt 301.

25 Paid the $70 electric bill, Check 715.

28 Purchased on credit an additional disk drive for the computer from Premier Processors for $540, Invoice C457.

31 Received a check from Lisa Logan for $1,600 to apply on her account, Receipt 302.

Problem 5-5 Recording General Journal Transactions

Doug Hawk opened Hawk's Heating and Air Conditioning on November 1. The following accounts are used to record the business's transactions.

Cash in Bank
Accounts Receivable—Carley Cole
Accounts Receivable—Lee Industries
Truck
Tools
Office Equipment
Accounts Payable—First National Bank

Accounts Payable—Lock-On Tool Co.
Doug Hawk, Capital
Doug Hawk, Withdrawals
Repair Revenue
Rent Expense
Utilities Expense

Instructions: Record the following transactions on page 1 of a general journal.

Nov. 1 Doug Hawk began business by investing the following assets in the business: Cash, $1,500; truck, $3,000; tools, $1,300; and office equipment, $200; Memorandum 101.

2 Paid the rent on the shop space, $400, Check 211.

4 Purchased a calculator from Marlo Equipment Co. for $150 by writing Check 212.

6 Completed repair work and received $600, Receipt 1001.

8 Bought $450 worth of tools on account from Lock-On Tool Co., Invoice 7872.

10 Doug Hawk withdrew $175 from the business for personal use, Check 213.

12 Completed $550 in repair work for Carley Cole on account, Invoice 10.

19 Received a check for $225 from Carley Cole to apply on account, Receipt 1002.

25 Wrote Check 214 to Lock-On Tool Co. for $450.

30 Completed repair work for $850 for Lee Industries. Accepted $425 cash (Receipt 1003) and a promise from Lee Industries to pay the balance in 30 days (Invoice 11).

With the growing importance of computers, businesses are becoming more conscious of security.

I'll use my initials. No one knows my middle name." Oh, sure. Check the company phone directory!)

Passwords should be easy to remember, but hard to decode. And they should be known to one person only. When several people share a computer, a company may want to add an extra protection product or method to the password system. Here are some devices companies can use.

- When the user logs on, *biometric devices* compare the user's fingerprints to those stored in its memory.
- *Key-reading devices* check a special identification card before allowing a user access to computer facilities.
- With *graphics passwords,* the computer screen might display, for example, a car. The user must then point to three parts in the correct sequence before gaining access to the system.
- A person calling in to a computer system may be connected to a *port protection device,* which requires the person to enter a password. If the password matches one in the device's memory, the caller is connected to the computer system. If it does not, the telephone call is terminated.
- *Encryption* changes the text into an unrecognizable form through character substitution or transposition. For example, GEORGE would be HFPSHF by simply substituting for each letter the letter that follows it in the alphabet. A caller who doesn't know the encryption scheme can't read the data.

If confidentiality isn't respected or security is lax, the last word may be TOOLATE.

Passwords to Computer Security

Before the computer revolution, companies kept highly sensitive and confidential data under lock and key. In today's world of electronic data management, the computer's hard disk is the "file cabinet" and the "key" is a password.

But convincing employees that a password is a security protection device is sometimes a dilemma. It's not uncommon to find a password taped to the computer. ("But I keep forgetting it!") Or hearing a shared password shouted across a crowded office. ("Hey, Clare, run that password by me one more time.") Or making it so obvious that anyone would guess it. ("I know!

Posting Journal Entries to General Ledger Accounts

In Chapter 5, you learned how to analyze business transactions and enter those transactions in a general journal. The general journal is an all-purpose journal in which the details of a business's transactions are recorded. These details include the date, the accounts affected, the debit and credit amounts, and a source document reference.

After the information about a business's transactions has been journalized, that information is transferred to the specific accounts affected by each transaction. The process of transferring this information is called posting. Posting is the fourth step in the accounting cycle.

After posting has been completed, the balances of all the accounts must be proved to make sure the accounting system is still in balance. This is done by preparing a trial balance, the fifth step in the accounting cycle.

LEARNING OBJECTIVES

When you have completed this chapter, you should be able to
1. Describe the steps followed in the posting process.
2. Accurately post business transactions from a general journal to the accounts in the ledger.
3. Prepare a trial balance.
4. Record correcting entries in the general journal.
5. Define the accounting terms introduced in this chapter.

NEW Terms

posting • trial balance • ledger • ledger account form • proving the ledger • transposition error • slide • correcting entry

The Fourth and Fifth Steps in the Accounting Cycle

Earlier, we referred to the general journal as a sort of business diary in which all of a business's transactions are recorded. However, you cannot easily see the increases and decreases taking place in the business's accounts by looking at these journal entries. To provide a clear picture of how each account is affected by a business transaction, the information in a journal entry must be recorded in the accounts themselves. The process of transferring the information in a journal entry to an individual account is called **posting.** The purpose of posting is to show the effects of business transactions on the business's accounts.

After posting has been completed, a trial balance is prepared. A **trial balance** is a proof of the equality of total debits and total credits. As you can see in Figure 6-1, posting is the fourth step in the accounting cycle. Preparing a trial balance is the fifth step in the accounting cycle.

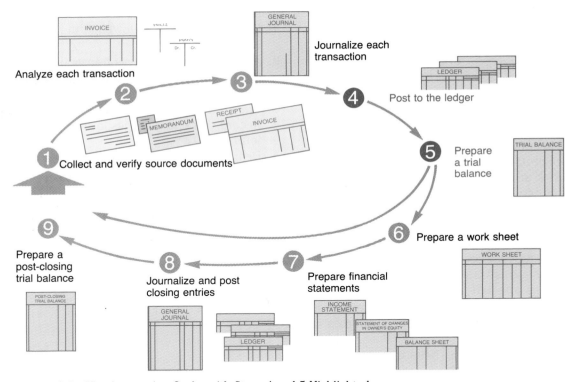

Figure 6-1   The Accounting Cycle, with Steps 4 and 5 Highlighted

The General Ledger

In a manual accounting system, the accounts used by a business are kept on separate pages or cards. These pages or cards are kept together in a book or file called a **ledger.** In a computerized accounting system, accounts are kept on magnetic tapes or disks, but the accounts as a group are

A company's general ledger accounts may be maintained on separate sheets in a ledger book.

still referred to as the ledger, or the ledger accounts. In either system, the ledger is often called a *general ledger*.

Posting to the ledger accounts creates a record of the effects of business transactions on each account used by a business. After journal entries have been posted, a business owner or manager can look at a specific account and easily find its current balance. If, for example, Jan Harter wants to know how much money Global Travel has in its bank account, she can simply look at the balance of the Cash in Bank account.

Before journal entries can be posted, however, all the accounts used in a business's accounting system must be opened in the ledger.

The Four-Column Ledger Account Form

In a manual accounting system, the accounting stationery used to record financial information about specific accounts is a **ledger account form.** There are several common ledger account forms. These forms—as well as other accounting stationery—are usually described by the number of amount columns they have. In other words, the number of columns refers only to those columns on the forms in which dollar amounts are recorded. For example, the ledger account form used for Global Travel's accounts is a four-column account form.

The four-column account form has spaces to enter certain information such as the account title, the account number, the date, an explanation of the entry, and the posting reference. It also has four columns in which to record dollar amounts. Look at the four-column account form shown in Figure 6-2 on page 110. Notice the four amount columns: the debit column, the credit column, the debit balance column, and the credit balance column. The first two amount columns are used to enter debit and credit amounts from journal entries. The last two amount columns are used to enter the new account balance after a journal entry has been posted. Which balance column is used depends on the type of account. For example, the balance of an account having a normal debit balance—such as an asset or expense account—is entered in the debit balance column. The balance of an account having a normal credit balance—such as a liability or revenue account—is entered in the credit balance column. The balance column shows the current balance in the account. Thus, the ledger account balances are kept up to date.

Figure 6-2 Four-Column Ledger Account Form

Opening Accounts in the Ledger

Before journal entries can be posted to the accounts in the ledger, an account must be opened for each account that appears on the chart of accounts. There are two steps to opening an account: (1) writing the account title on the account form and (2) writing the account number on the account form. Each account form will hold several entries, so it is not necessary to write the account title and number again until the first page is filled and a new page is needed. The accounts opened for Global Travel Agency's first three asset accounts are shown in Figure 6-3 as an example.

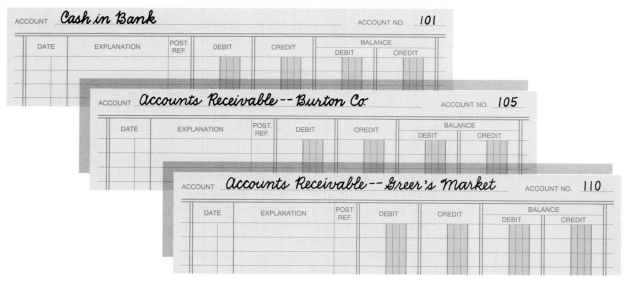

Figure 6-3 Opened General Ledger Accounts

In a computerized accounting system, the procedure is similar. An account is opened by entering the account title and number for each account on the chart of accounts. Computerized accounting systems vary, but all of them require that such information as the account numbers and titles be entered into the computer files.

The Posting Process

How often posting occurs depends on the size of a business, the number of its transactions, and whether posting is done manually or by computer. Large businesses must post daily to keep their accounts up to date. Smaller businesses may be able to post weekly or even monthly. The posting process remains the same, though, regardless of how often it is done.

As in journalizing a transaction, posting to the accounts is completed from left to right. Let's look at the first journal entry for Global Travel to be posted to a ledger account.

Global Travel's first transaction affected two accounts: Cash in Bank and Jan Harter, Capital. The information in the journal entry for this transaction is transferred item by item from the journal to each of the accounts affected. As you read about each step in the posting process, refer to Figure 6-4.

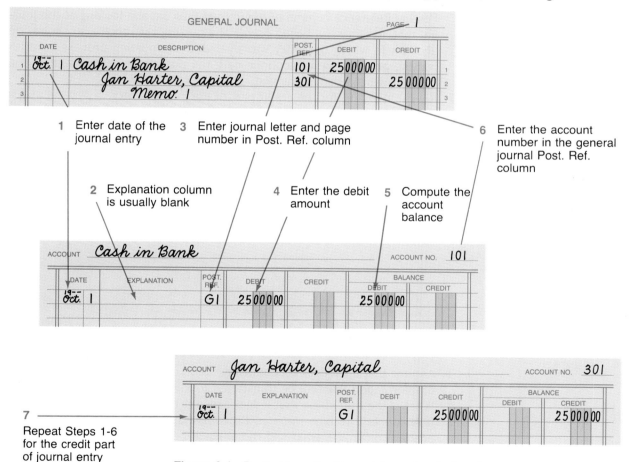

Figure 6-4 Posting from the General Journal to Ledger Accounts

1. Write the date of the journal entry in the Date column of the account debited. Use the date of the journal entry, not the date on which the posting is done. Write the year and month in the left side of the Date column. It is not necessary to write the year and month for other postings to the same account unless one or both change. The day, however, is always entered.

2. The Explanation column is usually left blank on the ledger account. Some businesses use this space to write in the source document number.

3. In the Posting Reference (Post. Ref.) column, write a letter for the journal from which the entry is being posted and the page number on which the journal entry is recorded. Use the letter "G" for the general journal.

4. Enter the debit amount in the Debit column of the ledger account.

5. Compute and record the new account balance in the appropriate balance column. Every amount posted will either increase or decrease the balance of that account. Remember that asset, withdrawals, and expense accounts have normal debit balances. Liability, owner's capital, and revenue accounts have normal credit balances.

6. Return to the journal and record the number of the account to which you just posted the debit part of the journal entry. Write the account number in the Posting Reference column on the same line as the debit entry.

   This step in the posting process is very important. The notation in the Posting Reference column of the journal tells anyone looking at the journal that an entry has been posted. The posting reference also shows the account to which the entry was posted. If the posting process is interrupted, perhaps by a telephone call, the posting reference signals the point at which posting stopped.

7. Repeat steps 1-6 for the credit part of the journal entry.

Before reading further, complete the following activity.

Check Your Learning

Use the following journal entry to answer the questions below.

		GENERAL JOURNAL				PAGE 6	
	DATE	DESCRIPTION	POST. REF.	DEBIT		CREDIT	
1	19-- June 6	Accounts Payable—Monroe Products		1 0 0 0 00			1
2		Cash in Bank				1 0 0 0 00	2
3		Check 610					3

1. Assume that the ledger accounts have been opened. What is the first item of information that will be transferred to a ledger account?

2. What is the title of the first ledger account to which you will post?

3. If Accounts Payable—Monroe Products has a current balance (before posting) of $1,250, what will the balance be after this journal entry has been posted? Does this account have a debit balance or a credit balance?

4. If the accounts to which this entry will be posted are numbered 101 and 210, which number will be written in the Posting Reference column of the journal after the credit part of the entry has been posted?

Compare your answers to those in the answers section. Re-read the preceding part of the chapter to find answers to any questions you may have missed.

The journal entries made in Chapter 5 for Global Travel's business transactions are shown in Figure 6-5. The postings made to the general ledger accounts from these entries are shown in Figure 6-6 on pages 114-115. Study these illustrations to check your understanding of the posting process.

GENERAL JOURNAL   PAGE __1__

	DATE	DESCRIPTION	POST. REF.	DEBIT	CREDIT	
1	19-- Oct. 1	Cash in Bank	101	25000 00		1
2		Jan Harter, Capital	301		25000 00	2
3		Memo. 1				3
4	2	Computer Equipment	120	8000 00		4
5		Cash in Bank	101		8000 00	5
6		Check 101				6
7	4	Office Equipment	130	200 00		7
8		Jan Harter, Capital	301		200 00	8
9		Memo. 2				9
10	9	Office Equipment	130	1500 00		10
11		Accts. Pay.—Modern Off. Supp.	205		1500 00	11
12		Invoice 200				12
13	11	Accts. Rec.—Greer's Market	110	200 00		13
14		Office Equipment	130		200 00	14
15		Memo. 3				15
16	14	Accts. Pay.—Modern Off. Supp.	205	750 00		16
17		Cash in Bank	101		750 00	17
18		Check 102				18
19	15	Rent Expense	520	550 00		19
20		Cash in Bank	101		550 00	20
21		Check 103				21
22	16	Advertising Expense	501	75 00		22
23		Accts. Payable—City News	201		75 00	23
24		Invoice 129				24
25	18	Cash in Bank	101	1200 00		25
26		Fees	401		1200 00	26
27		Receipt 1				27
28	20	Accts. Rec.—Burton Company	105	450 00		28
29		Fees	401		450 00	29
30		Invoice 1000				30
31	26	Cash in Bank	101	200 00		31
32		Accts. Rec.—Greer's Market	110		200 00	32
33		Receipt 2				33
34	28	Utilities Expense	530	125 00		34
35		Cash in Bank	101		125 00	35
36		Check 104				36

GENERAL JOURNAL   PAGE __2__

	DATE	DESCRIPTION	POST. REF.	DEBIT	CREDIT	
1	19-- Oct. 29	Maintenance Expense	510	450 00		1
2		Cash in Bank	101		450 00	2
3		Check 105				3
4	31	Jan Harter, Withdrawals	305	400 00		4
5		Cash in Bank	101		400 00	5
6		Check 106				6

Figure 6-5 General Journal Entries for October Business Transactions

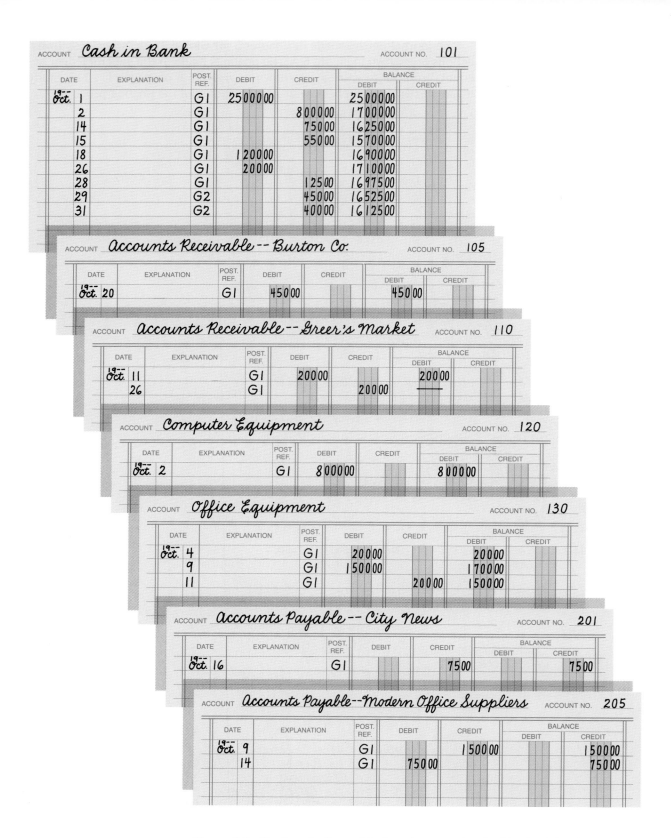

Figure 6-6 Postings to General Ledger Accounts for the Month of October

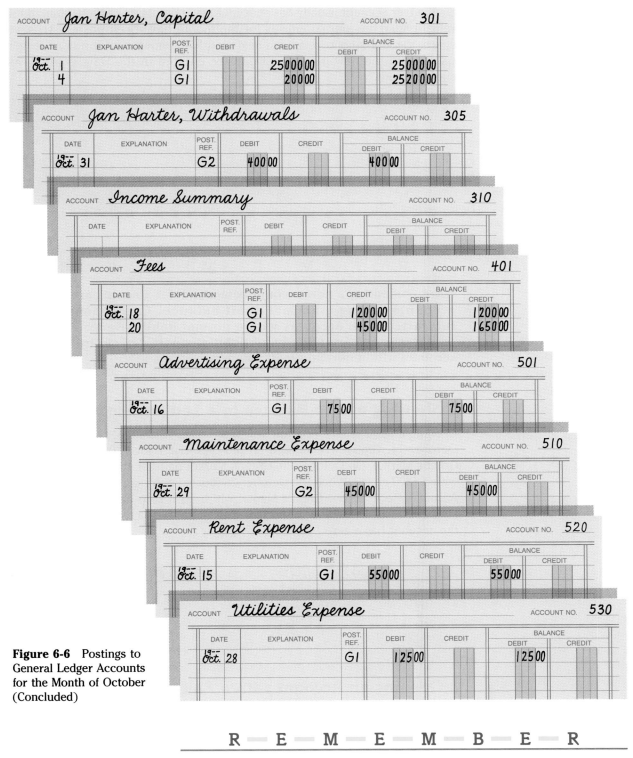

Figure 6-6 Postings to General Ledger Accounts for the Month of October (Concluded)

R—E—M—E—M—B—E—R

For every journal entry, you will post to at least two ledger accounts. You will post to one account for the debit part of the entry and then to another account for the credit part.

A ledger account usually has space for several postings. Often, blank lines remain after the journal entries for the month have been posted. To save space, the journal entries for the next month are entered on the same ledger page. Both the new month and day are entered in the Date column, as shown below.

ACCOUNT	Cash in Bank				ACCOUNT NO. 101	
DATE	EXPLANATION	POST. REF.	DEBIT	CREDIT	BALANCE DEBIT	CREDIT
19-- Oct. 1		G1	25 000 00		25 000 00	
31		G2		400 00	16 125 00	
Nov. 1		G2		50 00	16 075 00	

R—E—M—E—M—B—E—R

When computing a new account balance, debit amounts are added to accounts having a normal debit balance. Credit amounts are subtracted from accounts with a normal debit balance. Likewise, credit amounts are added and debit amounts are subtracted from accounts with a normal credit balance.

Showing a Zero Balance in a Ledger Account

Sometimes a ledger account will have a zero balance. For example, on October 11, Global Travel sold an old typewriter for $200 on account to Greer's Market. On October 26, Greer's Market paid for the typewriter in full with a $200 check. When the October 26 journal entry is posted, the account Accounts Receivable—Greer's Market will have a zero balance. Look at the ledger account below. The dash across the debit balance column means that the account has a zero balance.

ACCOUNT	Accounts Receivable—Greer's Market				ACCOUNT NO. 110	
DATE	EXPLANATION	POST. REF.	DEBIT	CREDIT	BALANCE DEBIT	CREDIT
19-- Oct. 11		G1	200 00		200 00	
26		G1		200 00	—	

Opening an Account with a Balance

When the first page of an account is filled, a second page must be opened. To transfer information from one page of an account to the next, follow these steps.

1. Write the account title at the top of the new page.
2. Enter the account number.
3. Enter the complete date (year, month, and day) of the *last* entry on the previous account page.

4. Write the word "Balance" in the Explanation column of the new account page.
5. Place a check mark (✔) in the Posting Reference column to show that the amount entered on this line is not being posted from a journal.
6. Enter the amount of the balance in the appropriate balance column of the new page.

The following illustration shows an example of an entry made to open an account with a balance.

ACCOUNT Cash in Bank					ACCOUNT NO. 101	
DATE	EXPLANATION	POST. REF.	DEBIT	CREDIT	BALANCE DEBIT	CREDIT
19-- Nov. 15	Balance	✔			26 470 00	

Posting in a Computerized Accounting System

In a computerized accounting system, the posting process is completed automatically by the computer. After entering the journal entries into the computer, the computer operator simply instructs the computer to post the entries to the accounts stored in the computer files. After posting has been completed, the operator can obtain a trial balance to prove the equality of total debits and credits.

Before continuing, complete the following activity to check your understanding of the posting process.

Check Your Learning

Write your answers to the following questions on a sheet of notebook paper.

1. What is recorded in the Posting Reference column of a ledger account?
2. Cash in Bank has a balance of $4,350. If a credit of $150 is posted to the account, what is the new balance of Cash in Bank?
3. What does a dash in a Balance column of a ledger account indicate?
4. When is a check mark entered in the Posting Reference column of a ledger account?
5. You are opening a new page for Accounts Payable—Apex Systems. In which column would you enter the balance of $1,650?

Compare your answers with those in the answers section. Re-read the preceding part of the chapter to find the correct answers to any questions you may have missed.

Proving the Equality of the Ledger

After the journal entries have been posted to the accounts in the general ledger, the total of all the debit balances should equal the total of all the credit balances. Adding all the debit balances and all the credit balances and then comparing the two totals to see whether they are equal is called **proving the ledger.**

In earlier chapters, you proved the equality of total debits and credits simply by listing each account title and its balance and then adding all the debit balances and all the credit balances. This proof of the equality of total debits and credits is called a trial balance. As you recall, preparing a trial balance is the fifth step in the accounting cycle. The trial balance for Global Travel Agency for the month of October is shown in Figure 6-7.

ACCOUNTING

Tips

When preparing a trial balance, be sure to list all the general ledger accounts, in the order in which they appear in the ledger and on the chart of accounts. List even those accounts with a zero balance. Every account is listed to avoid omitting an account— and its balance— from the trial balance.

Global Travel Agency Trial Balance October 31, 19--		
Cash in Bank	16 125 00	
Accts. Rec. – Burton Co.	450 00	
Accts. Rec. – Greer's Market		
Computer Equipment	8 000 00	
Office Equipment	1 500 00	
Accts. Pay. – City News		75 00
Accts. Pay. – Modern Office Suppliers		750 00
Jan Harter, Capital		25 200 00
Jan Harter, Withdrawals	400 00	
Income Summary		
Fees Income		1 650 00
Advertising Expense	75 00	
Maintenance Expense	450 00	
Rent Expense	550 00	
Utilities Expense	125 00	
Totals	27 675 00	27 675 00

Figure 6-7 Trial Balance

Notice that this trial balance has been prepared on two-column accounting stationery. All of the debit balances are entered in the first amount column and all of the credit balances are entered in the second amount column. A trial balance may also be handwritten on plain paper, typed, or prepared on a computer.

If the total debits equal the total credits on the trial balance, the ledger has been proved. If the two amounts are not equal, an error has been made either in journalizing or posting. You must find the error and correct it before continuing with the next step in the accounting cycle.

Finding Errors

Most trial balance errors can be located easily and quickly by following the steps below.

1. Re-add the trial balance columns. One or both of the columns may have been added incorrectly.
2. Determine the amount that you are out of balance by finding the difference between the trial balance debit and credit columns. If the difference

UNIT 2   The Basic Accounting Cycle

between the columns is 10, 100, 1,000, and so on, you have probably made an addition error. Suppose, for example, you have a debit column total of $35,245 and a credit column total of $35,345. The difference between the debit and credit columns is $100. Re-add the columns to find the error.

3. If the columns are added correctly, divide the column difference by 9. For example, suppose the difference between two totals is $27. That number is evenly divisible by 9 ($27 \div 9 = 3$). If the difference between the columns is evenly divisible by 9, you may have made a transposition error. A **transposition error** results when two numbers are accidentally reversed. If you have written the amount $325 as $352, for example, you have made a transposition error.

   A difference divisible by 9 may also indicate a slide error. A **slide** occurs when a decimal point is moved by mistake. For example, if you write $1,800 as either $180 or $18,000, you have made a slide error.

   To find the error, check the trial balance amounts against the balances in the general ledger accounts to make sure you have copied the balances correctly.

4. Check to make sure that you have not omitted one of the general ledger accounts. Look in the general ledger for an account balance equal to the amount of the column difference. For example, if the difference between the two columns is $725, look in the general ledger for an account having a balance of $725.

5. If all the general ledger accounts and their balances have been included in the trial balance, one of the account balances may be recorded in the wrong column. To find out if this is the case, divide the difference between the column totals by 2. For example, suppose that the difference between the two columns is $300; that amount divided by 2 is $150. Look in the debit and credit columns for an account balance matching this amount. Check to see whether a balance of $150 was entered in the wrong column.

6. If you still have not found the error, recompute the balance in each ledger account. You may have made an addition or subtraction error.

7. Finally, check the postings to verify that the correct amounts were posted from the journal entries. Also check to make sure that the amounts were posted to the correct amount columns.

Correcting Entries

Accounting workers understand very well the truth in the saying, "To err is human. . . ." When mistakes are made in accounting, one rule applies: *Never erase an error.* Erasures look suspicious. Honest mistakes should be honestly corrected.

The method for correcting an error depends on when the error is found. You learned in Chapter 5 that when an error in a journal entry is discovered *before* posting, it may be corrected by drawing a single line through the incorrect item and writing the correction directly above. However, when an error in a journal entry is discovered *after* posting, the correction is made by a **correcting entry.**

On November 15, Global Travel's accountant found an error in a journal entry made on November 2. A $100 check written to pay the electric bill had been journalized and posted to the Maintenance Expense account by mistake. The original journal entry is shown below in T-account form.

Maintenance Expense		Cash in Bank	
Dr.	Cr.	Dr.	Cr.
+	–	+	–
$100			$100

The T accounts below show how the transaction *should* have been recorded.

Utilities Expense		Cash in Bank	
Dr.	Cr.	Dr.	Cr.
+	–	+	–
$100			$100

As you can see, the $100 credit to Cash in Bank was correct. The error is in the debit part of the November 2 transaction. Maintenance Expense was incorrectly debited for $100. To correct the error, it must now be credited for that same amount. Utilities Expense should have been debited for $100. To correct the error, it is debited now.

The accountant wrote Memorandum 70 to notify the accounting clerk of the mistake. The correcting entry, recorded in the general journal, is shown below.

GENERAL JOURNAL   PAGE 3

	DATE	DESCRIPTION	POST. REF.	DEBIT	CREDIT	
1	19-- Nov. 15	Utilities Expense		10000		1
2		Maintenance Expense			10000	2
3		Memo. 70				3

Posting a correcting entry is similar to any other posting. However, in the Explanation column of the ledger accounts the words "Correcting Entry" are written. The illustration below and at the top of page 121 shows how the correcting entry was posted to the Maintenance Expense and Utilities Expense accounts.

ACCOUNT Maintenance Expense   ACCOUNT NO. 510

DATE	EXPLANATION	POST. REF.	DEBIT	CREDIT	BALANCE DEBIT	BALANCE CREDIT
19-- Oct. 29		G2			45000	
Nov. 2		G2	10000		55000	
15	Correcting Entry	G3		10000	45000	

ACCOUNT Utilities Expense						ACCOUNT NO. 530	
DATE	EXPLANATION	POST. REF.	DEBIT	CREDIT	BALANCE		
					DEBIT	CREDIT	
19-- Oct. 28		G1	125 00		125 00		
nov. 15	Correcting Entry	G3	100 00		225 00		

SUMMARY OF KEY POINTS

1. Posting is the fourth step in the accounting cycle. It is the process of transferring the information in a journal entry to the specific accounts in the ledger affected by that entry.
2. The accounts used by a business are kept in the ledger. In a manual accounting system, the ledger accounts are kept on pages or cards. In a computerized accounting system, the accounts are stored on magnetic tapes or disks.
3. The accounts in the ledger must be opened before posting can begin. An account is opened by writing the account title and its number at the top of the ledger account form.
4. A four-column ledger account form has four amount columns: one for a debit entry, one for a credit entry, one for a debit balance, and one for a credit balance.
5. After posting has been completed, the equality of the ledger must be proved. A proof of the equality of total debits and credits is called a trial balance. Preparing a trial balance is the fifth step in the accounting cycle.
6. The most common errors made in accounting records are addition or subtraction errors, transpositions, slides, omissions, and incorrect debiting or crediting.
7. Errors discovered after a transaction has been journalized and posted must be corrected by a correcting entry recorded in the general journal.

REVIEW AND APPLICATIONS

Building Your Accounting Vocabulary

In your own words, write the definition of each of the following accounting terms. Use complete sentences for your definitions.

correcting entry
ledger
ledger account form

posting
proving the ledger
slide

transposition error
trial balance

Reviewing Your Accounting Knowledge

1. What is the purpose of posting?
2. In what way can the information posted in the ledger accounts be helpful to the business owner?
3. What two steps are required to open a ledger account?
4. What determines the frequency of posting?
5. List the steps followed in posting.
6. What two things does the posting reference in a journal indicate?
7. How is a zero balance indicated in a ledger account?
8. List the steps you should follow to open the second page of a ledger account.
9. What steps would you follow to locate a trial balance error?
10. How should an accounting clerk correct an incorrect journal entry that has not yet been posted?
11. How should an accounting clerk correct a transaction that has been incorrectly journalized and posted?

Improving Your Communications Skills

Often the way we say things has a big impact on how our listeners respond to us. Angry words can bring an equally angry response, and no real communication will have taken place. Communication occurs when one person is able to express an idea in words and tone that are heard *and understood* in the way the speaker intended. See if you can identify why communication did not take place in the following examples. How would you have said things differently?

1. *Supervisor:* (Angrily) "You're late again, Wiley. If you're not here on time every day from now on, you're out of a job."
   Employee: "Aw, man. Get off my back. I'm tryin' as hard as I can."
2. *First Person:* "I'm tired of you always making the decisions on our projects. You never listen to what I want to do."
   Second Person: Well, you don't have to work with me anymore. I'll find someone else."

Applying Accounting Procedures

Exercise 6-1 Posting to Ledger Accounts

Kati Karl operates an alterations business called Kati's Custom Alterations. Listed below are several transactions that took place during the fiscal period.

Instructions: Use a form similar to the one that follows. For each transaction below,

(1) Enter the title of the account affected (indicated in parentheses at the end of the transaction) on the form.

(2) Indicate whether the transaction amount would be posted to the debit column or the credit column of the ledger account.

(3) Indicate in which balance column (debit or credit) the new account balance would be recorded. The first transaction is given as an example.

Transactions:

1. Paid the telephone bill. (Utilities Expense)
2. Received cash for altering a coat for a customer. (Alterations Revenue)
3. Purchased thread, paying cash. (Supplies)
4. Ms. Karl withdrew cash from the business. (Kati Karl, Withdrawals)
5. Paid a creditor a portion of the amount owed. (Accounts Payable—ALCO, Inc.)
6. Received cash from Alvin Jones on account. (Accounts Receivable—A. Jones)

				Balance	
Trans.	Account Affected	Debit	Credit	Debit	Credit
1	Utilities Expense	✔		✔	

Exercise 6-2 Determining Account Balances

The transactions that follow affect the account Accounts Receivable—Pat Downey.

Instructions:

(1) Open the ledger account by writing in the account title and account number, 115.

(2) Record the account balance of $350 as of June 1 of the current year.

(3) Post the following transactions to the ledger account. All of the transactions were recorded on general journal page 1.

Transactions:

June 2 Received $200 from Pat Downey on account.
      5 Completed services for Pat Downey and billed her $70.
     21 Received a check for $220 from Pat Downey.
     29 Sent Invoice 417 to Pat Downey for services completed, $90.

Exercise 6-3 Correcting Errors

Several errors are described below. Use a form similar to the one that follows. For each error,

(1) Determine whether the error will affect the totals of the trial balance.

(2) Indicate whether the error requires a correcting entry. The first one has been completed as an example.

Error	Does Error Affect Trial Balance Totals?	Correcting Entry Required?
1	Yes	No

Errors:

1. A $50 debit was not posted to the Office Supplies account.
2. A $200 purchase of store equipment was journalized and posted to Store Supplies.
3. A $30 job completed for Sarah James was recorded and posted to James Scott's account.
4. A $500 check received as payment for services was journalized and posted to the capital account.
5. A $69 debit to the withdrawals account was posted as $96.
6. A $100 debit to Cash in Bank was posted as $10.
7. After posting a $75 credit to a creditor's account, the account balance was incorrectly calculated.
8. A $25 debit to the Store Supplies account was posted as a credit.

Problem 6-1   Posting General Journal Transactions

Giles Gilbert, an orthodontist, operates Gilbert's Dental Services. The accounts used by the business have been opened and are included in the working papers accompanying this textbook. The general journal entries for the September business transactions are also included in the working papers.

Instructions: Post the transactions recorded in the general journal to the accounts in the general ledger.

Problem 6-2   Preparing a Trial Balance

Instructions: Use the general ledger accounts from Problem 6-1 to prepare a trial balance for the month ended September 30.

Problem 6-3   Journalizing and Posting
Business Transactions

You will need the general ledger from Problem 6-1 to complete this problem. During the month of October, Gilbert's Dental Services completed the transactions that follow.

Instructions:

(1) Journalize the transactions on page 2 of the general journal.
(2) Post the journal entries to the same general ledger accounts used in Problem 6-1.
(3) Prove the accuracy of the ledger by preparing a trial balance. Compare the totals to be certain they are in agreement.

Transactions:

Oct. 1   Bought several chairs and tables for the waiting room for $560, issuing Check 104.

Oct. 3 Received a $490 check from Rod McCune on account, Receipt 103.

5 Issued Check 105 for $1,350 to Dental Distributors on account.

8 Sarah Ashley sent a check for $375 to apply on her account, Receipt 104.

10 Giles Gilbert withdrew $600 from the business, Check 106.

15 Purchased $480 worth of dental supplies for cash, Check 107.

17 Bought dental equipment costing $1,300 from Dental Distributors on account, Invoice AB629.

20 Paid the electric bill for the month of $180, Check 108.

22 Completed dental work for several patients receiving $3,330, Receipts 105-108.

25 Giles Gilbert invested an office desk, valued at $75, in the business, Memorandum 3.

31 Completed dental services for Rod McCune and billed him $300, Invoice 102.

Problem 6-4 Journalizing and Posting Business Transactions

Chris Courtney started a business to provide legal services to the community. The chart of accounts for Chris Courtney, Attorney at Law, is as follows.

ASSETS		OWNER'S EQUITY	
101	Cash in Bank	301	Chris Courtney, Capital
105	Accounts Receivable—Jenny Simms	305	Chris Courtney, Withdrawals
110	Legal Supplies	310	Income Summary
120	Professional Library		
125	Office Furniture		REVENUE
		401	Legal Fees
	LIABILITIES		EXPENSES
201	Accounts Payable—Office Interiors	501	Salaries Expense

Instructions:

(1) Open an account in the general ledger for each account in the chart of accounts.

(2) Record the February transactions on page 1 of the general journal.

(3) Post each journal entry to the appropriate accounts in the ledger.

(4) Prove the ledger by preparing a trial balance.

Transactions:

Feb. 1 Chris Courtney invested $5,000 in the business, Memorandum 1.

3 Invested law books valued at $1,200 in the business, Memorandum 2.

5 Issued Check 101 for $300 for the purchase of legal supplies.

7 Bought a desk, chair, and table on account for $1,800 from Office Interiors, Invoice LX201.

9 Completed legal work for Jenny Simms on account, $400, Invoice 100.

12 Paid Office Interiors $900 on account, Check 102.

15 Issued Check 103 for $200 to pay the office secretary's salary.

18 Chris Courtney withdrew $500 cash from the business, Check 104.

20 Completed legal work for a client and received $800 cash, Receipt 100.

Feb. 24   Wrote Check 105 for $400 to Office Interiors on account.
       26   Received a check for $100 from Jenny Simms, Receipt 101.
       28   Chris Courtney took home $15 worth of supplies for personal use, Memorandum 3.

Problem 6-5   Recording and Posting Correcting Entries

An auditor reviewed the accounting records of Lopez's Chiropractic Service. The auditor wrote a memo, outlined below, about a number of errors discovered in the June records. The general journal for June and a portion of the general ledger are included in the working papers.

Instructions:

(1) Record whatever correcting entries are required on general journal page 22. Some errors will not require correcting entries, but will require a general ledger correction. Use Memorandum 50 as the source document for all correcting entries and June 30 as the date.

(2) Post all correcting entries to the appropriate general ledger accounts.

Errors:

June 3   The purchase was for store supplies.
       7   A $200 payment to a creditor, Vicki Dash, was not posted to the account.
       9   The Furniture and Fixtures account should have been debited for $500.
      13   Trina Lopez withdrew $1,200 from the business for personal use.
      17   Cash totaling $2,000 was received for professional services completed for patients.
      19   A $75 receipt from Suzanne Sharpe was posted as $57.
      27   Trina Lopez invested an additional $3,000 in the business.

Careers

Accounting Clerks: Patient, Persistent, Good with Figures

If you have these qualities—along with a high school diploma—clerical accounting could be in your future.

In today's work force, there are about two million clerical accounting workers—also known as accounting clerks or bookkeepers. Their tasks vary widely depending upon the size of the company that employs them. Generally speaking, accounting clerks are responsible for maintaining accurate records for all financial transactions (journalizing and posting) and preparing material for reports that measure the company's financial position or reports that facilitate corporate decision making.

Clerical accounting workers perform a wide variety of tasks.

In small companies, the clerical accounting worker performs many of the steps in the accounting cycle: analyzing and recording business transactions, posting to ledgers, preparing a trial balance. They might also perform a wide variety of other accounting tasks: computing payrolls, writing checks to pay bills, making deposits to the business's checking account, reconciling bank statements, handling telephone inquiries about orders and bills, preparing statements for customers, placing orders for supplies or equipment, maintaining records of merchandise purchased and sold, and being responsible for change or petty cash funds.

In larger companies, there may be many accounting clerks. Since there are more people to perform basic accounting tasks, the accounting clerks tend to specialize. For example, an accounting clerk might only handle activities involving the purchase of items used or sold by the business. Other specialized clerical accounting positions include cash clerk, payroll clerk, accounts receivable or accounts payable clerk.

In today's business world, many companies use computers to process and maintain their accounting records. Even smaller businesses have access to microcomputers. So be sure you can add this line to your resume: Can perform accounting tasks on a computer.

Setting Up Accounting Records for a Sole Proprietorship

You have just completed your study of the first five steps in the accounting cycle. Now you will have the opportunity to apply what you have learned by setting up the accounting records for Jack Hires, Attorney-at-Law. The accounting stationery needed to complete this activity is included in the working papers accompanying this textbook.

When you have completed this activity, you will have

1. analyzed business transactions
2. used the general journal to journalize business transactions
3. posted journal entries to the general ledger accounts
4. prepared a trial balance

Jack Hires, Attorney-at-Law

Jack Hires, Attorney-at-Law, is organized as a sole proprietorship. The business is fully owned and operated by Jack Hires. The firm provides a wide range of legal services to local businesses and to individuals who live in the community. These services include criminal defense, personal injury, family law, bankruptcy, and general practice. Revenue earned by the firm is in the form of professional fees.

Chart of Accounts

The chart of accounts for Jack Hires, Attorney at Law, follows.

JACK HIRES, ATTORNEY-AT-LAW
Chart of Accounts

ASSETS	101	Cash in Bank
	105	Accounts Receivable—Andrew Hospital
	110	Accounts Receivable—Indiana Trucking
	115	Accounts Receivable—Sunshine Products
	130	Office Supplies
	135	Office Equipment
	140	Office Furniture
	145	Professional Library
LIABILITIES	205	Accounts Payable—Legal Services, Inc.
	210	Accounts Payable—Office Systems
OWNER'S EQUITY	301	Jack Hires, Capital
	305	Jack Hires, Withdrawals
REVENUE	401	Professional Fees
EXPENSES	505	Professional Expenses
	510	Rent Expense
	515	Utilities Expense

Business Transactions

Jack Hires, Attorney-at-Law, began business operations on May 1 of this year. During the month of May, the business completed the transactions that follow.

Instructions: Use the accounting stationery in the working papers accompanying this textbook to complete this activity.

(1) Open a general ledger account for each account in the chart of accounts.

(2) Analyze each business transaction.

(3) Enter each business transaction in the general journal. Begin on journal page 1.

(4) Post each journal entry to the appropriate accounts in the general ledger.

(5) Prove the general ledger by preparing a trial balance.

Transactions:

May 1 Jack Hires invested $30,000 in the business by opening a checking account in the name of the business at City National Bank, Memorandum 1.

   2 Bought a computer for the office for $3,500, Check 101.

   2 Issued Check 102 for $125 for the purchase of office supplies.

   3 Bought office furniture for $2,700 on account from Office Systems, Invoice 457.

   7 Mr. Hires invested his personal law library worth $2,350 in the business, Memorandum 2.

   9 Received $675 from Mr. and Mrs. James Market for representing them in court, Receipt 101.

  11 Completed legal work for Andrew Hospital and agreed to be paid later, Invoice 101 for $750.

  12 Bought additional law books on account from Legal Services, Inc., Invoice 876, $1,325.

  14 Wrote Check 103 for $118 to pay the electric bill.

  15 Jack Hires withdrew $500 for personal expenses, Check 104.

  17 Completed legal services on account for Sunshine Products, Invoice 102, $1,250.

  18 Bought a filing cabinet (office equipment) for $275, Check 105.

  19 Received a check for $600 as payment legal services provided to a client, Receipt 102.

  20 Provided legal services on account to Indiana Trucking, Invoice 103 for $600.

  21 Prepared Receipt 103 for $625 received on account from Sunshine Products.

  22 Paid the telephone bill of $145, Check 106.

  25 Sent Check 107 for $1,350 to Office Systems as payment on account.

  26 Received $245 for legal services, Receipt 104.

  27 Paid the annual dues for membership in the American Bar Association, $350, Check 108.

  30 Wrote Check 109 for the monthly rent, $750.

  30 Withdrew $500 for personal expenses, Check 110.

CHAPTER 7

Preparing a Six-Column Work Sheet

In Chapter 6, you learned how to prepare a trial balance. At the end of a fiscal period, however, the owner of a business needs more information than a list of the account balances. The owner needs to know the business's financial position. In other words, has the business earned revenue greater than its expenses? Have expenses for the period increased or decreased? Has the business grown during the period?

The answers to such questions are found by preparing end-of-fiscal-period reports. Preparing a work sheet is the activity that begins the end-of-fiscal-period work. In this chapter, you will see how the work sheet is used to organize the information that has been recorded in the general ledger accounts during the fiscal period. You will also learn how to calculate the net income or the net loss for the fiscal period.

 LEARNING OBJECTIVES

When you have completed this chapter, you should be able to
1. Explain the purpose of the work sheet.
2. Describe the parts of a six-column work sheet.
3. Prepare a six-column work sheet.
4. Calculate net income and net loss amounts.
5. Define the accounting terms new to this chapter.

NEW Terms

work sheet • ruling • matching principle • net income • net loss

The Sixth Step of the Accounting Cycle

The length of a fiscal period varies from one company to another. However, the maximum period covered by the accounting cycle is one year. The first five steps of the accounting cycle are performed frequently during the cycle. The last four steps—preparing a work sheet, preparing financial statements, journalizing and posting closing entries, and preparing a post-closing trial balance—complete the accounting cycle. These steps begin the end-of-fiscal-period work. As you can see in Figure 7-1, this work begins with the sixth step of the accounting cycle: preparing a work sheet.

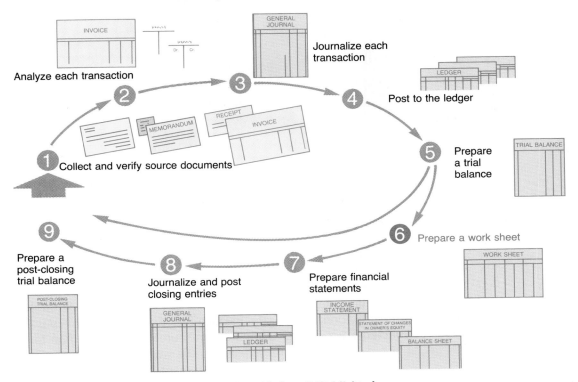

Figure 7-1 Steps in the Accounting Cycle, with Step 6 Highlighted

A **work sheet** is just what its name implies—a working paper used to collect information from the ledger accounts on one sheet of paper. Like the T account, the work sheet is a tool used by the accountant. The work sheet pulls together all the information needed to prepare the financial statements and complete the other end-of-fiscal-period activities.

Preparing a Work Sheet

A work sheet is prepared in pencil on standard multi-column accounting paper. The paper comes in several sizes and is usually printed without column headings. Blank spaces for column headings allow accounting clerks to write in headings needed by a particular business. The Global Travel Agency work sheet uses a six-column format with the column headings already filled in.

The work sheet is an accounting tool. Accountants use it to gather, on one document, all of the information needed to prepare end-of-period reports.

The Global Travel work sheet has five sections: (1) the heading, (2) the Account Title section, (3) the Trial Balance section, (4) the Income Statement section, and (5) the Balance Sheet section. The Account Title section includes a column for the account number and a column for the account name. Find each of these parts on the work sheet shown in Figure 7-2.

The Trial Balance, Income Statement, and Balance Sheet sections each have debit and credit amount columns. The six amount columns give this work sheet its name: the six-column work sheet.

		Global Travel Agency Work Sheet For the Month Ended October 31, 19--						
ACCT. NO.	ACCOUNT NAME	TRIAL BALANCE		INCOME STATEMENT		BALANCE SHEET		
		DEBIT	CREDIT	DEBIT	CREDIT	DEBIT	CREDIT	
1								1
2								2

Figure 7-2 Six-Column Work Sheet

The Heading

The heading of a work sheet is made up of three kinds of information, each centered on its own line. The heading includes:

1. the name of the business,
2. the name of the accounting form, and
3. the fiscal period covered by the work sheet.

It is easy to remember the function of the lines in the heading. Each line answers a "W" question: the name of the business (Who?), the name of the accounting form being prepared (What?), and the fiscal period covered (When?). Notice how these elements are positioned on the work sheet in Figure 7-2. Follow this format when preparing the heading of any work sheet.

The Account Title and Trial Balance Sections

Information for the Account Title and Trial Balance sections is taken from the general ledger accounts. In Chapter 6, as the fifth step of the accounting cycle, you prepared a trial balance by listing the account titles and their final balances. A trial balance can be prepared at any time during the fiscal period to prove the general ledger. When a trial balance is prepared at the end of a fiscal period, though, it is prepared as a part of the work sheet.

Look at the work sheet in Figure 7-3. The account numbers, titles, and balances were taken from Global Travel's general ledger. The account numbers and titles are listed on the work sheet in the same order as they appear in the general ledger. As you recall, asset accounts are placed first. After assets come the liability, owner's equity, revenue, and expense accounts. *All the general ledger accounts are listed on the work sheet, even those having a zero balance.* All the accounts are listed to avoid accidentally omitting an account and to ensure that the work sheet contains all the accounts needed to prepare the financial reports.

Global Travel Agency

Work Sheet

For the Month Ended October 31, 19--

	ACCT. NO.	ACCOUNT NAME	TRIAL BALANCE DEBIT	TRIAL BALANCE CREDIT	INCOME STATEMENT DEBIT	INCOME STATEMENT CREDIT	BALANCE SHEET DEBIT	BALANCE SHEET CREDIT	
1	101	Cash in Bank	16 125 00						1
2	105	Accts. Rec.–Burton Co.	450 00						2
3	110	Accts. Rec.–Greer's Market							3
4	120	Computer Equipment	8 000 00						4
5	130	Office Equipment	1 500 00						5
6	201	Accts. Pay.–City News		75 00					6
7	205	Accts. Pay.–Mod. Off. Supp.		750 00					7
8	301	Jan Harter, Capital		25 200 00					8
9	305	Jan Harter, Withdrawals	400 00						9
10	310	Income Summary							10
11	401	Fees		1 650 00					11
12	501	Advertising Expense	75 00						12
13	510	Maintenance Expense	450 00						13
14	520	Rent Expense	550 00						14
15	530	Utilities Expense	1 25 00						15

Figure 7-3 Work Sheet with Account Titles and Trial Balance Amounts

R — E — M — E — M — B — E — R

On the work sheet, be sure to enter the number, title, and final balance of every account that appears in the general ledger.

The final balance for each account is entered in the Trial Balance section in the column that corresponds to its normal balance side. In other words, the final balances of accounts with normal debit balances are entered in the Trial Balance debit column. The final balances for accounts with normal credit balances are entered in the Trial Balance credit column. If an account has a zero balance at the end of the period, a dash is entered in the normal balance column. Notice in Figure 7-3 that a dash was entered in the Trial Balance debit column for Accounts Receivable—Greer's Market. Dashes were also recorded in the Trial Balance debit *and* credit columns for Income Summary. Income Summary does not have a normal balance side. You'll learn more about this account in Chapter 9.

Ruling and Totaling the Trial Balance Section

Ruling means "drawing a line." In accounting, a single rule drawn under a column of amounts means that the entries above the rule are to be added or subtracted. After all account titles and their balances have been entered on the work sheet, a single line is drawn under the last entry and across the entire Trial Balance section (see Figure 7-4). The debit and credit columns are now ready for totaling. If the ledger is in balance, the total debits will equal the total credits. Look again at Figure 7-4. The totals match, with each column totaling $27,675.00. Since total debits equal total credits, a double rule is drawn across both amount columns just beneath the totals, as shown in Figure 7-4. This double rule means that the amounts just above are totals and that no other entries will be made in the Trial Balance columns.

If the total debits do not equal the total credits, an error has been made. The error must be found and corrected before the work sheet can be completed. Procedures for locating errors were discussed in Chapter 6.

Global Travel Agency
Work Sheet
For the Month Ended October 31, 19--

ACCT. NO.	ACCOUNT NAME	TRIAL BALANCE		INCOME STATEMENT		BALANCE SHEET		
		DEBIT	CREDIT	DEBIT	CREDIT	DEBIT	CREDIT	
101	Cash in Bank	16 125 00						1
105	Accts. Rec.—Burton Co.	450 00						2
110	Accts. Rec.—Greer's Market	—						3
120	Computer Equipment	8 000 00						4
130	Office Equipment	1 500 00						5
201	Accts. Pay.—City News		75 00					6
205	Accts. Pay.—Mod. Off. Supp.		750 00					7
301	Jan Harter, Capital		25 200 00					8
305	Jan Harter, Withdrawals	400 00						9
310	Income Summary	—	—					10
401	Fees		1 650 00					11
501	Advertising Expense	75 00						12
510	Maintenance Expense	450 00						13
520	Rent Expense	550 00						14
530	Utilities Expense	125 00						15
		27 675 00	27 675 00					16

Figure 7-4 Work Sheet with Trial Balance Section Completed

Before you read about the Income Statement and Balance Sheet sections of the work sheet, complete the following activity.

Check Your Learning

Answer the following questions about the work sheet on a sheet of notebook paper.

1. What part of the work sheet answers the questions who?, what?, when?
2. The account titles are listed on the work sheet in the same order as in the general ledger. What determines the order of the accounts in the general ledger?
3. How is a zero account balance indicated on the work sheet?

Compare your answers with those in the answers section. Re-read the preceding part of the chapter to find the correct answers to any questions you may have missed.

The Balance Sheet Section

The Balance Sheet section of the work sheet contains the balances of the asset, liability, and owner's equity accounts. As a result, these accounts are called the "balance sheet accounts." Once the Trial Balance section has been proved, the next step is to *extend*, or transfer, the amounts to the Balance Sheet section. In other words, the Trial Balance amounts for the asset, liability, and owner's equity accounts are simply copied to the appropriate Balance Sheet amount columns. Start on line 1 and extend each account balance in order. Debit amounts are extended to the Balance Sheet debit column, credit amounts to the Balance Sheet credit column. The work sheet in Figure 7-5 shows the balances extended to the Balance Sheet section.

Global Travel Agency
Work Sheet
For the Month Ended October 31, 19--

	ACCT. NO.	ACCOUNT NAME	TRIAL BALANCE DEBIT	TRIAL BALANCE CREDIT	INCOME STATEMENT DEBIT	INCOME STATEMENT CREDIT	BALANCE SHEET DEBIT	BALANCE SHEET CREDIT	
1	101	Cash in Bank	16125 00				16125 00		1
2	105	Accts. Rec. – Burton Co.	450 00				450 00		2
3	110	Accts. Rec. – Greer's Market	—				—		3
4	120	Computer Equipment	8000 00				8000 00		4
5	130	Office Equipment	1500 00				1500 00		5
6	201	Accts. Pay. – City News		75 00				75 00	6
7	205	Accts. Pay. – Mod. Off. Supp.		750 00				750 00	7
8	301	Jan Harter, Capital		2520 00				2520 00	8
9	305	Jan Harter, Withdrawals	400 00				400 00		9
10	310	Income Summary	—						10
11	401	Fees		1650 00					11
12	501	Advertising Expense	75 00						12
13	510	Maintenance Expense	450 00						13
14	520	Rent Expense	550 00						14
15	530	Utilities Expense	125 00						15
16			27675 00	27675 00					16

Figure 7-5 Work Sheet with Trial Balance Amounts Extended to Balance Sheet Section

The next step in completing the work sheet is to extend the account balances to the Income Statement section.

The Income Statement Section

The Income Statement section of the work sheet contains the balances of the revenue and expense accounts. These accounts are listed on the work sheet after the asset, liability, and owner's equity accounts. Therefore, they are extended to the Income Statement section *after* the accounts are extended to the Balance Sheet section. Revenue accounts have a normal credit balance. The account balances for revenue accounts are therefore extended to the credit column of the Income Statement section. Since expense accounts have a normal debit balance, account balances for expenses are extended to the Income Statement debit column. Notice the amounts in the debit and credit columns of the Income Statement section in Figure 7-6.

Global Travel Agency
Work Sheet
For the Month Ended October 31, 19--

ACCT. NO.	ACCOUNT NAME	TRIAL BALANCE DEBIT	TRIAL BALANCE CREDIT	INCOME STATEMENT DEBIT	INCOME STATEMENT CREDIT	BALANCE SHEET DEBIT	BALANCE SHEET CREDIT	
101	Cash in Bank	16 125 00				16 125 00		1
105	Accts. Rec.—Burton Co.	450 00				450 00		2
110	Accts. Rec.—Greer's Market	—				—		3
120	Computer Equipment	8 000 00				8 000 00		4
130	Office Equipment	1 500 00				1 500 00		5
201	Accts. Pay.—City News		75 00				75 00	6
205	Accts. Pay.—Mod. Off. Supp.		750 00				750 00	7
301	Jan Harter, Capital		25 200 00				25 200 00	8
305	Jan Harter, Withdrawals	400 00				400 00		9
310	Income Summary	—		—				10
401	Fees		1 650 00		1 650 00			11
501	Advertising Expense	75 00		75 00				12
510	Maintenance Expense	450 00		450 00				13
520	Rent Expense	550 00		550 00				14
530	Utilities Expense	125 00		125 00				15
		27 675 00	27 675 00					16

Figure 7-6 Work Sheet with Trial Balance Amounts Extended to Income Statement Section

Totaling the Income Statement and Balance Sheet Sections

After all the amounts in the Trial Balance section have been extended to the Balance Sheet and Income Statement sections, those sections are totaled. As in the Trial Balance section, a single rule is drawn across the four debit and credit columns to indicate that the columns are ready to be added. Look now at Figure 7-7 on page 137. After the four columns are totaled, notice that the debit and credit columns in each section are *not* equal. Unlike the Trial Balance debit and credit totals, the column totals in these two sections will not be equal until the net income or net loss for the fiscal period is added.

Showing Net Income on the Work Sheet

Businesses must spend money to provide goods and services for customers and to pay the costs of operating the business. The costs of operating a business (such as telephone bills and rent) are expenses. In

Global Travel Agency
Work Sheet
For the Month Ended October 31, 19--

ACCT. NO.	ACCOUNT NAME	TRIAL BALANCE		INCOME STATEMENT		BALANCE SHEET		
		DEBIT	CREDIT	DEBIT	CREDIT	DEBIT	CREDIT	
101	Cash in Bank	16 125 00				16 125 00		1
105	Accts. Rec. - Burton Co.	450 00				450 00		2
110	Accts. Rec.-Greer's Market	—						3
120	Computer Equipment	8 000 00				8 000 00		4
130	Office Equipment	1 500 00				1 500 00		5
201	Accts. Pay.-City News		75 00				75 00	6
205	Accts. Pay.-Mod. Off. Supp.		750 00				750 00	7
301	Jan Harter, Capital		25 200 00				25 200 00	8
305	Jan Harter, Withdrawals	400 00				400 00		9
310	Income Summary							10
401	Fees		1 650 00		1 650 00			11
501	Advertising Expense	75 00		75 00				12
510	Maintenance Expense	450 00		450 00				13
520	Rent Expense	550 00		550 00				14
530	Utilities Expense	125 00		125 00				15
		27 675 00	27 675 00	1 200 00	1 650 00	26 475 00	26 025 00	16
								17

Figure 7-7 Work Sheet with Income Statement and Balance Sheet Sections Totaled

accounting, expenses are always matched against revenue for the same period. This is referred to as the **matching principle.** Matching the expenses of a period to the revenue earned during the same period provides a more reliable measure of profit. Matching expenses to revenue provides information on the cost (expense) of producing revenue for the period. This information helps the business owner or manager make decisions about such things as whether expenses are too high compared to the amount of revenue those expenses produced.

The Income Statement section of the work sheet includes both the revenue and the expenses for the fiscal period. After the columns have been totaled, total expenses (the debit column total) are subtracted from total revenue (the credit column total) to find the net income. **Net income** is the amount left after expenses for the period have been subtracted from revenue for the period. Global Travel Agency has a net income of $450.00 for the month of October.

$1,650.00
−1,200.00
$ 450.00

The amount of the net income must also be reflected in the Balance Sheet section of the work sheet. Remember, revenue and expense accounts are temporary capital accounts. Both revenue and expenses affect capital. Revenue increases capital, while expenses decrease capital. A net income, therefore, increases capital since total revenue is greater than total expenses. During the fiscal period, revenue and expense amounts are recorded in the temporary capital accounts set up for this purpose. At the end of the fiscal period, the net income — the difference between total revenue and total expenses — is transferred to the owner's capital account. Since the capital account is increased by credits, the amount of the net income is shown on the work sheet as an addition to the total of the Balance Sheet *credit* column.

$26,475.00
−26,025.00
$ 450.00

To check the accuracy of the net income amount, subtract the total of the Balance Sheet credit column from the total of the Balance Sheet debit column. Your answer should equal the amount of the net income. If the two amounts match, enter the net income on the work sheet. If the amounts do not match, an error has been made. That error must be found and corrected. Check to be sure that all amounts have been extended correctly from the Trial Balance section and that the totals of all columns were added correctly.

To record the net income on the work sheet, follow these steps.

1. Skip a line after the last account title and then write the words "Net Income" in the Account Name column.   A
2. On the same line, enter the net income amount in the Income Statement debit column.   B
3. On the same line, enter the net income amount in the Balance Sheet credit column.   C

Look at the partial work sheet shown in Figure 7-8 to see how net income is recorded.

Global Travel Agency
Work Sheet
For the Month Ended October 31, 19--

ACCT. NO.	ACCOUNT NAME	TRIAL BALANCE		INCOME STATEMENT		BALANCE SHEET	
		DEBIT	CREDIT	DEBIT	CREDIT	DEBIT	CREDIT
11 401	*Fees*		1 650 00		1 650 00			11
12 501	*Advertising Expense*	75 00		75 00				12
13 510	*Maintenance Expense*	450 00		450 00				13
14 520	*Rent Expense*	550 00		550 00				14
15 530	*Utilities Expense*	125 00		125 00				15
16		2 767 5 00	2 767 5 00	1 200 00	1 650 00	26 475 00	26 025 00	16
17 A	*Net Income*			B 450 00			C 450 00	17

Figure 7-8   Partial Work Sheet Showing Net Income

Completing the Work Sheet

ACCOUNTING Tips

Use a rule to draw single and double rules neatly. A single rule means that the column of figures is to be added or subtracted. Double rules mean that the last figure is a total and that no more entries are to be made.

To complete the Income Statement and Balance Sheet sections, follow these steps. The completed work sheet for Global Travel is shown in Figure 7-9 on page 139.

1. Draw a single rule across all four columns on the line under the net income amount.   D
2. Add the net income amount to the previous total of the Income Statement debit column. Enter the new total and bring down the total of the Income Statement credit column to the same line. Total debits should equal total credits.   E
3. Repeat this process for the Balance Sheet section. Again, the total debit amount should equal the total credit amount.   F
4. Draw a double rule under the column totals and across all four columns. The double rule indicates that the debit and credit columns are equal and that no more amounts are to be entered in these columns.   G

Showing a Net Loss on the Work Sheet

When total expenses are greater than total revenue, a **net loss** occurs. A net loss decreases owner's equity. This decrease is shown as a debit to the capital account. When a net loss occurs, the Income Statement debit column

Global Travel Agency
Work Sheet
For the Month Ended October 31, 19--

ACCT. NO.	ACCOUNT NAME	TRIAL BALANCE DEBIT	TRIAL BALANCE CREDIT	INCOME STATEMENT DEBIT	INCOME STATEMENT CREDIT	BALANCE SHEET DEBIT	BALANCE SHEET CREDIT	
101	Cash in Bank	16125 00				16125 00		1
105	Accts. Rec.-Burton Co.	450 00				450 00		2
110	Accts. Rec.-Greer's Market	—						3
120	Computer Equipment	8000 00				8000 00		4
130	Office Equipment	1500 00				1500 00		5
201	Accts. Pay.-City News		75 00				75 00	6
205	Accts. Pay.-Mod. Off. Supp.		750 00				750 00	7
301	Jan Harter, Capital		25200 00				25200 00	8
305	Jan Harter, Withdrawals	400 00				400 00		9
310	Income Summary	—	—					10
401	Fees		1650 00		1650 00			11
501	Advertising Expense	75 00		75 00				12
510	Maintenance Expense	450 00		450 00				13
520	Rent Expense	550 00		550 00				14
530	Utilities Expense	125 00		125 00				15
		27675 00	27675 00	1200 00	1650 00	26475 00	26025 00	16
A	Net Income			B 450 00			C 450 00	17
				D G 1650 00	1650 00	26475 00	26475 00	18
				↑ E		↑ F		

Figure 7-9 Completed Work Sheet

$4,132.00
−3,904.00
$ 228.00

total (total expenses) is greater than the Income Statement credit column total (total revenue). The partial work sheet in Figure 7-10 shows a net loss. Expenses exceed revenue by $228.00.

To enter a net loss on the work sheet, follow the same general procedure as for entering net income.

1. Skip a line after the last account title and write the words "Net Loss" in the Account Name column.   **A**
2. On the same line, enter the net loss amount in the *credit* column of the Income Statement section.   **B**   Enter this same amount in the *debit* column of the Balance Sheet section.   **C**   (Remember to check the accuracy of the net loss amount by subtracting the Balance Sheet debit total from the Balance Sheet credit total. The difference should be the same as the amount of the net loss.)
3. Draw a single rule across all four columns.   **D**
4. Add the net loss amount to the previous totals and enter the new totals. Bring down the totals of the other two columns.   **E**   Draw a double rule under the column totals across all four columns.   **F**

	ACCT.	ACCOUNT NAME							
13	510	Maintenance Expense	1600 00		1600 00				13
14	520	Rent Expense	1400 00		1400 00				14
15	530	Utilities Expense	525 00		525 00				15
16			58241 00	58241 00	4132 00	3904 00	31242 00	31470 00	16
17	A	Net Loss				B 228 00	C 228 00		17 D
18					E 4132 00	4132 00	31470 00	31470 00	18 F

Figure 7-10 Partial Work Sheet Showing a Net Loss

Check Your Learning

Answer the following questions about the Income Statement and Balance Sheet sections of the work sheet.

1. Balances from the Trial Balance section of the work sheet are extended first to the ___?___ section.
2. The difference between total revenue and total expenses is ___?___ .
3. When the Balance Sheet debit and credit columns are first totaled, the totals are not equal. The totals are not equal because the amount of the net income or net loss for the period is not reflected in the ___?___ account.
4. If the difference between the Income Statement debit and credit totals does not match the difference between the Balance Sheet debit and credit totals, what should you do to find the error?

Compare your answers to those in the answers section. Re-read the preceding part of the chapter to find the correct answers to any questions you may have missed.

A Review of the Steps in Preparing a Six-Column Work Sheet

Follow the steps below—in order—when preparing a six-column work sheet.

1. Write the heading on the work sheet.
2. In the Account Title and Trial Balance sections, list all account numbers and titles and each account balance from the general ledger.
3. Prove the equality of total debits and total credits in the Trial Balance section.
4. Extend the amounts of the Trial Balance section to the appropriate Balance Sheet and Income Statement columns.
5. Total the columns in the Income Statement and Balance Sheet sections.
6. Determine the amount of the net income or the net loss for the fiscal period.
7. Enter the amount of the net income or the net loss in the appropriate columns in the Income Statement and Balance Sheet sections.
8. Total and rule the Income Statement and Balance Sheet sections.

SUMMARY OF KEY POINTS

1. The preparation of a work sheet is the sixth step in the accounting cycle.
2. A work sheet is prepared to pull together all the information needed to complete the end-of-fiscal-period work.
3. The Trial Balance section of the work sheet is completed first. The Income Statement and Balance Sheet sections cannot be completed until the debit and credit totals in the Trial Balance section are equal.
4. Amounts are extended from the Trial Balance section to the Balance Sheet section and then to the Income Statement section.
5. The work sheet is used to calculate the net income or net loss for the fiscal period. Net income results when revenue is greater than the expenses. A net loss results when expenses are greater than revenue.

REVIEW AND APPLICATIONS

Building Your Accounting Vocabulary

In your own words, write the definition of each of the following accounting terms. Use complete sentences for your definitions.

matching principle   net loss   work sheet
net income   ruling

Reviewing Your Accounting Knowledge

1. Explain why a work sheet is prepared.
2. Name and briefly describe the five parts of a six-column work sheet.
3. In what order are the account titles listed on the work sheet?
4. Why are all accounts, including those with zero balances, listed on the work sheet?
5. What does the Trial Balance section of the work sheet prove when it has been totaled and ruled?
6. Which account balances are extended to the Balance Sheet section of the work sheet?
7. Which account balances are extended to the Income Statement section of the work sheet?
8. Why is the matching principle important?
9. Explain how net income and net loss are recorded on the work sheet.
10. What does a double rule on the work sheet indicate?

Improving Your Math Skills

Many types of work require you to convert fractions into decimals and vice versa. Practice your skills at converting decimals and fractions in the following problems.

Convert the following fractions into decimals.

1. $\frac{1}{2}$ 2. $\frac{1}{5}$ 3. $\frac{1}{3}$
4. $\frac{4}{5}$ 5. $\frac{7}{8}$ 6. $\frac{3}{10}$

Convert the following decimals into fractions.

7. 0.889   8. 0.60   9. 0.375
10. 0.25   11. 0.667   12. 0.75

Applying Accounting Procedures

Exercise 7-1   Entering Account Balances on the Work Sheet

The following accounts appear in the Account Title section of the work sheet.

Store Equipment	Advertising Expense
Rent Expense	Accounts Receivable—John Long
Service Fees	Vincent Lee, Withdrawals
Accounts Payable—Panters Supply	Maintenance Expense
Vincent Lee, Capital	Office Supplies

Instructions: Use a form similar to the one that follows. For each account,
(1) Classify the account.
(2) Use a check mark to indicate whether the account balance will be entered in the debit or the credit column of the Trial Balance section of the work sheet. The first account is shown as an example.

Account Title	Account Classification	Trial Balance	
		Debit	Credit
Store Equipment	Asset	✔	

Exercise 7-2   Extending Amounts

Instructions: Use the same account titles listed in Exercise 7-1. On a form similar to the one that follows, indicate to which column on the work sheet the account balance will be extended. The first account has been completed as an example.

Account Title	Income Statement		Balance Sheet	
	Debit	Credit	Debit	Credit
Store Equipment			✔	

Exercise 7-3   Calculating Net Income or Net Loss

The totals of the Income Statement debit and credit columns of several different work sheets are listed below. Calculate the amount of the net income or net loss for each set of work sheet amounts.

	Income Statement	
	Debit	Credit
1.	$2,342.00	$1,814.00
2.	914.00	1,173.00
3.	1,795.00	1,424.00
4.	6,933.00	8,256.00
5.	9,125.00	7,258.00
6.	1,182.00	2,089.00

Problem 7-1   Preparing a Six-Column Work Sheet

The final balances in the ledger accounts of the Snowbird Playhouse for the fiscal period ended September 30 appear on page 144.

		Debit Balances	Credit Balances
101	Cash in Bank	$7,469.00	
105	Stage Equipment	8,396.00	
110	Concession Equipment	5,340.00	
205	Accounts Payable—Atlas, Inc.		$ 1,920.00
210	Accounts Payable—King Co.		834.00
301	Sue Wellen, Capital		13,760.00
305	Sue Wellen, Withdrawals	1,200.00	
310	Income Summary		
401	Ticket Revenue		17,663.00
501	Advertising Expense	3,405.00	
505	Maintenance Expense	1,483.00	
510	Rent Expense	4,500.00	
515	Utilities Expense	2,384.00	

Instructions: Using the preceding account titles and balances, prepare a work sheet for the month ended September 30.

(1) Write the heading on the work sheet.

(2) List all of the account numbers, account titles, and each account balance in the Trial Balance section.

(3) Total and rule the Trial Balance section. (Remember, the two totals must equal before you can continue the work sheet.)

(4) Extend the amounts to the Balance Sheet section.

(5) Extend the amounts to the Income Statement section.

(6) Total the amount columns in the Income Statement and Balance Sheet sections.

(7) Enter the amount of net income or net loss in the appropriate columns in the Income Statement and Balance Sheet sections.

(8) Total and rule the Income Statement and Balance Sheet sections.

Problem 7-2   Preparing a Six-Column Work Sheet

The ledger for the Four Star Travel Center shows the following account balances on June 30, the end of the fiscal period.

101	Cash in Bank	$10,589.00
105	Accounts Receivable—Frank Perkins	476.00
110	Accounts Receivable—Judy Mudre	385.00
115	Office Equipment	15,395.00
120	Computer Equipment	7,459.00
125	Office Furniture	2,486.00
201	Accounts Payable—Turner Co.	4,396.00
205	Accounts Payable—Spencer Corp.	2,840.00
210	Accounts Payable—LKH Co.	1,036.00
301	Karen Hart, Capital	27,500.00
305	Karen Hart, Withdrawals	2,500.00
310	Income Summary	
401	Commissions Revenue	14,957.00
501	Advertising Expense	3,940.00
505	Entertainment Expense	1,836.00
510	Miscellaneous Expense	924.00
515	Rent Expense	3,500.00
520	Utilities Expense	1,239.00

Instructions: Using the preceding account numbers, account titles, and balances, prepare a work sheet for the Four Star Travel Center. The Center operates on a three-month fiscal period.

Problem 7-3 Preparing a Six-Column Work Sheet

The final balances in the ledger of the Tower Movie Theatre at the end of November are as follows.

101	Cash in Bank	$13,394.50
105	Accounts Receivable—Kline, Inc.	357.00
110	Concession Equipment	9,305.75
115	Projection Equipment	4,395.00
120	Office Equipment	5,497.58
125	Office Furniture	1,385.70
205	Accounts Payable—K & D Supply	3,945.65
210	Accounts Payable—Janson Co.	2,846.90
215	Accounts Payable—Top Movie, Inc.	1,923.00
301	Pat Morganstern, Capital	30,426.48
305	Pat Morganstern, Withdrawals	2,500.00
310	Income Summary	
401	Admissions Revenue	11,596.00
405	Concession Revenue	4,496.00
501	Advertising Expense	3,675.00
505	Maintenance Expense	2,658.55
510	Miscellaneous Expense	864.59
515	Rent Expense	7,500.00
520	Telephone Expense	753.96
525	Utilities Expense	2,946.40

Instructions: Prepare a work sheet for the month ended November 30 for the Tower Movie Theatre.

Problem 7-4 Locating and Correcting Work Sheet Errors

A-1 Computer Repair Co.'s work sheet for the month ended September 30 appears in the working papers. The Trial Balance section of the work sheet has been completed, and the total debits and total credits are equal. The amounts have also been extended to the Balance Sheet and Income Statement sections. Unfortunately, as the amounts were extended, several errors were made.

Instructions:

(1) Locate and correct all errors in the Income Statement and Balance Sheet sections. Cross out incorrect amounts and write the correct amount above the crossed-out amount or in the correct column.

(2) Complete the work sheet and determine the net income or net loss for the month.

Problem 7-5 Completing the Work Sheet

The work sheet for Matt's Cleaning Service appears on page 146. Several amounts have been deleted from various columns.

Instructions: Calculate all missing amounts and complete the work sheet.

Matt's Cleaning Service
Work Sheet
For the Month Ended March 31, 19--

ACCT. NO.	ACCOUNT NAME	TRIAL BALANCE DEBIT	TRIAL BALANCE CREDIT	INCOME STATEMENT DEBIT	INCOME STATEMENT CREDIT	BALANCE SHEET DEBIT	BALANCE SHEET CREDIT	
101	Cash in Bank	1486240				1486240		1
105	Accts. Rec.-Lynn Tarok	271491				271491		2
110	Accts. Rec.-Jeffrey Holden					160400		3
115	Office Furniture	988140						4
120	Office Equipment					301745		5
125	Computer Equipment							6
130	Delivery Equipment					914650		7
201	Accts. Pay.- Peterson Supply		601319				601319	8
205	Accts. Pay.- Atlas Co.							9
210	Accts. Pay.- New Mark, Inc.		568309				568309	10
301	Jason Stone, Capital						3245000	11
305	Jason Stone, Withdrawals	200000						12
310	Income Summary	—	—	—	—			13
401	Commissions Revenue		1431980		1431980			14
501	Advertising Expense	360500		360500				15
505	Entertainment Expense			39491				16
510	Maintenance Expense			183140				17
515	Miscellaneous Expense	43265						18
520	Rent Expense			500000				19
525	Utilities Expense	21324		21324				20
								21
	Net Income			284260				22
							5108145	23

Computers

Proper planning may mean the difference between continuing operations or going out of business if a disaster strikes.

Planning for Disasters

Sarah was feeling proud of herself. After weeks of entering accounting data into her company's computer, she expected to reach the end of her project by the end of the day. As she was opening up the document for the final data entry, she accidentally wiped out everything. And there were no backup disks. Disaster #1: Data Loss.

Greg, bookkeeper for *The Good Earth Gardeners,* got a promotion—to another company. No one else knew the system. Disaster #2: Personnel Loss.

Carlos's restaurant on the Florida Keys managed to bear the brunt of the hurricane. The building was still standing, but it was standing in several feet of water. The computer was inoperable and inaccessible. Disaster #3: Site Loss.

In the age of computer data management, companies need to ask themselves these questions: Have we assessed the short-term and long-term effects of data or computer loss? Do we have contingency plans? Is the plan in writing and has it been communicated to all who share the system?

For starters, here are some guidelines for disaster planning:

- Install computer locks and passwords.
- Always make backup disks of important data. How often data is saved should be measured by how much the company can afford to lose.
- Keep a fireproof safe on the premises or elsewhere for storing backup records.
- Appoint a security administrator who's responsible for communicating risks and alternative procedures, and reviewing them regularly with users.
- Keep an inventory of all hardware and software—and a list of suppliers that can supply and install compatible systems quickly. Establish alternative sites.
- Use surge protectors to safeguard against sudden electrical surges.
- Train personnel in order to minimize software errors.

Whether the computer disaster results from a fire or flood, theft, vandalism, power failure, or employee absenteeism, a company needs to plan for the worse case—because according to Murphy's Law, "If anything can go wrong, it will."

Preparing Financial Statements for a Sole Proprietorship

At the end of a fiscal period, financial reports are prepared to show the effects of business transactions for the period. In Chapter 7, you learned how to prepare a work sheet to summarize the financial information needed to prepare the financial reports. In this chapter, you will learn how to prepare those reports: namely, the income statement, the statement of changes in owner's equity, and the balance sheet.

Financial reports are prepared to give the business owner information on how successfully the business is operating. By comparing current financial reports with those from previous fiscal periods, the owner can make more informed decisions about how to run the business.

 LEARNING OBJECTIVES

When you have completed this chapter, you should be able to

1. Explain the purpose of the income statement.
2. Prepare an income statement.
3. Explain the purpose of the statement of changes in owner's equity.
4. Prepare a statement of changes in owner's equity.
5. Explain the purpose of a balance sheet.
6. Prepare a balance sheet in report form.
7. Define the accounting terms new to this chapter.

NEW Terms

financial statements • income statement • statement of changes in owner's equity • balance sheet • report form

The Seventh Step of the Accounting Cycle

To operate a business profitably, a business owner needs to have up-to-date financial information. Financial statements are prepared to provide such information. **Financial statements** are reports prepared to summarize the changes resulting from business transactions that have occurred during a fiscal period. As you can see from Figure 8-1, the preparation of financial statements is the seventh step in the accounting cycle. By analyzing these statements, a business owner can tell whether the business is on course, experiencing some difficulty, or headed for serious trouble.

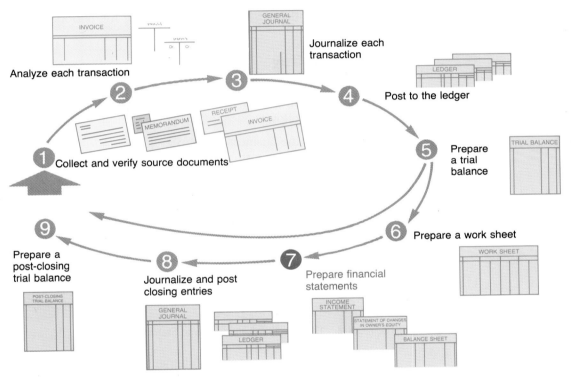

Figure 8-1   The Accounting Cycle, with Step 7 Highlighted

Comparing information shown on the financial statements for different fiscal periods helps owners spot trends that indicate the "health" of a business. Are total assets or total liabilities increasing or decreasing? Is owner's equity increasing or decreasing? Is net income increasing or decreasing? If there is a net loss, is it a one-time occurrence or has it been going on for some time? If owner's equity and net income have decreased, or if the business has shown a net loss, an owner must find out the cause and try to correct the problem. Any business that shows losses over several reporting periods is in trouble, often severe trouble.

The primary financial statements prepared for a sole proprietorship are the income statement and the balance sheet. A third statement, the statement of changes in owner's equity, is also often prepared. Let's look now at how these reports are prepared and the information that is shown on each of them.

The Income Statement

The **income statement** reports the net income or net loss for the fiscal period it covers. As you recall from Chapter 7, net income or net loss is the difference between total revenue and total expenses. The main purpose of the income statement is to provide a report of the revenue earned and the expenses incurred over a specific period of time. For this reason, it is sometimes called a "profit-and-loss statement" or an "earnings statement."

The income statement may be handwritten, typed, or prepared on a computer. Since it is a formal report, the income statement is prepared in ink if it is done by hand. The income statement contains the following sections: (1) the heading, (2) the revenue for the period, (3) the expenses for the period, and (4) the net income or net loss for the period.

The Heading

Like the work sheet heading, the heading of an income statement has three parts, which answer the questions who? what? when? The parts of the heading are as follows:

1. the name of the business (who?)
2. the name of the report (what?)
3. the period covered (when?)

The heading for Global Travel Agency's income statement is shown in Figure 8-2. Notice that each line of the heading is centered on the stationery.

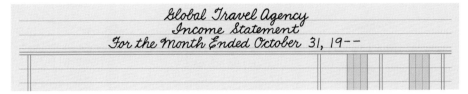

Figure 8-2 The Heading for an Income Statement

When preparing an income statement, be sure to follow the wording, capitalization, and punctuation shown in Figure 8-2. The wording of the date line is especially important. The reporting period on the income statement must be clearly identified. The reporting period covered by the income statement is the entire fiscal period. The net income (or loss) reported on the income statement is the profit (or loss) for the entire fiscal period.

The wording of the date line will vary from business to business. For Global Travel, the reporting period is one month. The heading therefore reads "For the Month Ended October 31, 19—." For a three-month period, the heading would read "For the Quarter Ended March 31, 19—." The date line for an income statement covering a full year would read "For the Year Ended June 30, 19—."

A business must be consistent in the fiscal period it uses as the basis for its financial reports. Owners want to be able to compare the data on financial statements from one fiscal period to the next. This is difficult to do if one statement covers a period of, say, one month while another covers a period of six months.

Owners use the information on financial statements to help them make more informed business decisions.

The Revenue Section

After the heading has been completed, the revenue earned for the period is entered on the income statement. This information is taken from the Income Statement section of the work sheet. Look at the income statement for Global Travel Agency shown in Figure 8-3 on page 152. The Income Statement section of the work sheet has been included to show you the source of the information used in preparing the income statement.

The income statement for Global Travel Agency is prepared on standard accounting stationery having a column for account titles and two amount columns. The two amount columns, however, are *not* used for debit and credit entries. Rather, they are used to separate individual account balances from totals. The first amount column is used to enter the balances of the individual revenue and expense accounts. The second amount column is used to enter totals: total revenue, total expenses, and net income (or net loss).

Refer to Figure 8-3 as you read the procedures for preparing an income statement.

1. Write the classification "Revenue:" on the first line at the left side of the form.   A
2. Enter the titles of the accounts classified as revenue accounts. Enter the account titles beginning on the second line, indented about a half inch from the left edge of the column.   B
3. Enter the balance of the revenue account(s)—in this case, the balance of the Fees account. Since Global Travel has only one revenue account, total revenue is the same as the balance of the one revenue account. The balance is thus written in the second, or totals, column.   C

Global Travel Agency
Work Sheet
For the Month Ended October 31, 19--

	ACCT. NO.	ACCOUNT NAME	TRIAL BALANCE DEBIT	TRIAL BALANCE CREDIT	INCOME STATEMENT DEBIT	INCOME STATEMENT CREDIT	BALANCE SHEET DEBIT	BALANCE SHEET CREDIT	
1	101	Cash in Bank	16 125 00				16 125 00		1
2	105	Accts. Rec. – Burton Co.	450 00				450 00		2
3	110	Accts. Rec. – Greer's Market							3
4	120	Computer Equipment	8 000 00				8 000 00		4
5	130	Office Equipment	1 500 00				1 500 00		5
6	201	Accts. Pay. – City News		75 00				75 00	6
7	205	Accts. Pay. – Mod. Off. Supp.		750 00				750 00	7
8	301	Jan Harter, Capital		25 200 00				25 200 00	8
9	305	Jan Harter, Withdrawals	400 00				400 00		9
10	310	Income Summary							10
11	401	Fees		1 650 00		1 650 00			11
12	501	Advertising Expense	75 00		75 00				12
13	510	Maintenance Expense	450 00		450 00				13
14	520	Rent Expense	550 00		550 00				14
15	530	Utilities Expense	125 00		125 00				15
16			27 675 00	27 675 00	1 200 00	1 650 00	26 475 00	26 025 00	16
17		Net Income			450 00			450 00	17
18					1 650 00	1 650 00	26 475 00	26 475 00	18

Global Travel Agency
Income Statement
For the Month Ended October 31, 19--

Revenue: A			
B Fees		1 650 00	← C
Expenses: D			
Advertising Expense	75 00		
E Maintenance Expense	450 00		
Rent Expense	550 00		
Utilities Expense	F 125 00		
Total Expenses G		H 1 200 00	I
Net Income K		J 450 00	L

Figure 8-3 Preparing an Income Statement

Global Travel uses only one revenue account, Fees. Many businesses, however, have more than one revenue account, with a separate account for each different source of revenue. For example, a tennis club might have such revenue accounts as Membership Fees, Court Rental Fees, and Instruction Fees.

If a business has more than one revenue account, the individual account balances are entered in the first amount column. The total revenue is then written on a separate line in the second amount column. Figure 8-4 illustrates the revenue section for a business that has more than one revenue account. Notice that the words "Total Revenue" are indented about one inch from the left edge of the form.

R E M E M B E R

The information needed to prepare the income statement is taken from the Income Statement section of the work sheet.

Revenue:		
Membership Fees	1000000	
Service Fees	350000	
Total Revenue		1350000

Figure 8-4 Income Statement with More Than One Revenue Account

The Expenses Section

After total revenue has been entered, the expenses incurred during the period must be reported. The expense account titles and the balances shown in the Income Statement section of the work sheet are used to prepare this section of the income statement. The listing of expenses on the income statement is shown in Figure 8-3. Refer to this illustration as you read the instructions that follow.

1. On the line following the entry for total revenue, write the classification "Expenses:" at the left side of the form.   **D**
2. Write the titles of the expense accounts, indented half an inch, in the order they appear on the work sheet. Since there are several expense accounts, enter the individual balances in the first amount column.   **E**
3. Draw a single rule under the last expense account balance.   **F**
4. Write the words "Total Expenses" on the line following the last expense account title, indented about one inch.   **G**
5. Add the balances for all the expense accounts. Write the total expense amount in the second amount column, one line below the last expense account balance.   **H**

The Net Income Section

After the amount of total expenses has been entered in the second amount column, the net income is entered. A net income, remember, occurs when total revenue is greater than total expenses.

1. Draw a single rule under the total expenses amount.   **I**
2. Subtract the total expenses from the total revenue to find net income. Enter the amount of the net income in the second amount column under total expenses.   **J**
3. On the same line in the wide column, write the words "Net Income" at the left edge of the form.   **K**
4. If the amount of net income matches the amount shown on the work sheet, draw a double rule under the net income amount.   **L**   The income statement is now complete.

If the amount of net income shown on the work sheet and the amount shown on the income statement do not agree, an error has been made. Since the work sheet has been balanced and ruled, it is safe to assume that the error has occurred while preparing the income statement. An account balance may have been omitted or entered on the income statement incorrectly, or an error in addition or subtraction may have been made. The error must be found and corrected before the income statement can be completed (double ruled).

ACCOUNTING
Tips

To lessen the chance of error, write all numbers clearly. Be especially careful with numbers that look alike. For example, do not write 4's that look like 9's or 3's that look like 8's.

Showing a Net Loss

If the total expenses are greater than the total revenue for the period, the result is a net loss. To determine the amount of net loss, subtract total revenue from total expenses. Enter the amount in the second amount column under total expenses. Write the words "Net Loss" on the same line at the left edge of the form. An illustration of how to report a net loss is shown in Figure 8-5.

Revenue:		
Fees		2765 00
Expenses:		
Advertising Expense	750 00	
Maintenance Expense	295 00	
Miscellaneous Expense	164 00	
Rent Expense	1400 00	
Utilities Expense	393 00	
Total Expenses		3002 00
Net Loss		237 00

Figure 8-5 Income Statement Showing a Net Loss

R — E — M — E — M — B — E — R

The net income or net loss amount reported on the income statement must match the amount calculated on the work sheet.

Before reading about the statement of changes in owner's equity, complete the following activity to check your understanding of the income statement.

Check Your Learning

Answer the following questions about the income statement. Write your answers on notebook paper.

1. What are the three "W" questions answered by the heading of the income statement?
2. What is the date line for an income statement prepared for the three months of April, May, and June?
3. The first amount column on the income statement is used to report ____?____ . The second amount column on the income statement is used to report ____?____ .
4. If expenses for a period are $19,351 and revenue is $19,587, does the business have a net income or a net loss? What is the amount of net income or net loss?

Compare your answers to those in the answers section. Re-read the preceding part of the chapter to find the correct answers to any questions you may have missed.

The Statement of Changes in Owner's Equity

One of the most important things an owner wants to know is whether her or his equity in the business has increased or decreased during the fiscal period. Increases in owner's equity mean *increases* in assets, which in turn means the business has grown. Decreases in owner's equity mean *decreases* in assets and in turn a reduction in the size of the business.

During the period, transactions involving investments by the owner are recorded in the capital account. However, transactions affecting revenue, expenses, and withdrawals are recorded in separate accounts. At the end of the period, a financial statement is prepared to summarize the effects on the capital account of the various business transactions that occurred during the period. This statement is called the **statement of changes in owner's equity.**

The statement of changes in owner's equity is completed as a supporting document for the balance sheet. The information needed to prepare this statement is found in three places: the work sheet, the income statement, and the capital account in the general ledger. Look at Figure 8-6 below to see the statement of changes in owner's equity prepared by Global Travel Agency for the month ended October 31.

Global Travel Agency				
Statement of Changes in Owner's Equity				
For the Month Ended October 31, 19--				
Beginning Capital, October 1, 19-- A			B —
Add: Investment	D	2520000	
Net Income	E	45000	
Total Increase in Capital			F 2565000
Subtotal			G 2565000
Less: Withdrawals			H 40000
Ending Capital, October 31, 19-- I			J 2525000

Figure 8-6 Statement of Changes in Owner's Equity

The statement shows the changes in capital from the beginning of the fiscal period through the end of the period. As a result, the heading of the statement is similar to that for the income statement.

Follow these steps to complete the statement of changes in owner's equity.

1. On the first line, write the words "Beginning Capital," followed by the first day of the fiscal period. For Global Travel, that date is October 1, 19—. **A**

2. In the second amount column, enter the balance of the capital account at the beginning of the fiscal period. The source of this information is the capital account in the general ledger. Since Global Travel began operations during this fiscal period, there is no beginning capital balance. Enter a dash in the second amount column. **B**

3. Next, enter the *increases* to the capital account, namely, investments by the owner and net income. First, write the word "Add:" at the left side of the form. **C**

The first addition would be any investments by the owner during the period. This information is found in the capital account in the general ledger. Jan Harter, the owner of Global Travel, invested a total of $25,200 in the business in the month of October. Write "Investment" following the word "Add." Enter the amount of the investment in the first amount column.   **D**

On the next line, write the words "Net Income." Enter the amount of the net income—taken from the income statement—in the first amount column. Draw a single rule under the investment and net income amounts.   **E**

4. Write the words "Total Increase in Capital" on the next line at the left edge of the form. Add the total investments and net income amounts and enter the total in the second amount column. Then draw a single rule under the amount.   **F**

5. Write "Subtotal" on the next line, at the left edge of the form. Add the amounts for beginning capital and total increase in capital. Enter the total in the second amount column.   **G**   Since Global Travel did not have a beginning capital balance, this amount is the same as the total increase in capital amount.

6. The next section of the statement lists the *decreases* to the capital account: withdrawals and net loss. Since Global Travel did not have a net loss for the period, write the words "Less: Withdrawals" at the left edge of the account title column. Enter the amount of withdrawals for the period (taken from the work sheet) in the second amount column. Then draw a single rule under the amount.   **H**

7. On the next line, write the words "Ending Capital," followed by the last day of the fiscal period.   **I**

8. Subtract the withdrawals amount from the subtotal to determine the new, ending balance of the capital account. Finally, draw a double rule below the ending capital amount.   **J**

The statement of changes in owner's equity is now complete. The ending capital balance determined on this statement will be used in preparing the balance sheet.

A statement of changes in owner's equity for an ongoing business that had a net loss for the period is shown in Figure 8-7. Notice that the investment by the owner increases the capital account, while the withdrawals and net loss decrease the capital account.

Beginning Capital, May 1, 19--			46 300 00
Add: Investment			1 000 00
Subtotal			47 300 00
Less: Withdrawals	2 100 00		
Net Loss	675 00		
Total Decrease in Capital			2 775 00
Ending Capital, May 31, 19--			44 525 00

Figure 8-7   Statement of Changes in Owner's Equity Showing a Net Loss

Before reading about the preparation of the balance sheet, complete the following activity to check your understanding of the statement of changes in owner's equity.

Check Your Learning

Answer the following questions about the statement of changes in owner's equity. Write your answers on notebook paper.

1. The statement of changes in owner's equity is prepared to reflect the changes in the ___?___ from the beginning of the period to the end.
2. The wording in the date line for the statement of changes in owner's equity is the same as that used for the ___?___ .
3. If the owner invested $20,000 during the period covered by this statement, and net income was $3,200, the ending balance in the capital account is ___?___ .
4. The information on the statement of changes in owner's equity is used in preparing the ___?___ .

Compare your answers to those in the answers section. Re-read the preceding part of the chapter to find the correct answers to any questions you may have missed.

The Balance Sheet

The **balance sheet** is a report of the final balances in all the asset, liability, and owner's equity accounts at the end of the fiscal period. These accounts, you'll remember, are the permanent accounts. The main purpose of the balance sheet is to provide a record of the business's assets and a summary of the claims (of both creditors and owners) against those assets *on a specific date*. In other words, the balance sheet states the financial position of a business at a specific point in time. It pinpoints what a business owns, owes, and is worth. For this reason, the balance sheet is sometimes called a "position statement."

Like the income statement and the statement of changes in owner's equity, the balance sheet may be handwritten, typed, or prepared by computer. A handwritten balance sheet is prepared in ink since it is a formal record.

The balance sheet prepared by Global Travel Agency is prepared in report form. In **report form,** the classifications of balance sheet accounts are shown one under the other.

The balance sheet is prepared from the information in the Balance Sheet section of the work sheet and from the statement of changes in owner's equity. Let's look now at the sections of the balance sheet: (1) the heading, (2) the assets section, and (3) the liabilities and owner's equity sections.

The Heading

Like the heading of the income statement, the heading of the balance sheet answers the questions who? what? when? The heading includes:

1. the name of the business (who?)
2. the name of the financial statement (what?)
3. the date of the balance sheet (when?)

As you recall, the income statement reports the amount of net income (or net loss) for the complete fiscal period. Unlike the income statement, the balance sheet refers to only one day in the fiscal period, usually the last day. The amounts shown on the balance sheet are the balances in the accounts as of that day. Look at the headings in Figure 8-8 to see the difference between the date lines on the income statement and on the balance sheet.

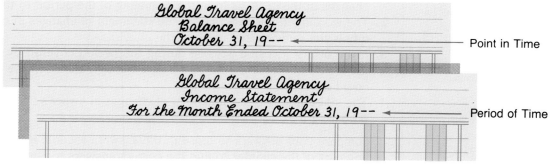

Figure 8-8 Headings of Financial Statements

The Assets Section

Refer to Figure 8-9 as you read the procedures for preparing the balance sheet. The work sheet and statement of changes in owner's equity have been included in the illustration to show the sources of the information used to prepare the balance sheet.

1. Write the word "Assets" in the center of the first line. **A**
2. Next, enter the asset account titles and their balances. The account titles and balances are listed on the balance sheet in the same order as they appear in the Balance Sheet section of the work sheet. Enter the individual account balances in the first amount column. Then draw a single rule under the last account balance. **B**
3. On the next line, write the words "Total Assets," indented about half an inch. Add the individual balances and enter the total assets amount in the second amount column. **C**

Do *not* draw a double rule under the total at this time. The double rule is not entered until the Liabilities and Owner's Equity sections have been completed and are shown to be equal to total assets.

The Liabilities and Owner's Equity Sections

The information for the Liabilities and Owner's Equity sections is taken from the work sheet *and* from the statement of changes in owner's equity. To complete these sections of the balance sheet, follow these steps.

1. Skip one line and then write the heading "Liabilities," centered. **D**
2. List the liability account titles and their balances, using the same order as they appear in the Balance Sheet section of the work sheet. Enter the account balances in the first amount column. Draw a single rule under the last account balance. **E**
3. On the next line, write the words "Total Liabilities," indented about half an inch. Total the individual balances and enter the total liabilities amount in the second amount column. **F**

4. Skip a line and write the heading "Owner's Equity," centering it on the line.   **G**
5. Write the title of the capital account and enter its balance in the second amount column. The balance is the amount of the ending balance shown on the statement of changes in owner's equity.   **H**

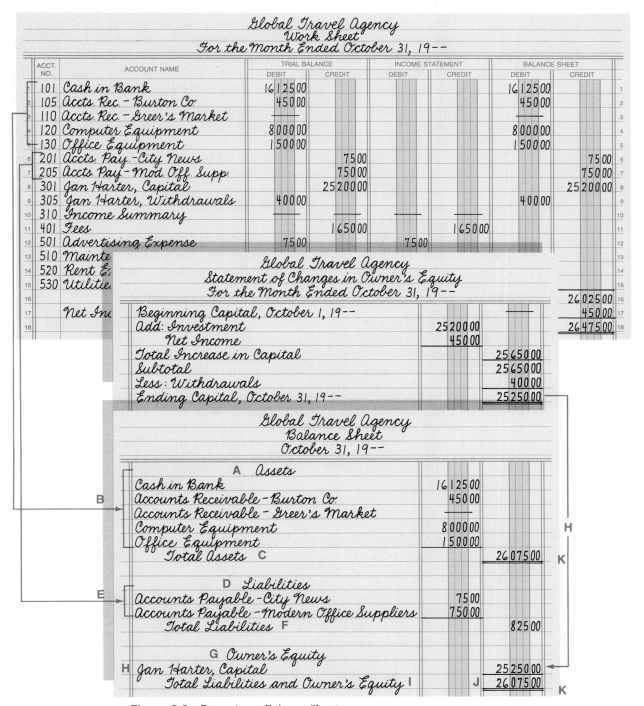

Figure 8-9   Preparing a Balance Sheet

Use the balance calculated on the statement of changes in owner's equity for the balance of the capital account on the balance sheet.

Proving the Equality of the Balance Sheet

You learned in earlier chapters that the basic accounting equation must always be in balance in a double-entry system of accounting. The balance sheet represents the basic accounting equation; thus the Assets section must balance the Liabilities and Owner's Equity sections. To prove the equality of the balance sheet, follow these procedures.

1. Draw a single rule under the balance of the capital account. Write the words "Total Liabilities and Owner's Equity," indented about half an inch, on the next line.   **I**

2. Add the total liabilities amount and the ending capital balance. Enter the total in the second amount column.   **J**   This total must agree with the total assets amount. If the totals are not equal, an error has been made— most likely in transferring amounts from the work sheet or from the statement of changes in owner's equity. Any errors must be found and corrected before the balance sheet can be completed.

3. If the totals are equal, draw a double rule under the total assets amount *and* under the total liabilities and owner's equity amount.   **K**   The balance sheet is now complete.

Check Your Learning

Answer the following questions about Figure 8-9 on notebook paper.

1. What is the wording used in the date line of the balance sheet?
2. What are the three sections of the balance sheet?
3. How are the accounts listed on the balance sheet?
4. What is the source of the balance reported for Jan Harter, Capital?

Compare your answers to those in the answers section.

Preparing Financial Statements on the Computer

As we mentioned earlier, financial statements may be handwritten, typewritten, or prepared using a computer. Regardless of how they are prepared, the information shown on the statements remains the same.

The balance sheet shown in Figure 8-10 is an example of a report prepared with a computer. In a computerized accounting system, the information for preparing financial statements is stored in the computer files. When financial reports are needed, it is not necessary to prepare a work sheet since all the information from business transactions is already stored in the

```
                    Global Travel Agency
                       Balance Sheet
                      October 31, 19--

                          Assets
Cash in Bank                          16125.00
Accts. Rec.--Burton Co.                 450.00
Accts. Rec.--Greer's Market               0.00
Computer Equipment                     8000.00
Office Equipment                       1500.00
                                      _____
     Total Assets                                 26075.00
                                                  =========


                        Liabilities
Accts. Pay.--City News                   75.00
Accts. Pay.--Modern Office Suppliers    750.00
                                      _____
     Total Liabilities                              825.00

                      Owner's Equity
Jan Harter. Capital                               25250.00
                                                 _____
     Total Liabilities and Owner's Equity         26075.00
                                                  =========
```

Figure 8-10 Balance Sheet
Prepared by Computer

computer. The computer operator simply gives a command indicating the
reports needed. The computer calculates the net income or net loss and ad-
justs the capital account to correctly report any changes that have occurred
during the period. Obviously, the information in the computer files must be
kept up to date through regular journal entries or the reports generated
from that information will not be accurate.

SUMMARY OF KEY POINTS

1. The preparation of financial reports is the seventh step in the accounting
    cycle. The primary reports are the income statement and the balance
    sheet. The statement of changes in owner's equity is also often prepared.
2. The income statement reports the net income or net loss for the period.
    Net income or net loss is the difference between total revenue and total
    expenses over a specific period of time.
3. The statement of changes in owner's equity summarizes the effects of the
    period's business transactions on the capital account.
4. The balance sheet reports the final balances of asset, liability, and
    owner's equity accounts at the end of the fiscal period.
5. The work sheet is the source of information for preparing the income
    statement. The statement of changes in owner's equity is prepared from
    the work sheet, the income statement, and the capital account in the
    general ledger. The balance sheet is prepared from the work sheet and
    the statement of changes in owner's equity.
6. Financial reports may be handwritten on accounting stationery, typewrit-
    ten, or prepared using a computer. If prepared by hand, the reports are
    written in ink.

REVIEW AND APPLICATIONS

Building Your Accounting Vocabulary

In your own words, write the definition of each of the following accounting terms. Use complete sentences for your definitions.

balance sheet

financial statements

income statement

report form

statement of changes in owner's equity

Reviewing Your Accounting Knowledge

1. Why are financial statements prepared?
2. What is the purpose of the income statement?
3. What other names can be given to an income statement?
4. Why does a business need to be consistent in the fiscal period it uses as the basis for its financial reports?
5. What is the source of information used to prepare the income statement?
6. What is the purpose of the statement of changes in owner's equity?
7. What are the sources of information used to prepare the statement of changes in owner's equity?
8. What is the purpose of the balance sheet?
9. What are the sources of the information needed to prepare the balance sheet?
10. How does the date in the heading of a balance sheet differ from the date in the heading of an income statement and a statement of changes in owner's equity?
11. Which financial statement represents the basic accounting equation?

Improving Your Decision-Making Skills

Anna Choi is the accounting clerk for George Damaris, owner of Colonial Bakery. For several months, Anna has tried to convince George to install a computer. Anna believes that a computer would save time, especially when financial statements are being prepared. She has explained to George that all of the information for preparing financial statements can be stored in the computer files. Then, when the financial statements are needed, it is not necessary to prepare a work sheet. George believes that a computer will cost too much money. He also believes that if just one mistake is made in entering an amount, the financial statements will not provide a true picture of the business. What would you say to convince George that a computer should be installed for use in the business?

Applying Accounting Procedures

Exercise 8-1 Reporting Accounts on Financial Statements

The following list contains some of the account titles from the general ledger of the Winter Theater.

Accounts Payable—Boyden Company	Clem Winter, Capital
Accounts Payable—Gail's Supplies	Clem Winter, Withdrawals
Accounts Receivable—Clinton Co.	Concession Revenue
Accounts Receivable—King Company	Miscellaneous Expense
Admissions Revenue	Office Furniture
Advertising Expense	Projection Equipment
Cash in Bank	Rent Expense

Instructions: Use a form similar to the one that follows. For each account listed,

(1) Write the classification of the account.

(2) Use a check mark to indicate whether the account balance will be entered in the Trial Balance debit or credit column of the work sheet.

(3) Use a check mark to indicate on which financial statement (income statement or balance sheet) the account will appear. The first account is shown as an example.

| Account Title | Account Classification | Trial Balance | | Financial Statements | |
		Debit	Credit	Income Statement	Balance Sheet
Accounts Payable— Boyden Co.	Liability		✔		✔

Exercise 8-2 Determining Ending Capital Amounts

The financial data affecting the capital accounts for several different businesses is summarized below.

Instructions: Use the form in your working papers or plain paper. Determine the ending capital balance for each business.

	Beginning Capital	Investments	Revenue	Expenses	Withdrawals
1.	$40,000	$ 500	$ 5,800	$3,400	$ 600
2.	24,075	0	14,980	6,240	900
3.	19,800	1,000	6,450	6,980	0
4.	0	26,410	5,920	4,790	200
5.	6,415	0	4,420	3,975	800
6.	20,870	1,200	12,980	9,240	1,200

Problem 8-1 Preparing an Income Statement

The work sheet for Matira's Delivery Service for the month ended April 30, 19—, appears on page 164.

Instructions: Using the work sheet, prepare an income statement for Matira's Delivery Service.

Problem 8-2 Preparing a Statement of Changes in Owner's Equity

Instructions: Using the work sheet for Matira's Delivery Service and the income statement prepared in Problem 8-1, prepare a statement of changes in owner's equity. Pat Matira made an additional investment in the business of $500 during the period.

ACCT. NO.	ACCOUNT NAME	TRIAL BALANCE DEBIT	TRIAL BALANCE CREDIT	INCOME STATEMENT DEBIT	INCOME STATEMENT CREDIT	BALANCE SHEET DEBIT	BALANCE SHEET CREDIT	
101	Cash in Bank	5391 00				5391 00		1
104	Accts. Rec. - J. Lincoln	423 00				423 00		2
106	Accts. Rec. - A. Jones	914 00				914 00		3
110	Office Equipment	2806 00				2806 00		4
115	Computer Equipment	6482 00				6482 00		5
120	Delivery Equipment	12361 00				12361 00		6
205	Accts. Pay. - Modern Supp.		4618 00				4618 00	7
210	Accts. Pay. - A + L Forms		2394 00				2394 00	8
301	Pat Matira, Capital		19589 00				19589 00	9
302	Pat Matira, Withdrawals	1500 00				1500 00		10
303	Income Summary	—	—	—	—			11
401	Delivery Fees		9309 00		9309 00			12
501	Advertising Expense	1852 00		1852 00				13
505	Delivery Expense	931 00		931 00				14
510	Miscellaneous Expense	246 00		246 00				15
515	Rent Expense	2400 00		2400 00				16
520	Utility Expense	604 00		604 00				17
		35910 00	35910 00	6033 00	9309 00	29877 00	26601 00	18
	Net Income			3276 00			3276 00	19
				9309 00	9309 00	29877 00	29877 00	20

Problem 8-3   Preparing a Balance Sheet

Instructions: Using the work sheet for Matira's Delivery Service and the statement of changes in owner's equity prepared in Problem 8-2, prepare a balance sheet in report form.

Problem 8-4   Preparing Financial Statements

The trial balance for the Joker Amusement Center has been prepared. It is included on the work sheet in the working papers accompanying this textbook.

Instructions:

(1) Complete the work sheet.
(2) Prepare an income statement for the quarter ended March 31.
(3) Prepare a statement of changes in owner's equity. Ken Graf made no additional investments during the period.
(4) Prepare a balance sheet in report form.

Problem 8-5   Preparing Financial Statements

The general ledger accounts for Jenkins Caterers follow. The balance in each account at the end of the fiscal period is also given.

101	Cash in Bank	$ 3,956
110	Accounts Receivable—Brian Doonan	1,328
114	Accounts Receivable—Fran Ullman	1,204
120	Catering Supplies	1,968
125	Office Equipment	10,957
130	Delivery Equipment	8,396

210	Accounts Payable — Adams Supply	3,976
215	Accounts Payable — Graham Co.	2,946
220	Accounts Payable — King Supply	1,285
301	Judy Jenkins, Capital	22,336
302	Judy Jenkins, Withdrawals	1,900
303	Income Summary	
401	Catering Revenue	4,989
403	Party Revenue	1,420
505	Advertising Expense	934
510	Delivery Expense	803
520	Maintenance Expense	1,483
525	Miscellaneous Expense	748
530	Rent Expense	1,850
535	Repair Expense	589
540	Utility Expense	836

Instructions:

(1) Prepare a work sheet for the month ended October 31.

(2) Prepare an income statement for the period.

(3) Prepare a statement of changes in owner's equity. Judy Jenkins made an additional investment of $1,000 during the period.

(4) Prepare a balance sheet.

Problem 8-6   Preparing a Statement of Changes in Owner's Equity

You are the accounting clerk at the Raintree Company. The financial statements for the month of November have already been prepared. Unfortunately, the statement of changes in owner's equity was damaged when someone accidentally spilled a cup of coffee. Mary Fienwald, the accountant, has asked you to reconstruct that statement. Ms. Fienwald reminded you that the owner, Tyler Best, made an additional investment of $4,000 and withdrew $1,500 during the period.

Instructions: Use the balance sheet and income statement shown below and on page 166 to prepare a new statement of changes in owner's equity.

Raintree Company
Balance Sheet
November 30, 19--

Assets		
Cash in Bank	8 297 00	
Accounts Receivable – Lester Maltese	693 00	
Accounts Receivable – Brian Cropp	478 00	
Store Equipment	16 204 00	
Video Equipment	24 869 00	
Total Assets		50 541 00
Liabilities		
Accounts Payable – C & L Amusements	4 013 00	
Accounts Payable – Gotham Company	3 192 00	
Total Liabilities		7 205 00
Owner's Equity		
Tyler Best, Capital		43 336 00
Total Liabilities and Owner's Equity		50 541 00

Raintree Company
Income Statement
For the Month Ended November 30, 19--

Revenue:			
Concession Revenue	1930 00		
Game Revenue	8295 00		
Total Revenue		10225 00	
Expenses:			
Advertising Expense	1854 00		
Miscellaneous Expense	831 00		
Rent Expense	2350 00		
Utility Expense	752 00		
Total Expenses		5787 00	
Net Income		4438 00	

Problem 8-7   Interpreting Financial Information

You are applying for a job with Foran Tree Service. The job includes preparing financial statements. In order to determine your ability to do the job, the owner, Carl Foran, has given you the following information.

At the beginning of the last fiscal period, the account Carl Foran, Capital had a balance of $46,105. At the end of the period, the account showed a balance of $49,386. During the period, Mr. Foran made an additional investment of $2,000 and had withdrawals of $500. The revenue for the period was $13,248.

Instructions: Use the stationery provided in the workbook or plain paper. Based on the information just given, determine the total expenses for the period.

The microprocessor in this man's camera controls shutter speed, flash, and film advancement.

Invisible Computers

Fifty years ago, the word *computer* referred, not to a machine, but to a person who did calculating for a living. Just a quarter of a century ago, there were very few people who had actually seen a computer "face to face." That was the era of the large mainframe computers that were kept in huge, air-conditioned rooms and run by teams of data-processing scribes.

Today, computers are everywhere. They're versatile and often so discreet that we don't even know they're there. Small *embedded microprocessor chips* can be programmed to control functions in a range of everyday items. Here are just a few examples.

- Thermostats are programmed to control the daytime and nighttime temperatures in your home.
- Video cassette recorders can tape one program while you're watching a different program or even while you're away.
- Telephone answering machines can be programmed to answer the phone, take messages, and play back all the calls when you return.
- Lifesaving pacemakers regulate a person's heartbeat.
- Wristwatches can be programmed to wake you, time a morning jog, or check your pulse rate.
- Electronic exercise cycles record time, speed, and distance of exercise intervals.
- Microprocessors in cars adjust the fuel flow, provide safe braking, and display information on the dashboard about how the car is operating.
- Television sets contain microprocessors to control channel selection.
- Security systems with delicate sensors detect intruders and alert the local police station.
- And to raise consumer awareness of the national economy, one entrepreneur has created a desktop calculator that displays the time, date, and—at the push of a button—the national debt, programmed to rise $8,000 a second from an October 1, 1987, base of $2.35 trillion.

Check any direct-mail catalogue or department store and witness the booming field of computer-driven small appliances. Who knows what someone will think of next!

Completing the Accounting Cycle for a Sole Proprietorship

In Chapter 8, you learned how to prepare the end-of-period financial statements for a sole proprietorship service business. The income statement reports the business's revenue, expenses, and net income or net loss for a fiscal period. The statement of changes in owner's equity summarizes the effects of the business transactions for the period on the owner's capital account. The balance sheet reports the financial position of the business as of the end of the fiscal period.

In this chapter, you will complete the accounting cycle for Global Travel Agency. The accounting cycle is completed by journalizing the closing entries and preparing a post-closing trial balance.

 LEARNING OBJECTIVES

When you have completed this chapter, you should be able to

1. Explain why the temporary capital accounts are closed at the end of the fiscal period.
2. Explain the purpose of the Income Summary account.
3. Explain the relationship between the Income Summary account and the capital account.
4. Analyze and journalize closing entries.
5. Post closing entries to accounts in the general ledger.
6. Prepare a post-closing trial balance.
7. Define the accounting terms new to this chapter.

NEW Terms

closing entries • post-closing trial balance • Income Summary account • compound entry

The Eighth and Ninth Steps in the Accounting Cycle

During a fiscal period, the temporary capital accounts are used to record transactions involving revenue, expenses, and withdrawals. At the end of the period, the balances in these accounts are transferred to the capital account to summarize the changes in owner's equity and to bring that account up to date.

The balances in the temporary capital accounts are transferred by recording a series of closing entries. **Closing entries** are journal entries made to close out, or reduce to zero, the balances in the temporary capital accounts and to transfer the net income or net loss for the period to the capital account.

After the closing entries have been journalized and posted, a trial balance is prepared to prove the equality of the general ledger after the closing process. The trial balance prepared after closing is called a **post-closing trial balance.** As you can see in Figure 9-1, the closing process and the post-closing trial balance complete the accounting cycle.

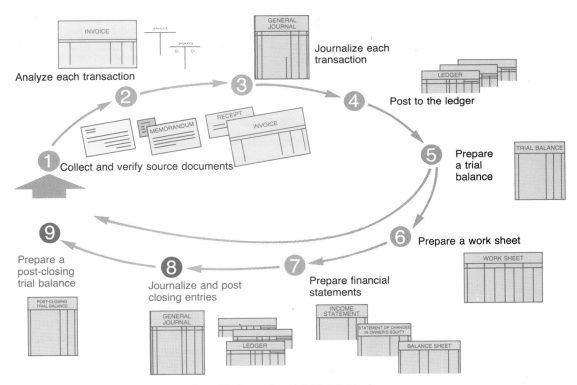

Figure 9-1   The Accounting Cycle, with Steps 8 and 9 Highlighted

The Closing Process

Preparing financial records for the start of another fiscal period is a little like keeping the records for a basketball team. Although individual and team scores are kept and tallied at the end of every game, each new game starts with a score of zero. Similarly, although entries are recorded in the accounts during the fiscal period, the temporary capital accounts start each new fiscal period with zero balances.

In Chapter 8, you learned how to prepare an income statement. The income statement, you'll remember, reports the net income or net loss for *one accounting period.* The statement is prepared from information recorded and accumulated in the revenue and expense accounts. At the end of the period, then, the revenue and expense accounts must be closed or cleared because their balances apply to only one fiscal period. Closing entries are prepared to reduce the balances in the revenue and expense accounts to zero, thus preparing them for use during the next fiscal period.

Closing entries are also used to transfer the net income or net loss for the period to the capital account. Earlier you learned how to calculate the net income or loss on the work sheet. The net income or loss is then reported on the income statement and reflected in the ending balance of the capital account reported on the balance sheet. This ending capital balance is calculated on the statement of changes in owner's equity. But no journal entries have yet been recorded to update the balance of the capital account in the general ledger. For example, the balance for Jan Harter, Capital shown on the work sheet is $25,200. The balance for Jan Harter, Capital reported on the balance sheet is $25,250. These two amounts are different because the withdrawals and the net income for the period have not yet been recorded in the capital account in the general ledger. This is done during the closing process.

The Income Summary Account

Before the closing entries are journalized and posted, there is no single account in the general ledger that shows the revenue and expenses for the fiscal period. This information appears in the balances of the individual revenue and expense accounts, but it is not shown in any one account in the general ledger.

There is, however, one general ledger account that, up to this point, has not been used. That is the Income Summary account. The **Income Summary account** is used to accumulate and summarize the revenue and expenses for the period. The account, then, serves as a simple income statement in the ledger. That is, the balance of the account equals the net income or net loss for the fiscal period.

Income Summary	
Dr.	Cr.
Expense Account Balances	Revenue Account Balances

Look at the T account for Income Summary. Expenses, which have debit balances, are transferred as debits to Income Summary. Revenues, which have credit balances, are transferred as credits to Income Summary.

Look back at the chart of accounts for Global Travel on page 40. You will notice that Income Summary is located in the owner's equity section of the general ledger. It is located there because of its relationship to the owner's capital account. Remember, revenue and expenses actually represent increases and decreases to owner's equity. The balance of Income Summary (the net income or net loss for the period) must be transferred to the capital account at the end of the closing process.

Like the withdrawals account, Income Summary is a temporary capital account. Income Summary is quite different, however, from the other temporary capital accounts. First, Income Summary is used only at the end of the fiscal period. It is used only to summarize the balances from the revenue and expense accounts. Second, Income Summary does not have a normal balance, which means that it does not have an increase side or a decrease side. The debit and credit sides of the account are simply used to summarize the period's revenue and expenses. If the business has a net income, Income Summary will have a credit balance because the revenue recorded on the credit side will exceed the expenses recorded on the debit side. If the business has a net loss, the account will have a debit balance because the expenses recorded on the debit side will exceed the revenue recorded on the credit side.

Journalizing the Closing Entries

Four separate journal entries are prepared to close the temporary capital accounts for Global Travel.

ACCOUNTING Notes....

Closing entries are sometimes called clearing entries because one of their functions is to *clear* the revenue and expense accounts and leave them with zero balances.

1. The balance of the revenue account is transferred to the credit side of the Income Summary account.
2. The expense account balances are transferred to the debit side of the Income Summary account.
3. The balance of the Income Summary account is transferred to the capital account (net income to the credit side; net loss to the debit side).
4. The balance of the withdrawals account is transferred to the debit side of the capital account.

The work sheet is the source of the information for the closing entries.

Closing the Balance of the Revenue Account into Income Summary

The first step in the closing procedure is to transfer the balance of the revenue account to Income Summary. The account balance for the revenue account is taken from the Income Statement section of the work sheet. Global Travel has only one revenue account, Fees, so the accounts affected by this first closing entry are Fees and Income Summary.

The balance for Fees shown on the work sheet is $1,650. To close Fees, the balance must be reduced to zero. Since Fees has a credit balance of $1,650, a debit of $1,650 to that account will result in a balance of zero. The closing entry for revenue is therefore a debit of $1,650 to Fees and a credit of $1,650 to Income Summary. This closing entry reduces the balance of the Fees account to zero and transfers the amount of total income to the Income Summary account.

Fees		Income Summary	
Dr.	Cr.	Dr.	Cr.
−	+		
Clo. $1,650	Bal. $1,650		Clo. $1,650

The journal entry to close the revenue account into Income Summary is shown in Figure 9-2. To record the closing entry in the general journal:

	DATE	DESCRIPTION	POST. REF.	DEBIT	CREDIT	
		GENERAL JOURNAL			PAGE 3	
1		Closing Entries				1
2	19-- Oct. 31	Fees		1 65000		2
3		Income Summary			1 65000	3

Figure 9-2 Closing the Revenue Account

1. Write the words "Closing Entries" in the center of the Description column. If you are recording the closing entries on a journal page that contains other entries, skip a line after the last entry. If you begin the closing entries on a new journal page, write the heading "Closing Entries" on the first line. This heading is the explanation for *all* the closing entries.
2. Enter the date (the last day of the fiscal period) in the Date column.
3. Enter the title of the account(s) debited and the amount of the debit.
4. Enter the title of the account credited and the amount of the credit.

Closing the Balances of the Expense Accounts into Income Summary

The second closing entry is made to transfer the balances of the expense accounts into Income Summary. The balances of the expense accounts are taken from the Income Statement section of the work sheet. The expense accounts used by Global Travel are Advertising Expense, Maintenance Expense, Rent Expense, and Utilities Expense.

Look at the T accounts that follow. Each expense account must be credited for the amount of its debit balance. (It is not necessary to use a separate closing entry for each expense account.) Income Summary then is debited for the total amount of expenses, $1,200.

Income Summary		Advertising Expense		Maintenance Expense	
Dr.	Cr.	Dr.	Cr.	Dr.	Cr.
		+	−	+	−
Clo. $1,200	Clo. $1,650	Bal. $75	Clo. $75	Bal. $450	Clo. $450

Rent Expense		Utilities Expense	
Dr.	Cr.	Dr.	Cr.
+	−	+	−
Bal. $550	Clo. $550	Bal. $125	Clo. $125

The journal entry to close the expense accounts appears in Figure 9-3.

Look again at the second closing entry. You will notice that it has one debit and four credits. A journal entry having two or more debits or two or more credits is called a **compound entry.** The compound entry saves both space and posting time. For example, each expense account could have been closed into Income Summary separately. However, that would have required four entries, and postings, to Income Summary instead of one.

	DATE	DESCRIPTION	POST. REF.	DEBIT	CREDIT	
1		*Closing Entries*				1
4	31	*Income Summary*		1 200 00		4
5		*Advertising Expense*			75 00	5
6		*Maintenance Expense*			450 00	6
7		*Rent Expense*			550 00	7
8		*Utilities Expense*			1 250 00	8

Figure 9-3 Closing the Expense Accounts

R — E — M — E — M — B — E — R

To close revenue accounts, debit each revenue account for the amount of its credit balance. Credit Income Summary for the amount of total revenue. To close expense accounts, debit Income Summary for the amount of total expenses. Credit each expense account for the amount of its debit balance.

Before going on, complete the following activity to make certain you understand how to close the revenue and expense accounts.

Check Your Learning

Write your answers to the following questions on a sheet of paper.

1. A closing entry must be made for the account Ticket Revenue, which has a balance of $6,000.
   a. What is the title of the account debited?
   b. What is the title of the account credited?
   c. What is the amount of the debit? the credit?
2. A business has three expense accounts: Gas and Oil Expense (balance, $700), Miscellaneous Expense (balance, $600), and Utilities Expense (balance, $1,800). The end of the business's fiscal period is June 30.
   a. The date of the journal entry to close these accounts is ___?___ .
   b. The account debited is ___?___ .
   c. The amount of the debit is ___?___ .
   d. The accounts credited are ___?___ .
   e. The amounts of the credits are ___?___ .

Compare your answers to those in the answers section. Re-read the preceding part of the chapter to find the answers to any questions you missed.

Closing the Balance of the Income Summary Account into Capital

The next journal entry is made to close the balance of the Income Summary account into the capital account. After closing the revenue and expense accounts, Income Summary has a credit balance of $450. This balance is the amount of the net income for the period. It is the same amount that was calculated on the work sheet.

The first part of this closing entry is a debit of $450 to Income Summary. As you can see from the following T account, a debit of $450 to Income Summary reduces the balance of that account to zero. The amount of net income must be closed into the owner's capital account, so the second part of this closing entry is a credit of $450 to Jan Harter, Capital.

Income Summary		Jan Harter, Capital	
Dr.	Cr.	Dr.	Cr.
		−	+
Clo. $1,200	Clo. $1,650		Bal. $25,200
Clo. 450			Clo. 450

The journal entry to close the balance of Income Summary (the net income for the period) into the capital account is illustrated in Figure 9-4.

	GENERAL JOURNAL			PAGE 3	
DATE	DESCRIPTION	POST. REF.	DEBIT	CREDIT	
31	Income Summary		450 00		9
	Jan Harter, Capital			450 00	10

Figure 9-4 Closing the Income Summary Account

If a business reports a net loss for the period, Income Summary would have a debit balance. The third closing entry, then, would be a debit to the capital account and a credit to Income Summary for the amount of the net loss. This situation is shown in Figure 9-5.

	GENERAL JOURNAL			PAGE 3	
DATE	DESCRIPTION	POST. REF.	DEBIT	CREDIT	
31	Jan Harter, Capital		250 00		9
	Income Summary			250 00	10

Figure 9-5 Closing Income Summary for the Amount of Net Loss

Closing the Balance of the Withdrawals Account into Capital

The last closing entry made is to close the balance of the withdrawals account into capital. As you recall, withdrawals decrease owner's equity. The balance of the withdrawals account must be transferred to the capital account at the end of the period to show the decrease it causes in owner's equity. Therefore, to close the withdrawals account, the amount of its balance — taken from the Balance Sheet section of the work sheet — is debited to capital. The withdrawals account is credited for the same amount to reduce its balance to zero. Therefore, Jan Harter, Capital is debited for $400, and Jan Harter, Withdrawals is credited for $400.

Jan Harter, Capital		Jan Harter, Withdrawals	
Dr.	Cr.	Dr.	Cr.
−	+	+	−
Clo. $400	Bal. $25,200	Bal. $400	Clo. $400
	450		

This journal entry is shown in Figure 9-6.

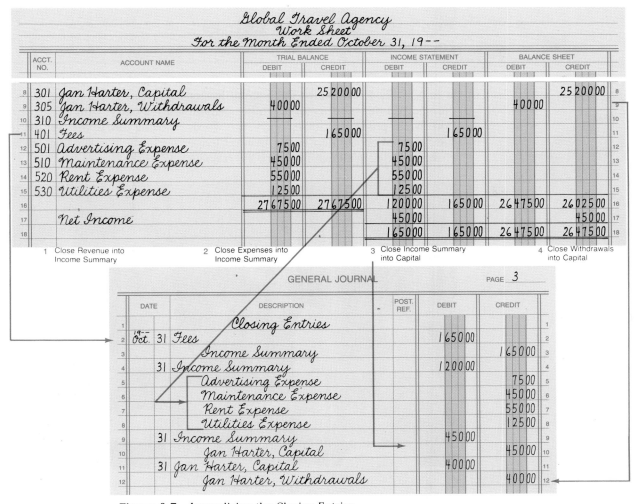

GENERAL JOURNAL   PAGE _3_

	DATE	DESCRIPTION	POST. REF.	DEBIT	CREDIT	
11	31	Jan Harter, Capital		40000		11
12		Jan Harter, Withdrawals			40000	12

Figure 9-6   Closing the Withdrawals Account

The work sheet and the journal entries made to close the temporary capital accounts for Global Travel are shown in Figure 9-7.

Global Travel Agency
Work Sheet
For the Month Ended October 31, 19− −

ACCT. NO.	ACCOUNT NAME	TRIAL BALANCE DEBIT	TRIAL BALANCE CREDIT	INCOME STATEMENT DEBIT	INCOME STATEMENT CREDIT	BALANCE SHEET DEBIT	BALANCE SHEET CREDIT	
301	Jan Harter, Capital		25 200 00				25 200 00	8
305	Jan Harter, Withdrawals	400 00				400 00		9
310	Income Summary							10
401	Fees		1 650 00		1 650 00			11
501	Advertising Expense	75 00		75 00				12
510	Maintenance Expense	450 00		450 00				13
520	Rent Expense	550 00		550 00				14
530	Utilities Expense	125 00		125 00				15
		27 675 00	27 675 00	1 200 00	1 650 00	26 475 00	26 025 00	16
	Net Income			450 00			450 00	17
				1 650 00	1 650 00	26 475 00	26 475 00	18

1 Close Revenue into Income Summary   2 Close Expenses into Income Summary   3 Close Income Summary into Capital   4 Close Withdrawals into Capital

GENERAL JOURNAL   PAGE _3_

	DATE	DESCRIPTION	POST. REF.	DEBIT	CREDIT	
1		Closing Entries				1
2	19−− Oct. 31	Fees		1 650 00		2
3		Income Summary			1 650 00	3
4	31	Income Summary		1 200 00		4
5		Advertising Expense			75 00	5
6		Maintenance Expense			450 00	6
7		Rent Expense			550 00	7
8		Utilities Expense			125 00	8
9	31	Income Summary		450 00		9
10		Jan Harter, Capital			450 00	10
11	31	Jan Harter, Capital		400 00		11
12		Jan Harter, Withdrawals			400 00	12

Figure 9-7   Journalizing the Closing Entries

Before you read any further, complete the following activity to check your understanding of closing entries.

Check Your Learning

Use notebook paper and answer the following questions on Figure 9-7.

1. What is the source of information for the closing entries?
2. How many expense accounts are affected by the closing entries?
3. Which account serves as a "clearinghouse" during the closing process?
4. In the third closing entry, is the capital account being increased or decreased?
5. How many closing entries affect the Income Summary account?

Compare your answers to those in the answers section. Re-read the preceding part of the chapter to find the correct answers to any questions you may have missed.

Posting the Closing Entries to the General Ledger

After journalizing the closing entries, the next step in the closing process is to post those entries to the general ledger accounts. The posting procedure here is the same as for any other general journal entry, with one exception. When posting a closing entry, the words "Closing Entry" are written in the Explanation column of the general ledger account. The posting of the closing entries is shown in Figure 9-8 on pages 177-178.

Closing entries divide the accounting activities of one fiscal period from those of another. This process provides financial data with which the owner or manager can evaluate the business's success.

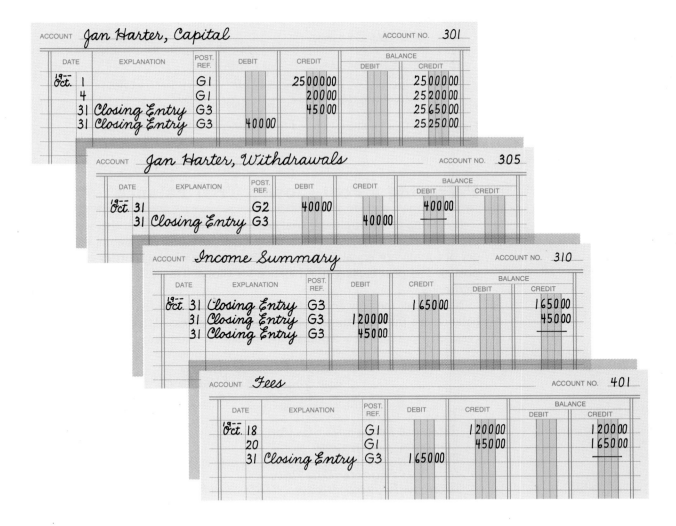

Figure 9-8 Closing Entries Posted to the General Ledger

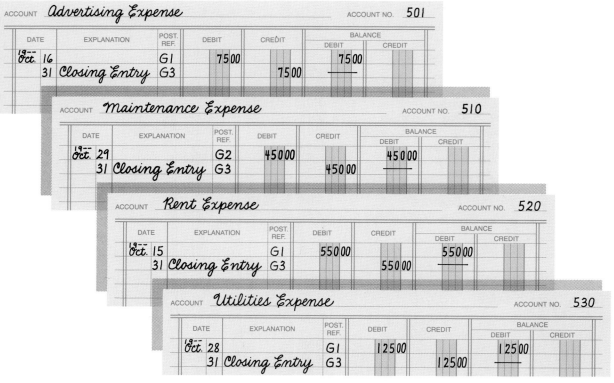

Figure 9-8   Closing Entries Posted to the General Ledger (Continued)

Preparing a Post-Closing Trial Balance

Preparing the post-closing trial balance is the last step in the accounting cycle. This trial balance is prepared to make sure the total debits in the ledger accounts are equal to total credits after the closing entries have been posted. The post-closing trial balance for Global Travel Agency is shown in Figure 9-9.

Notice that the only accounts and balances listed on the post-closing trial balance are the permanent accounts of the business. After the closing process, only permanent accounts have balances. Temporary capital accounts

Global Travel Agency Post-Closing Trial Balance October 31, 19--		
Cash in Bank	16 125 00	
Accounts Receivable - Burton Co.	450 00	
Computer Equipment	8 000 00	
Office Equipment	1 500 00	
Accounts Payable - City News		75 00
Accounts Payable - Modern Office Suppliers		750 00
Jan Harter, Capital		25 250 00
Total	26 075 00	26 075 00

Figure 9-9   Post-Closing Trial Balance

have zero balances, so there is no need to list those accounts on the post-closing trial balance.

The Computer and Closing Entries

The closing entries we just discussed were prepared manually. In a computerized accounting system, closing entries may be completed entirely by the computer. A command from the computer operator instructs the computer to close the general ledger. The computer will close the temporary capital accounts, determine the amount of net income or net loss, and update the owner's capital account. After the closing is complete, the operator can instruct the computer to prepare a post-closing trial balance. The post-closing trial balance prepared by the computer lets the accounting clerk know that the temporary capital accounts have zero balances. A computer-prepared post-closing trial balance is illustrated in Figure 9-10.

```
                    Global Travel Agency
                  Post-Closing Trial Balance
                      October 31, 19--

Cash in Bank                        16125.00
Accts. Rec.--Burton Co.               450.00
Computer Equipment                   8000.00
Office Equipment                     1500.00
Accts. Pay.--City News                                  75.00
Accts. Pay.--Mod. Off. Supp.                           750.00
Jan Harter, Capital                                  25250.00

      Total                         26075.00         26075.00
                                    ========         ========
```

Figure 9-10   Post-Closing Trial Balance Prepared by Computer

You have now completed an accounting cycle for a service business organized as a sole proprietorship.

SUMMARY OF KEY POINTS

1. The eighth and ninth steps in the accounting cycle are to record and post the closing entries and to prepare a post-closing trial balance. These steps complete the accounting cycle.
2. Closing is the process of transferring the balances in the temporary capital accounts to the capital account. The work sheet is the source of the balances of the temporary capital accounts.

3. Only temporary capital accounts are closed. The asset, liability, and owner's capital account are never closed.
4. The first closing entry transfers the balance of the revenue account(s) into Income Summary. The balances of the expense accounts are then closed into Income Summary. The balance of the Income Summary account (the net income or net loss for the period) is then closed into the capital account. The last closing entry transfers the balance of the withdrawals account into the capital account.
5. After the closing entries have been journalized, they are posted to the general ledger. A post-closing trial balance is then prepared to test the equality of total debits and credits in the ledger.

REVIEW AND APPLICATIONS

Building Your Accounting Vocabulary

In your own words, write the definition of each of the following accounting terms. Use complete sentences for your definitions.

closing entries
compound entry

Income Summary
 account

post-closing trial
 balance

Reviewing Your Accounting Knowledge

1. Why are the temporary capital accounts closed at the end of the fiscal period?
2. What is the purpose of the Income Summary account?
3. Explain the relationship between the Income Summary account and the capital account.
4. How is the Income Summary account different from the other temporary capital accounts?
5. List the steps involved in closing the temporary capital accounts.
6. What is the source of information for the closing entries?
7. How does the closing procedure for a net loss differ from the closing procedure for a net income?
8. In what way is the posting procedure for closing entries different from the posting procedure for other general journal entries?
9. What is the purpose of preparing a post-closing trial balance?
10. Why do only the balances of permanent accounts appear on the post-closing trial balance?

Improving Your Human Relations Skills

Recently Elena, a new employee, was assigned to work with you on several important projects in your office. You have found that Elena is not very well organized and often has to redo her part of an assignment. As a result of her poor work, you have already missed your first deadline.

1. What should you say to Elena?
2. How would you explain this problem to your supervisor?
3. What can be done to make sure you do not miss future deadlines?

Applying Accounting Procedures

Exercise 9-1   Understanding the Accounting Cycle
The nine steps in the accounting cycle are listed at the top of page 182, but not in the proper order.

Instructions: Rearrange these steps in the order in which they would be completed by a business during an accounting period. Use the form in the workbook or plain paper. Place a number (from 1 to 9) on the line preceding the step.

a. Complete the work sheet.
b. Analyze business transactions.
c. Prepare a post-closing trial balance.
d. Journalize and post the closing entries.
e. Collect and verify data on source documents.
f. Prepare a trial balance.
g. Post each entry to the general ledger.
h. Journalize business transactions.
i. Prepare the financial statements.

Exercise 9-2   Determining Accounts Affected by Closing Entries

The following list contains some of the accounts used by the Living Well Health Spa.

Accounts Payable — The Fitness Shop
Accounts Receivable — Linda Brown
Advertising Expense
Cash in Bank
Exercise Class Revenue
Exercise Equipment
Income Summary
Laundry Equipment
Maintenance Expense

Membership Fees
Miscellaneous Expense
Office Furniture
Rent Expense
Repair Tools
Ted Chapman, Capital
Ted Chapman, Withdrawals
Utilities Expense

Instructions: Use a form similar to the one that follows. For each account,
(1) Indicate the statement on which each account is reported by writing "Balance Sheet" or "Income Statement" in the space provided.
(2) In the next column, use "Yes" or "No" to indicate whether the account is closed.
(3) In the last column, use "Yes" or "No" to indicate whether the account is included in the post-closing trial balance. The first account is shown as an example.

Account Title	Financial Statement	Is the account affected by a closing entry?	Does the account appear on the post-closing trial balance?
Accounts Payable— The Fitness Shop	Balance Sheet	No	Yes

Problem 9-1   Preparing Closing Entries

A portion of the work sheet for Holmes Accounting Service for the period ended September 30 appears on page 183.

Instructions: Using the information from the work sheet, prepare the journal entries to close the temporary capital accounts. Use journal page 7.
(1) Record the closing entry for the revenue account.
(2) Record the closing entry for the expense accounts.
(3) Record the closing entry for the Income Summary account.
(4) Record the closing entry for the withdrawals account.

ACCT. NO.	ACCOUNT NAME	INCOME STATEMENT DEBIT	INCOME STATEMENT CREDIT	BALANCE SHEET DEBIT	BALANCE SHEET CREDIT	
101	Cash in Bank			7000 00		1
105	Accts. Rec. - Betty Foley			3000 00		2
115	Office Equipment			12000 00		3
120	Accounting Library			6000 00		4
201	Accts. Pay. - Ron Williams				900 00	5
301	Robert Holmes, Capital				19775 00	6
305	Robert Holmes, Withdrawals			2350 00		7
310	Income Summary					8
401	Accounting Fees		15865 00			9
501	Entertainment Expense	3400 00				10
510	Miscellaneous Expense	560 00				11
520	Rent Expense	1000 00				12
530	Utilities Expense	1230 00				13
		6190 00	15865 00	30350 00	20675 00	14
	Net Income	9675 00			9675 00	15
		15865 00	15865 00	30350 00	30350 00	16

Problem 9-2 Preparing a Post-Closing Trial Balance

Shown below are the accounts of Carrier's Repair Shop on June 30 after the closing entries have been journalized and posted.

Cash in Bank	
Dr.	Cr.
+	–
$8,000	

Accounts Receivable— Kathy Clarke	
Dr.	Cr.
+	–
$875	

Accounts Receivable— Malcolm, Inc.	
Dr.	Cr.
+	–
$5,050	

Accounts Receivable— James Moreaux	
Dr.	Cr.
+	–
$1,275	

Shop Equipment	
Dr.	Cr.
+	–
$6,000	

Tools	
Dr.	Cr.
+	–
$9,000	

Accounts Payable— Beste Tool & Die Co.	
Dr.	Cr.
–	+
	$1,000

Accounts Payable— Oliver Equipment	
Dr.	Cr.
–	+
	$2,500

J. C. Carrier, Capital	
Dr.	Cr.
–	+
$1,500	$21,000
	7,200

J. C. Carrier, Withdrawals	
Dr.	Cr.
+	–
$1,500	$1,500

Income Summary	
Dr.	Cr.
$7,800	$15,000
7,200	

Repair Revenue	
Dr.	Cr.
–	+
$15,000	$15,000

Rent Expense	
Dr.	Cr.
+	–
$5,000	$5,000

Utilities Expense	
Dr.	Cr.
+	–
$2,800	$2,800

Instructions: Use the information in the T accounts to prepare the June 30 post-closing trial balance for Carrier's Repair Shop.

Problem 9-3   Journalizing Closing Entries

The following account titles and balances appeared on the work sheet for Whitman Contractors. The work sheet was for the month ended July 31.

	Income Statement		Balance Sheet	
	Debit	Credit	Debit	Credit
Cash in Bank			9,300	
Accounts Receivable—Projean Co.			3,000	
Accounts Receivable—Ford Bakery			10,000	
Office Equipment			8,000	
Construction Equipment			60,000	
Accounts Payable—Joseph's Elec.				5,000
Accounts Payable—Moran Cement Co.				1,500
Accounts Payable—Stoll Bldg. Supp.				15,000
C. Whitman, Capital				64,500
C. Whitman, Withdrawals			7,000	
Income Summary				
Construction Revenue		20,000		
Advertising Expense	1,700			
Gas and Oil Expense	4,300			
Miscellaneous Expense	700			
Repairs Expense	1,200			
Utilities Expense	800			

Instructions: Using the above information, record the closing entries for Whitman Contractors. Use general journal page 11.

Problem 9-4   Posting Closing Entries and
Preparing a Post-Closing Trial Balance

Instructions: Use the closing entries prepared in Problem 9-3 to complete this problem.

(1) Post the closing entries recorded in Problem 9-3 to the appropriate general ledger accounts. The general ledger accounts for Whitman Contractors are included in the working papers accompanying this textbook.

(2) Prepare a post-closing trial balance.

Problem 9-5   Completing End-of-Period Activities

At the end of April, the general ledger for Tsung Management Company shows the following account balances.

110	Cash in Bank	$12,000	220	Accounts Payable—	
120	Accounts Receivable—			The Computer Shop	$15,500
	Hatter Company	3,000	301	Alan Tsung, Capital	54,675
130	Accounts Receivable—		302	Alan Tsung,	
	Jackson Co.	900		Withdrawals	4,000
140	Accounts Receivable—		303	Income Summary	
	Zest Realty Co.	1,800	401	Management Fees	9,600
150	Office Supplies	500	510	Advertising Expense	1,000
160	Office Equipment	13,000	520	Miscellaneous Expense	400
170	Computer Equipment	42,000	530	Rent Expense	1,200
210	Accounts Payable—		540	Utilities Expense	375
	Fox Office Supply	400			

Instructions: Using the preceding account titles and balances,

(1) Prepare the six-column work sheet. The period covered is one month.

(2) Prepare the financial statements. Alan Tsung made an investment of $10,000 during the month.

(3) Record the closing entries on page 12 of a general journal.

(4) Post the closing entries.

(5) Prepare a post-closing trial balance.

Problem 9-6   Correcting Errors in the Closing Entries

The work sheet and financial statements for Bennett Company for the month of November have been completed. They show that during this one-month period:

a. The net income for the period was $1,800.

b. The owner, Dale Bennett, made an additional investment of $5,000.

c. Dale Bennett withdrew $2,000.

d. The November 30 balance of Dale Bennett, Capital that appeared on the work sheet was $30,000.

e. Expenses for the month were as follows: Advertising Expense, $900; Miscellaneous Expense, $300; Rent Expense, $1,400; and Utilities Expense, $600.

The closing entries for the month were entered in the general journal as shown below.

	DATE	DESCRIPTION	POST. REF.	DEBIT	CREDIT	
		GENERAL JOURNAL			PAGE 14	
1		*Closing Entries*				1
2	19-- Nov. 30	*Fees*		5 000 00		2
3		*Income Summary*			5 000 00	3
4	30	*Income Summary*		3 200 00		4
5		*Advertising Expense*			9 00 00	5
6		*Miscellaneous Expense*			3 00 00	6
7		*Rent Expense*			1 4 00 00	7
8		*Utilities Expense*			6 00 00	8
9	30	*Income Summary*		3 000 00		9
10		*Dale Bennett, Capital*			3 000 00	10
11	30	*Dale Bennett, Capital*		2 000 00		11
12		*Dale Bennett, Withdrawals*			2 000 00	12

Instructions: Based on these closing entries, answer the following questions.

(1) What error has been made in recording the closing entries?

(2) After posting the entries shown, will Income Summary have a debit or a credit balance?

(3) After posting these entries, what will the balance of the capital account be?

(4) What *should* the balance of Dale Bennett, Capital be?

(5) Why does the additional investment of $5,000 *not* appear in the closing entries?

Make corrections in the journal entries in your working papers.

Computer analysis of the serve may improve this tennis player's performance.

Computers in Sports: New Angles on the Winning Performance

When mere hundredths of inches, seconds, or points separate winning performances from second-place finishes, coaches of world-class athletes are adopting state-of-the-art coaching assistants: computers.

At the U.S. Olympic Committee sports science lab in Colorado Springs, Colorado, researchers videotape an athlete's performance. They then process and digitize the performance frame-by-frame to create multidimensional images that can be analyzed from different angles. The analysis can point out flaws in the athlete's technique that might not otherwise be noticed. The computer can even be told to look for a specific flaw and highlight it throughout the analysis.

This $35,000 motion-analysis system was created by Phillip Cheetham, a former Olympic gymnast from Australia. Cheetham withdrew from competition as the result of an injury. His injury led him to develop another system used by the U.S. Olympic Committee to analyze how gymnastic injuries can be prevented.

Young Tom Eldredge, junior world figure-skating champion, believes motion-analysis helped him become one of only a dozen figure skaters in the United States to perform a triple-axel (three and a half revolutions in the air).

As this technology becomes more widely used, will world records fall even faster? Will athletes be able to leap higher and longer, run faster, score more perfect 10s than ever before? How much does technique contribute to the winning performance? And how much is the result of conditioning, training, body type, and the competitive spirit?

Cash Control and Banking Activities

An important part of the recordkeeping for any business involves the records kept on the cash received and paid out. Cash is a business's most liquid asset. It is the asset needing the greatest protection, or control, to prevent its loss or waste.

In this chapter, you will learn about the controls businesses use to protect their cash. One of the most commonly used controls is a checking account. The use of a checking account not only helps protect cash but also provides a separate record of the cash transactions of the business.

 LEARNING OBJECTIVES

When you have completed this chapter, you should be able to

1. Describe the internal controls used to protect cash.
2. Describe the forms used to open and use a checking account.
3. Accurately record information on check stubs.
4. Prepare a check correctly.
5. Reconcile a bank statement.
6. Journalize and post entries relating to bank service charges.
7. Define the terms new to this chapter.

NEW Terms

internal controls • external controls • checking account • check • depositor • signature card • deposit slip • endorsement • restrictive endorsement • payee • drawer • drawee • voiding a check • bank statement • canceled checks • reconciling the bank statement • outstanding checks • outstanding deposits • bank service charge • stop payment order • NSF check • electronic funds transfer system

One way a business can control, or protect, its cash is by making all payments by check and depositing all cash received in a bank account.

Protecting Cash

In any business, ready cash (bills, coins, and checks) is used daily for a large number of transactions. A business receives cash in return for its goods or services. It pays out cash to purchase goods and services or to pay its expenses.

You learned in an earlier chapter that cash is a business's most liquid asset. It is important to protect that asset from loss, waste, theft, forgery, and embezzlement. Cash can be protected through internal controls and external controls. **Internal controls** refer to those steps the business takes to protect cash and other assets. For example, internal controls may include

1. limiting the number of persons handling cash,
2. separating accounting tasks involving cash (such as, not allowing the person who handles cash receipts and cash payments to also keep the accounting records showing the amounts received or paid out),
3. bonding (insuring) employees who handle cash or cash records,
4. using a safe or a cash register,
5. depositing cash receipts in the bank daily, and
6. using checks to make all cash payments.

External controls are those controls provided outside the business. For example, banks maintain controls to protect the funds deposited by their customers. These controls include verifying the accuracy of signatures on checks and maintaining records of the transfer of money into and out of each customer's checking account.

Opening a Checking Account

A **checking account** is a bank account that allows a bank customer to deposit cash and to write checks against the account balance. A **check** is a written order from a depositor telling the bank to pay a stated amount of cash to the person or business named on the check. A **depositor** is a person or business that has cash on deposit in a bank. To open a checking account, a business owner must fill out a signature card and deposit cash in the bank.

A **signature card** contains the signature(s) of the person(s) authorized to write checks on the bank account. The signature card is kept on file by the bank so that it can be matched against signed checks presented for payment. The use of a signature card helps protect both the account holder and the bank against checks with forged signatures.

The signature card signed by Jan Harter to open the checking account for Global Travel Agency is shown in Figure 10-1.

ACCOUNTING Notes.....

Modern banking began in Italy over 500 years ago. Our word *bank* comes from the Italian word *banco*, meaning "bench." Why? In early times, Italian bankers set up benches along the streets to do business.

ACCT. NO. 303443	ACCOUNT NAME *Global Travel Agency*
ACCT. TYPE: ☑CKG. ☐ SAV. ☐ C.R.	
☐ OTHER _____	
NO. SIGNATURES REQUIRED __1__	SIGNATURE *Jan Harter*
SOC. SEC. NO. OR TAXPAYER I.D. NO.	
1	SIGNATURE
2	SIGNATURE

THE INDIVIDUALS WHO HAVE SIGNED ABOVE ARE AUTHORIZED TO USE THIS ACCOUNT ACCORDING TO THE RULES AND REGULATIONS THAT APPLY TO IT **AND** ANY SPECIAL INSTRUCTIONS ON FILE WITH THE BANK. EACH PERSON WHO SIGNS ACKNOWLEDGES THAT THESE RULES AND REGULATIONS HAVE BEEN RECEIVED AND AGREES TO THEIR TERMS. EACH PERSON ALSO AUTHORIZES THE BANK TO REQUEST A CONSUMER REPORT FROM ANY CONSUMER REPORTING AGENCY.

FOR BANK USE

IDENTIFICATION PRESENTED *Mass. State License*

COMMENTS *Sole Proprietorship – travel agency*

ACCOUNT ADDRESS *200 Brattle Street, Cambridge, MA 02138*

HOME PHONE *258-4512* BUSINESS PHONE *258-2020*

☑NEW ACCOUNT ☐ CAPTION CHANGE ☐ NEW SIGNATURE ☐ ADDITIONAL SIGNATURE

☐ INDIVIDUAL ☐ JOINT ☐ CORPORATE ☑BUSINESS ☐ FIDUCIARY

☐ OTHER _____

NCPS OPENED BY *GLC* BRANCH

DATE OPENED OR CHANGED *10/1* AMOUNT DEPOSITED $ *25,000.00*

Figure 10-1 Checking Account Signature Card

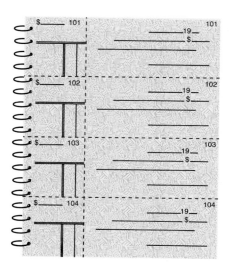

When a depositor opens a checking account, checks are printed for the sole use of that depositor. Printed checks are packaged together in *checkbooks*. The checkbook chosen by Jan Harter is typical of those used by businesses. It looks like a spiral-bound notebook. Its pages are made up of detachable checks attached to check stubs. Each check—and its stub—is numbered in sequence. Prenumbered checks help a business keep track of every check that is written. Using checks with printed numbers is an important part of the internal control of cash.

In addition to the check number, each check is printed with the business's account number and an American Bankers Association (ABA) number. The ABA number is the fractional number printed in the upper right corner of a check, just below the check number. The ABA number is a code that identifies exactly where a check comes from. For example, look at the ABA number on the check in Figure 10-2.

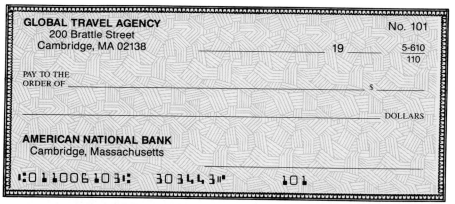

Figure 10-2   Printed Check

The part of the number above the line and to the left of the hyphen stands for the city or state in which the bank is located. The number to the right of the hyphen indicates the specific bank on which the check is written. The number below the line is a code for the Federal Reserve district in which the bank is located.

The ABA number was developed to speed the sorting of checks by hand. An updated version of the ABA number is also printed on the bottom of each check for use in electronic sorting. The ABA number, the depositor's account number, and perhaps the check number are printed at the bottom of the check in a special ink and typeface. These specially printed numbers are referred to as MICR (*m*agnetic *i*nk *c*haracter *r*ecognition) numbers. Can you identify the MICR number on the check in Figure 10-2?

Making Deposits to a Checking Account

A business should make regular deposits to protect the currency and checks it receives. Most businesses make daily deposits. A **deposit slip** is a bank form on which the currency (bills and coins) and checks to be deposited are listed. The deposit slip, also called a deposit ticket, gives both the depositor and the bank a detailed record of a deposit. Most banks provide their depositors with deposit slips on which the depositor's name, address, and account number are printed. A deposit slip for Global Travel Agency is shown in Figure 10-3. To complete a deposit slip, follow these steps.

1. Write the date on the Date line.
2. On the Cash line, list the total amount of bills and coins being deposited.
3. List checks separately by their ABA numbers. If many checks are being deposited, list the checks by amount on a calculator tape and attach the tape to the deposit slip. On the first Checks line, write "See tape listing," followed by the total amount of the checks.
4. Total the cash and checks, and write the total amount being deposited on the Total line.

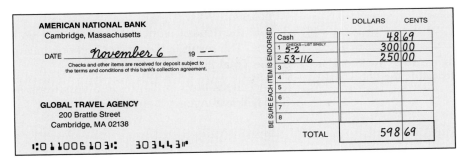

Figure 10-3 Deposit Slip

The deposit slip and the cash and checks being deposited are handed to a bank teller. Checks should be arranged in the order listed on the deposit slip. The teller verifies the deposit and gives the depositor a receipt. The deposit receipt may be a stamped and initialed (by the teller) copy of the deposit slip or a machine-printed form.

R E M E M B E R

On the deposit slip, list checks being deposited by their ABA numbers.

Endorsing Checks

When a business receives a check in payment for a product or service, it acquires the right to that check. The check is a form of property. To deposit the check in a checking account, the depositor endorses the check to transfer its ownership to the bank. An **endorsement** is an authorized signature that is written or stamped on the back of a check.

The endorsement on the check represents a promise to pay. For example, suppose the bank cannot collect the amount of the check from the account

FOR DEPOSIT ONLY IN

Global Travel
Agency

Acct. 303443

Figure 10-4 Restrictive Endorsement

$ _____		No. 104
DATE _____		19___
TO _____		
FOR _____		

	DOLLARS	CENTS
BAL. BRO. FWD.	15,700	00
ADD DEPOSITS *Oct. 18*	1,200	00
Oct. 26	200	00
TOTAL	17,100	00
LESS THIS CHECK		
BAL. CARR. FWD.		

Figure 10-5 Recording a Deposit in the Checkbook

Checks dated on a Sunday or written for amounts less than $1 are as valid as checks dated on weekdays or written for larger amounts. A check doesn't have to be written on a bank form, either. Checks written on a blank sheet of paper or even a log are negotiable.

on which the check is written. The endorsement of the depositor authorizes the bank to deduct the amount of the check from the depositor's account. The depositor, of course, can go back to the person or business that wrote the check to collect payment on it.

Types of endorsements vary, but most businesses use restrictive endorsements. A **restrictive endorsement** restricts, or limits, how a check may be handled. To protect checks from being cashed by anyone else, Global Travel Agency stamps a restrictive endorsement on each check as soon as it is received. For example, by writing "For Deposit Only" as part of its endorsement, Global Travel limits any other use of the check. A typical restrictive endorsement is shown in Figure 10-4.

Recording Deposits in the Checkbook

The check stubs in the checkbook are a duplicate record of the Cash in Bank account. That is, the completed stubs contain the records of all checking account transactions: withdrawals, deposits, and bank service charges.

To record a deposit in the checkbook, follow these procedures.

1. Enter the date of the deposit on the Add Deposits line of the next unused check stub.

2. Enter the total amount of the deposit on the same line in the amount column.

3. Add the deposit amount to the amount on the Balance Brought Forward line. The result is the new checkbook balance. Enter the new balance on the Total line.

The check stub in Figure 10-5 illustrates how deposits are recorded in Global Travel Agency's checkbook.

Writing Checks

Writing checks is a simple procedure governed by a few important rules. These rules must be followed to ensure correct recordkeeping and proper handling of the money represented by the check.

First, *always write checks in ink.* Typewritten checks are also acceptable. Checks written in pencil are *not* acceptable. Checks typed or written in ink are difficult to change, while those written in pencil may be easily altered.

Next, always complete the check stub *before* writing the check. Following this procedure reduces the chance of forgetting to complete the stub. After the check is removed from the checkbook, the stub serves as a permanent record of the check.

Completing the Check Stub

Global Travel's check stub is divided into two parts. The upper half summarizes the details of the cash payment transaction. The lower half is a record of the effects of the transaction on the checking account. It contains the balance before the transaction, any current deposits, the transaction amount, and the balance after the transaction. To complete the check stub, follow these steps.

Check Stub No. 104:

$125.00		No. 104
DATE Oct. 28		19 – –
TO Bay State Bell		
FOR Telephone bill		

	DOLLARS	CENTS
BAL. BRO. FWD.	15,700	00
ADD DEPOSITS Oct. 18	1,200	00
Oct. 26	200	00
TOTAL	17,100	00
LESS THIS CHECK	125	00
BAL. CARR. FWD.	16,975	00

Check Stub No. 105:

$		No. 105
DATE		19
TO		
FOR		

	DOLLARS	CENTS
BAL. BRO. FWD.	16,975	00
ADD DEPOSITS		
TOTAL		
LESS THIS CHECK		
BAL. CARR. FWD.		

1. In the upper half of the stub, enter the amount of the check, the date, the name of the payee (on the To line), and the purpose of the check (on the For line). A **payee** is the person or business to whom a check is written.
2. If you have not already done so, enter the total balance on the Total line on the bottom half of the stub.
3. Enter the amount of the check on the line marked "Less This Check." This amount must be the same as the amount shown on the first line in the upper half of the stub.
4. Subtract the check amount from the total balance. Enter the new balance on the line marked "Balance Carried Forward."
5. Enter the new balance on the first line of the *next* check stub on the line labeled "Balance Brought Forward."

R — E — M — E — M — B — E — R

Always complete the check stub *before* you write a check.

Filling Out the Check

After you have completed the check stub, write the check following the steps below. Remember to write the check in ink so that it cannot easily be changed.

1. Write the date on which the check is being issued.
2. Write the payee's name on the line marked "Pay To the Order Of." Start the payee's name as far left as possible.
3. Enter the amount of the check in numbers. Write clearly and begin the first number as close to the printed dollar sign as possible.
4. On the next line, write the dollar amount of the check *in words*. Start at the left edge of the line. Write any cents amount as a fraction. Draw a line from the cents fraction to the word "Dollars."
5. Sign the check. Only an authorized person—one who has signed the signature card for that account—may sign a check. The person who signs a check is the **drawer.** The bank on which the check is written is called the **drawee.**

The checkbook is now ready for the next transaction. A completed check and its stub are shown in Figure 10-6.

Figure 10-6 Completed Check and Stub

Some businesses use a check-writing machine when preparing a check. A check writer perforates the amount of the check in words on the Dollars line. These perforations protect a check from alteration, since the holes in the check are almost impossible to alter.

Voiding a Check

As a rule, if an error is made while writing a check, that check is not used. Corrected checks are not used because the corrections might look suspicious to banks. Instead, the incorrect check is marked "Void" and a new check is prepared. Writing the word "Void" in large letters across the front of a check (in ink) is known as **voiding a check.** When a check is voided, the stub is also voided.

The business needs to account for each check used, so a voided check is never destroyed. It is kept and filed in the business's records. One means of filing a voided check is to fold it and staple it to its check stub. A special file can also be set up for voided checks.

Before reading any further, complete the following activity to check your understanding of the information that appears on a check.

Check Your Learning

Study the check below and then answer the questions that follow. Write your answers on notebook paper.

Burton Company
101 Tremont Street
Boston, MA 02107

No. 324

November 12 19 – –

$\frac{5\text{-}3421}{110}$

PAY TO THE ORDER OF *Global Travel Agency* $ *450.00*

Four hundred fifty and $^{no}/100$ ———— DOLLARS

Patriot Bank
Boston, MA

Hilda H. Burton

⑈0110342131⑈ 293111⑈ 324

1. The payee of this check is ___?___ .
2. The drawer is ___?___ , and the drawee is ___?___ .
3. The number in the upper right corner, $\frac{5\text{-}3421}{110}$, is the ___?___ number.
4. The number 293111 at the bottom of the check is the ___?___ number.

Compare your answers to those in the answers section. Re-read the preceding part of the chapter to find the correct answers to any questions you may have missed.

Proving Cash

The balance in the Cash in Bank account in the general ledger is regularly compared with the balance in the checkbook. If all cash receipts have been deposited, all cash payments made by check, and all transactions journalized and posted, the Cash in Bank account balance should agree with the checkbook balance. Comparing these two cash balances regularly is part of the internal control of cash. Some businesses prove cash daily or weekly, while others prove cash on a monthly basis.

If the Cash in Bank balance does not agree with the checkbook balance, and the trial balance has been proved, the error is probably in the checkbook. A checkbook error is usually the result of: (1) faulty addition or subtraction, (2) failure to record a deposit or a check, or (3) a mistake in copying the balance brought forward amount.

If an error has been made in the checkbook, the proper place to enter the correction is on the next unused stub. For example, suppose Check 22 for $84.60 has been recorded on the check stub as $48.60. The error is found when cash is proved. By this time, several other checks have been written, so the next unused check stub is 31. In this case, the amount of the error ($84.60 − 48.60 = $36.00) should be subtracted from the balance brought forward amount on check stub 31. A note is written on check stub 22 to indicate that the error has been corrected on check stub 31.

The Bank Statement

A **bank statement** is an itemized record of all the transactions occurring in a depositor's account over a given period, usually a month. Typical bank statements include the following information: (1) the checking account

It is important to reconcile the bank statement to ensure that the business's cash records and the bank's records agree.

balance at the beginning of the period, (2) a list of all deposits made by the business during the period, (3) a list of all checks paid by the bank, (4) a list of any other deductions from the depositor's account, and (5) the checking account balance at the end of the period. Find each of these items on Global Travel Agency's bank statement in Figure 10-7 below.

When a bank sends a statement to a depositor, it also returns the checks paid by the bank and deducted from the depositor's account. These returned checks are called **canceled checks.** Canceled checks are stamped or marked with the word "Paid" and the date of payment.

Upon receiving the bank statement, a business should promptly check the statement against its checkbook. The process of determining any differences between the balance shown on the bank statement and the checkbook balance is called **reconciling the bank statement.** The ending balance on the bank statement seldom agrees with the balance in the checkbook. There are several reasons for this.

There is frequently a two- or three-day delay between the preparation and delivery of a bank statement. During that delay, the business may have written additional checks. Often, checks written in one statement period do not reach the bank for payment until the next period. A deposit made when the statement is being prepared may not be listed on the statement. Finally, the depositor does not know about some bank transactions, such as service charges, until the statement is received.

STATEMENT

Global Travel Agency 200 Brattle Street Cambridge, MA 02138		ACCOUNT NUMBER	303443
		DATE OF STATEMENT	10/30/--

PREVIOUS BALANCE	CHECKS AND CHARGES	NO. OF DEPOSITS	NO. OF CHECKS	DEPOSITS AND CREDITS	BALANCE AT THIS DATE
00.00	9,433.00	3	4	26,400.00	16,967.00

CHECKS AND OTHER CHARGES		DEPOSITS AND OTHER CREDITS	DATE	BALANCE
		25,000.00	10/1	25,000.00
8,000.00			10/4	17,000.00
750.00	550.00		10/16	15,700.00
		1,200.00	10/18	16,900.00
		200.00	10/26	17,100.00
8.00S	125.00		10/30	16,967.00

PLEASE EXAMINE YOUR STATEMENT AT ONCE. IF NO ERROR IS REPORTED IN 10 DAYS THE ACCOUNT WILL BE CONSIDERED CORRECT AND VOUCHERS GENUINE. ALL ITEMS ARE CREDITED SUBJECT TO FINAL PAYMENT.

C = Certified Check T = Ticket Debit or Credit S = Service Charge L = List CR = Overdraft R = Returned Check

Figure 10-7 Bank Statement

The three situations most frequently causing differences between the bank statement balance and the checkbook balance involve outstanding checks, outstanding deposits, and bank service charges.

Outstanding Checks and Deposits

In banking terms, the word "outstanding" simply means "not yet received." Therefore, **outstanding checks** are checks that have been written but not yet presented to the bank for payment. **Outstanding deposits** are deposits that have been made and recorded in the checkbook but that do not appear on the bank statement.

Bank Service Charges

The statement balance will also reflect any service charges made by the bank during the statement period. A **bank service charge** is a fee charged by the bank for maintaining bank records and for processing bank statement items for the depositor. This charge varies from bank to bank, but it is frequently based on the number of checks and deposits handled during the month or the balance kept in the depositor's account. The bank subtracts the service charge from the depositor's account and then notifies the depositor of the amount of the charge on the bank statement.

The checkbook balance must be adjusted to show the amount of the bank service charge. One way to adjust the balance in the checkbook is shown on the stub. The words "Less: Service Charge" are written on the line above the Total line. Next, the amount of the service charge is entered in the amount column—preceded by a minus sign. The balance is then recalculated and entered on the Total line.

R E M E M B E R

Before reconciling the bank statement, record in the checkbook any bank service charges or other deductions listed on the bank statement.

Reconciling a Bank Statement

Promptly reconciling the bank statement is a good way to guard against disorderly cash records or cash loss. Banks expect to be notified immediately of any error on the statement. Failure to do so within the time noted on the statement releases the bank from any responsibility for the error.

Most banks provide a form on the back of the bank statement for use in reconciling the bank statement. The reconciliation form for Global Travel's bank statement is shown in Figure 10-8 on page 198. This form documents the differences between the bank balance and the checkbook balance. Follow these steps when reconciling a bank statement.

1. Arrange the canceled checks in numerical order. Compare the canceled checks with those listed on the statement and with the stubs. As you find matching checks and stubs, place a check mark beside the check amount on the bank statement and on the check stub. Then list on the reconciliation form, by number and amount, all the stubs without check marks. These are the outstanding checks.

BANK RECONCILIATION FORM

PLEASE EXAMINE YOUR STATEMENT AT ONCE. ANY
DISCREPANCY SHOULD BE REPORTED TO THE BANK
IMMEDIATELY.

1. Record any transactions appearing on this statement but not listed in your checkbook.

2. List any checks still outstanding in the space provided to the right.

3. Enter the balance shown on this statement here. **16,967 00**

4. Enter deposits recorded in your checkbook but not shown on this statement. ———

5. Total Lines 3 and 4 and enter here. **16,967 00**

6. Enter total checks outstanding here. **850 00**

7. Subtract Line 6 from Line 5. This adjusted bank balance should agree with your checkbook balance. **16,117 00**

CHECKS OUTSTANDING	
Number	Amount
105	450 00
106	400 00
TOTAL	850 00

Figure 10-8 Bank Reconciliation

2. Enter the ending balance shown on the bank statement.
3. Compare deposits listed on the bank statement to deposits listed in the checkbook. Enter the total of any outstanding deposits on the reconciliation form. Add this total to the bank statement balance and enter the amount on the form.
4. Subtract the total of the outstanding checks from the amount calculated in Step 3. The result is the adjusted bank balance.
5. Compare the adjusted bank balance to the adjusted checkbook balance. The two amounts should match.

If the adjusted bank balance does not match the adjusted checkbook balance, the error must be found and corrected. If the bank has made an error on the bank statement, notify the bank immediately. It is more likely, however, that the error is in the checkbook. Check the addition and subtraction on the check stubs to be sure they are correct.

When the adjusted balances match, the bank statement has been reconciled. The bank fees shown on the bank statement must then be recorded in the accounting records of the business. Before you read about the recording of bank service charges, complete the following Check Your Learning activity.

R — E — M — E — M — B — E — R

If you are having problems reconciling a bank statement, double check for any outstanding checks or outstanding deposits that you may not have included in your calculations.

Valleyview Rental Center received its bank statement on April 27. The balance in the checkbook on April 27 is $2,944.20. The checking account balance shown on the statement is $3,085.95. A deposit of $345.00 was made on April 26, and on April 27 of $290.00. The service charge for the month was $5.25. Valleyview has these four outstanding checks.

Check 344	$202.00	Check 350	$ 25.00
Check 346	55.00	Check 351	500.00

1. What is the amount of the adjusted checkbook balance?
2. What is the amount of outstanding deposits?
3. What is the total amount of outstanding checks?
4. What is the amount of the adjusted bank balance?
5. Does the adjusted bank balance match the adjusted checkbook balance?

Compare your answers to those in the answers section. Re-read the preceding part of the chapter to find the answers to any questions you missed.

Recording Bank Service Charges

Like any other business, banks charge fees for their services. To the depositor, a service charge is an expense that must be recorded in the accounting records. Bank service charges are often recorded in the account Miscellaneous Expense. Since expenses decrease owner's equity, Miscellaneous Expense is debited for the amount of the service charge. Cash in Bank is also decreased by the amount of the service charge, so that account is credited. Remember, the amount of the service charge has already been deducted from the depositor's account, so it is not necessary to write a check for this expense. The journal entry for this transaction is shown in Figure 10-9. The bank statement is the source document for recording the bank service charge.

		GENERAL JOURNAL			PAGE 4	
	DATE	DESCRIPTION	POST. REF.	DEBIT	CREDIT	
1	19-- nov. 1	Miscellaneous Expense		8 00		1
2		Cash in Bank			8 00	2
3		Bank Statement				3

Figure 10-9 General Journal Entry for Bank Service Charge

Special Banking Procedures

Checks are usually written or received and deposited without any problems. However, a business may not want its bank to pay a check that it has written and sent out. Or, a business may receive a check from a customer who does not have enough money to cover the amount of the check.

Stopping Payment on a Check

Occasionally, a drawer will ask the bank (drawee) not to honor, or pay, a check. A **stop payment order** is a demand by the depositor that the bank not honor a certain check. The depositor must issue a stop payment order *before* the check has been presented to the bank for payment. Usually, the depositor must complete and sign a written stop payment order.

When payment is stopped on a check, the accounting clerk writes the words "Stopped Payment" on the appropriate check stub. The clerk must then *add* the amount of the stopped check to the current balance in the checkbook (on the next unused check stub). If appropriate, the accounting clerk then issues a new check.

Most banks charge a fee for stopping payment on a check. When this occurs, the amount of the fee must be subtracted from the checkbook balance and recorded in the business's accounting records. Most businesses record the amount of the fee as an expense in the Miscellaneous Expense account. The journal entry is similar to that made for the bank service charge.

Recording NSF Checks

An **NSF check** is one returned by the bank because there are *not* sufficient *f*unds in the drawer's checking account to cover the amount of the check. For example, suppose Global Travel received and deposited a check from a customer. If the customer does not have enough money in the bank to cover the check, the check will be returned to Global Travel. Global Travel will notify the customer that the check was returned by the bank. The customer must then deposit enough money in the bank to cover the check or find another means of paying its bill.

When the bank returns the NSF check to Global Travel, it deducts the amount of the check from Global Travel's checking account. Global Travel must then subtract the amount of the check from its checkbook balance.

A journal entry must also be made to record the return of the NSF check. Since the check represents payment for an amount owed to Global Travel, the amount of the check is recorded as an account receivable. Cash in Bank was originally debited for the amount of the check, so that account is now credited for the same amount. The journal entry is shown in Figure 10-10.

	GENERAL JOURNAL			PAGE 4	
DATE	DESCRIPTION	POST. REF.	DEBIT	CREDIT	
18	Accts. Rec. — Burton Company		450 00		
	Cash in Bank			450 00	
	NSF Check				

Figure 10-10 Recording the Return of an NSF Check

Electronic Funds Transfer System

As you learned earlier, when a bank sends a statement to a depositor, it also returns the checks paid by the bank. Let's look at the route a check follows from the time it is written until it is returned with the bank statement.

1. Global Travel Agency writes Check 103 to Abrams Real Estate for $550 for the month's rent.
2. Abrams Real Estate deposits the check in its acccount at the First National Bank.
3. First National Bank increases the balance in Abrams' checking account by $550.
4. First National Bank sends the $550 check to American National Bank, Global Travel Agency's bank, for collection.
5. American National Bank sends the First National Bank $550 and deducts this amount from Global Travel's account.
6. The paid check is returned to Global Travel Agency by American National Bank with the monthly bank statement.

As you can see, the exchange of checks and funds is a routine procedure. However, since the number of checks written each day is in the millions, this transferring of funds from one bank to another is quite a job if handled manually. Today, banks use the electronic funds transfer system (EFTS) to handle the details of exchanging funds. The **electronic funds transfer system** enables banks to transfer funds from the account of one depositor to the account of another quickly and accurately without the immediate exchange of checks.

The full development of the electronic funds transfer system is not now being used because the general public does not wish to move to a system that is completely checkless.

SUMMARY OF KEY POINTS

1. The use of a checking account is an important way for a business to protect cash. The checking account also serves as a duplicate record of all cash transactions.
2. Deposit slips are prepared when cash and checks are deposited in a bank account. Copies of deposit slips should be kept as proof of deposits.
3. Checks must be endorsed before they can be deposited. Most businesses stamp a restrictive endorsement on checks as soon as they are received. A restrictive endorsement limits how a check may be handled. The restrictive endorsement helps protect the checks received by a business from misuse.
4. Correctly written checks and accurate check stubs help prevent the loss of cash through carelessness or fraud.
5. As a part of its control of cash, a business regularly proves cash by comparing the Cash in Bank balance to the checkbook balance and finding the reason for any differences between the two amounts.
6. A bank statement is sent to each depositor, usually once a month. A bank statement should be reconciled promptly upon receipt. Any errors found on the bank statement must be reported to the bank immediately.
7. Bank service charges are recorded in the checkbook to keep the checkbook balance up to date.
8. After the bank statement has been reconciled, the service charges reported on the bank statement are journalized and then posted to the appropriate accounts.

REVIEW AND APPLICATIONS

Building Your Accounting Vocabulary

In your own words, write the definition of each of the following accounting terms. Use complete sentences for your definitions.

bank service charge
bank statement
canceled checks
check
checking account
deposit slip
depositor
drawee
drawer

electronic funds
   transfer system
endorsement
external controls
internal controls
NSF check
outstanding check
outstanding deposit
payee

reconciling the bank
   statement
restrictive
   endorsement
signature card
stop payment order
voiding a check

Reviewing Your Accounting Knowledge

1. Explain why it is important for businesses to protect their cash.
2. What internal controls can a business use to protect its cash?
3. What external controls can a business use to protect its cash?
4. Describe the types of forms that are needed to open and use a checking account.
5. What is the purpose of a check endorsement?
6. Why should you always complete the check stub *before* writing the check?
7. What information does a bank statement contain?
8. List the steps followed in reconciling a bank statement.
9. Explain how bank service charges and NSF checks are recorded in the accounting records of a business.
10. How is the bank service charge recorded in the checkbook?

Improving Your Analysis Skills

Maria Varga and John Wills are cashiers for Bacon Construction Co. Both Maria and John are responsible for receiving and paying out cash and are authorized to sign checks for the company. Maria is supposed to record all cash transactions in the company's accounting records, although John often helps. What is wrong with the cash control policies followed by Bacon Construction Co.? What suggestions can you make for improving these policies?

Applying Accounting Procedures

Exercise 10-1   Preparing a Deposit Slip

On August 14, Loretta Harper, owner of Harper Limousine Service, deposited the following items in the business's checking account.

Cash: $784.29
Checks: Charles Ling, drawn on American Bank of Commerce, Dallas, ABA No. 32-7091; $39.44

Keith Lopez, drawn on People's Bank, Baton Rouge, ABA No. 84-268; $249.82

Marjorie Luke, drawn on Horizon Federal Savings and Loan, Shreveport, ABA No. 84-6249; $846.19

Instructions: Using this information, complete a deposit slip.

Exercise 10-2   Writing a Check

Carey Video Rentals received a bill from Northeast Telephone for $214.80 for September telephone services.

Instructions: Prepare Check 41 to pay the telephone bill. Use October 12 as the date and sign your name as drawer.

Exercise 10-3   Recording Deposits in the Checkbook

On January 20, Jon Preston, owner of Preston Fitness Center, deposited $1,434.86 in the business's checking account.

Instructions: Record this deposit on check stub 44 in Preston Fitness Center's checkbook.

Exercise 10-4   Recording Bank Service Charges in the Checkbook

The December bank statement for the Century Advertising Agency listed a bank service charge of $19.80.

Instructions: Record this service charge in the checkbook on check stub 24.

Problem 10-1   Handling Deposits

On February 4, Stanford Mott, owner of Mott Furniture Rental, deposited the following items in the company's checking account at the First National Bank in Ocala, Florida.

Cash: Currency, $374.00; Coins, $7.42
Checks: Bob Warner, drawn on Consumers Bank, Ocala, ABA No. 63-706; $64.98

Joan Walkman, drawn on Sun Bank, Gainesville, ABA No. 63-699; $349.81

Ernesto Garcia, drawn on Progressive Savings and Loan, Tampa, ABA No. 63-710; $29.44

Instructions:

(1) Endorse the checks with a restrictive endorsement. Use the name "Mott Furniture Rental."
(2) Fill out a deposit slip. Use the ABA number to identify each check.
(3) Record the deposit in the checkbook on check stub 651.

Problem 10-2   Maintaining the Checkbook

As the accounting clerk for Currie Construction, you write and sign checks and make deposits. The current checkbook balance, shown on check stub 104, is $3,486.29.

Instructions: For each transaction,

(1) Record the necessary information on the check stub. Determine the new balance and carry the balance forward.

(2) Write checks where requested. Sign your name as drawer.

Transactions:

Mar. 3 Issued Check 104 for $868.45 to Custom Construction for construction supplies.

3 Deposited $601.35 in the checking account.

6 Purchased building materials for cash by issuing Check 105 for $299.60 to Cunningham Lumber.

7 Paid Laverne Brothers $1,000.00 for completing a painting job, Check 106.

10 Made a deposit of $342.80 in the checking account.

10 Wrote Check 107 to Union Utilities for the February electric bill of $175.50.

Problem 10-3   Reconciling the Bank Statement

On May 31, George Fister, the accountant for Anco Financial Services, received the bank statement dated May 30. After comparing the company's checkbook with the bank statement, George found:

1. The checkbook balance on May 31 was $960.

2. The ending bank statement balance was $1,380.

3. The bank statement showed a service charge of $10.

4. A deposit of $405 was made on May 30 but did not appear on the bank statement.

5. Check 468 for $529 and Check 472 for $306 were outstanding.

Instructions:

(1) Record the bank service charge in the checkbook.

(2) Reconcile the bank statement for Anco Financial Services.

(3) Journalize the entry for the bank service charge in the general journal.

(4) Post the bank service charge to the appropriate general ledger accounts.

Problem 10-4   Reconciling the Bank Statement

On July 31, June Hankins, owner of Hankins Photography Studio, received a bank statement dated July 30. After she compared the company's checkbook records with the bank statement, June found:

1. The checkbook had a balance of $2,551.34.

2. The bank statement showed a balance of $2,272.36.

3. The statement showed a bank service charge of $20.00.

4. A check from Ted Koonce for $62.44 that was deposited on July 18 was returned by the bank. There was no fee for handling the NSF check.

5. A deposit of $672.48 made on July 30 did not appear on the July bank statement.

6. These checks are outstanding:

Check 172 for $126.84   Check 183 for $192.80
Check 181 for $ 87.66   Check 187 for $ 68.64

Instructions: Using the preceding information,

(1) Record the service charge and the NSF check in the checkbook.
(2) Reconcile the bank statement for Hankins Photography Studio.
(3) Journalize the service charge and the NSF check on page 7 of a general journal.
(4) Post the journal entries to the appropriate general ledger accounts.

**Problem 10-5   Reconciling the Bank Statement
Using the T Account Form**

On February 20, the Northam Computer Service Co. received its bank statement dated February 18. After examining it and the checkbook, these facts were determined.

1. The checkbook balance on February 20 was $880.84.
2. The ending bank balance was $344.58.
3. There was a service charge of $14.00 for the month.
4. The following checks were outstanding:

| Check 164 | $ 88.41 | Check 171 | $129.88 |
| Check 169 | 69.34 | Check 173 | 14.25 |

5. A $68.42 check from Tom McCrary that was deposited on February 13 was returned by the bank for insufficient funds. The bank charged Northam's account $7.00 for handling the NSF check. No journal entry has yet been made for the NSF check.
6. A deposit of $938.72 made on February 9 does not appear on the bank statement.
7. A check for $200.00 made out to Fontenot, Inc., was lost in the mail and has never been cashed. A stop payment order, which cost $10.00, was issued on February 15. No new check has yet been issued.

Instructions: Reconcile the bank statement. Using the T account form in the working papers, list changes to the bank statement balance on the left side and changes to the checkbook balance on the right side.

Today's CPA

Do you have a flair for working with numbers? Do you like interpreting facts and solving problems? If you do, you might want to consider a career as a certified public accountant. These professionals offer accounting advice and assistance to the public for a fee.

To become a certified public accountant (CPA), you'll need a bachelor's degree, a passing grade on a two-and-a-half day examination, plus a certificate from a state accountancy board. In 48 states, the board also requires an additional 40 hours of continuing education classwork a year. And, while not a written requirement, computer literacy is indispensable.

Today's CPAs play leading roles in a wide variety of industries.

Over 300,000 CPAs practice in this country. Every year, about 10,000 new CPAs enter the field. Some are self-employed, but the majority work for accounting firms. And over half of the accountants entering the profession today are women.

CPAs have traditionally worked in the fields of taxation and auditing. Tax accountants prepare tax returns for their clients. Auditors verify the accuracy of financial statements prepared by business accountants.

Because tax laws are becoming more demanding and small businesses are growing, the demand for certified public accountants is increasing. And this consumer demand is moving CPAs toward fields such as financial planning, computer auditing, tax law, or consulting services. In addition to being experts in accounting, CPAs may also need to be experts in a particular industry. CPAs who perform consulting services are increasingly being asked to participate in long-range planning, to give advice on marketing plans, to implement and evaluate computer systems, or to evaluate management personnel for promotion.

Today's challenging business environment and computer technology are redefining the CPA profession. Public accounting firms that march to this different drummer are moving toward specialization. While this trend may require different employee qualifications, it can also present new opportunities to those of you who wish to enter the field in the coming years.

Completing the Accounting Cycle
for a Sole Proprietorship

You have just completed your study of the accounting cycle and the banking activities for a service business organized as a sole proprietorship. Now you will have the opportunity to apply what you have learned as you work through the accounting cycle for Jenny's Gymnastic Academy.

When you have completed this activity, you will have

1. analyzed business transactions
2. journalized business transactions in the general journal
3. posted journal entries to the general ledger accounts
4. prepared a trial balance and a work sheet
5. prepared financial statements
6. journalized and posted the closing entries
7. prepared a post-closing trial balance
8. prepared a reconciliation of the bank statement and recorded any bank service charges

Jenny's Gymnastic Academy

Jenny's Gymnastic Academy is owned and managed by Jennifer Rachael. The business is organized as a sole proprietorship. The academy provides gymnastic programs for children ages 4-18. The business earns revenue from membership fees and fees charged for special classes.

Chart of Accounts

The chart of accounts for Jenny's Gymnastic Academy appears at the top of the next page.

Business Transactions

Jenny's Gymnastic Academy began business operations on March 1 of this year. During the month of March, the business completed the transactions that follow.

Instructions: Use the accounting stationery in the working papers accompanying this textbook to complete this activity.

(1) Open a general ledger account for each account in the chart of accounts.
(2) Analyze each business transaction.
(3) Enter each business transaction in the general journal. Begin on journal page 1.
(4) Post each journal entry to the appropriate accounts in the general ledger.

JENNY'S GYMNASTIC ACADEMY
Chart of Accounts

ASSETS	101	Cash in Bank
	105	Accounts Receivable—Sally Chapin
	110	Accounts Receivable—Carla DiSario
	115	Accounts Receivable—George McGarty
	120	Accounts Receivable—Joyce Torres
	130	Office Supplies
	135	Office Furniture
	140	Office Equipment
	145	Gymnastic Equipment
LIABILITIES	205	Accounts Payable—Custom Designs
	210	Accounts Payable—The Gym House
	215	Accounts Payable—T & N Equipment
OWNER'S EQUITY	301	Jennifer Rachael, Capital
	305	Jennifer Rachael, Withdrawals
	310	Income Summary
REVENUE	401	Membership Fees
	405	Class Fees
EXPENSES	505	Maintenance Expense
	510	Miscellaneous Expense
	515	Rent Expense
	525	Utilities Expense

(5) Reconcile the bank statement that was received on March 31. The statement is dated March 30.
   a. The checkbook has a current balance of $19,580.00.
   b. The bank statement shows a balance of $19,831.00.
   c. The bank service charge is $15.00.
   d. A deposit of $140.00 made on March 30 does not appear on the bank statement.
   e. These checks are outstanding: Check 112 for $106.00 and Check 113 for $300.00.
(6) Make any necessary adjustments to the checkbook balance.
(7) Journalize and post the entry for the bank service charge.
(8) Prepare a trial balance and then complete the work sheet.
(9) Prepare an income statement.
(10) Prepare a statement of changes in owner's equity.
(11) Prepare a balance sheet.
(12) Journalize and post the closing entries.
(13) Prepare a post-closing trial balance.

Transactions:

Mar. 1 Jennifer Rachael invested $25,000 in Jenny's Gymnastic Academy, Memorandum 1, by opening a business checking account.

  2 Bought a cash register (office equipment) for $525, Check 101.

  2 Purchased $73 in office supplies and issued Check 102.

Mar. 3 Received Invoice 2348 from Custom Designs for office furniture bought on account, $2,680.

4 Jennifer Rachael invested a used typewriter worth $135 in the business, Memorandum 2.

5 Purchased gymnastic equipment for $3,924, Check 103.

5 Received $950 for membership fees, Receipt 1.

6 Bought $8,495 of gymnastic equipment on account from The Gym House, Invoice 395.

8 Carla DiSario completed two classes, $36, Invoice 101, to be paid later.

9 Wrote Check 104 for $850 for the March rent.

10 Charged George McGarty $175 for special classes, on account, Invoice 102.

10 Received Invoice 5495 for a $2,375 microcomputer system bought on account from T & N Equipment.

11 Prepared Receipt 2 for $695 in membership fees received.

13 Received $36 from Carla DiSario on account, Receipt 3.

14 Sent Check 105 for $200 to The Gym House on account.

14 Jennifer Rachael invested $800 worth of gymnastic equipment in the business, Memorandum 3.

15 Wrote Check 106 for $750 to repaint a section of the gym.

16 Completed classes totaling $250 with Joyce Torres, Invoice 103, on account.

18 Jennifer Rachael withdrew $500 for personal use, Check 107.

19 Sent Check 108 for the electric bill of $183.

20 Received a check from George McGarty for $75 to apply on his account, Receipt 4.

21 Issued Check 109 for $45 for stamps (Miscellaneous Expense).

22 Received membership fees, Receipt 5 for $550.

24 Sent Check 110 for $500 to Custom Designs on account.

25 Paid $85 for the cleaning of the office, Check 111.

26 Completed classes with Sally Chapin, $185, to be paid later, Invoice 104.

27 Paid the $106 electric bill, Check 112.

28 Sold a piece of gymnastic equipment to another gym for $175 cash, Receipt 6.

30 Paid T & N Equipment $300 on account, Check 113.

30 Received $140 on account from Joyce Torres, Receipt 7.

31 Bought additional office supplies on account for $227 from T & N Equipment, Invoice 5643.

AquaClean Pool Service

An Accounting Simulation Using a General Journal

AquaClean Pool Service is a business simulation based on a business that provides cleaning and maintenance services for swimming pools to local businesses and homeowners for a fee. AquaClean Pool Service is a sole proprietorship that is owned and managed by Keith Berger. The company records its business transactions in a general journal. This simulation is available from the publisher and can be completed manually or on a microcomputer.

When you have completed this business simulation, you will have

1. analyzed business transactions from source documents
2. maintained the business's checking account by writing checks, making deposits, and reconciling the bank statement
3. journalized business transactions in the general journal
4. posted journal entries to the general ledger accounts
5. prepared a trial balance and a work sheet
6. prepared financial statements
7. journalized and posted the closing entries
8. prepared a post-closing trial balance

ACCOUNTING FOR A PAYROLL SYSTEM

You have learned how to record transactions for businesses that provide services. Regardless of the type of business, all businesses that employ people must also keep records on the money paid to their employees and on the taxes paid to local, state, and federal governments. In this unit, you will learn how to keep records on employee earnings and how to record the payment of wages in the accounting records of the business.

CHAPTER 11

Payroll Accounting

Most businesses have employees who help keep the business operating. In a private enterprise economy, people are free to work for any business they choose so long as they meet the requirements for employment. Businesses in turn must follow certain guidelines in paying their employees for the services they perform. For example, both federal and state laws require businesses to keep accurate payroll records and to prepare various reports on those earnings.

Most companies set up a system to ensure that their employees are paid on time and that the employees' paychecks are accurate. In this chapter, you will learn about such a system. You will learn how employee earnings and deductions from those earnings are calculated, as well as how paychecks are prepared. You will also learn about the earnings records kept for each employee.

LEARNING OBJECTIVES

When you have completed this chapter, you should be able to
1. Explain the importance of accurate payroll records.
2. Calculate gross earnings and net pay.
3. Explain the types of deductions from employees' gross earnings.
4. Prepare a payroll register.
5. Prepare an employee's earnings record.
6. Define the accounting terms new to this chapter.

NEW Terms

payroll • pay period • payroll clerk • gross earnings • salary • wage • time card • electronic badge readers • piece rate • commission • overtime rate • deduction • exemption • payroll register • net pay • direct deposit • employee's earnings record • accumulated earnings

The Importance of Payroll Records

A **payroll** is a list of a business's employees and the payments due to each employee for a specific pay period. A **pay period** is the amount of time for which an employee is paid. Most businesses use weekly, biweekly, semimonthly, or monthly pay periods.

The employee payroll is a major expense for most companies. To ensure that they have accurate records of their payroll costs, most businesses set up a payroll system for use in recording and reporting employee earnings information. A payroll system should accomplish two basic goals: (1) the collection and processing of all the information needed to prepare and issue payroll checks, and (2) the production of the necessary payroll records for accounting purposes and for reporting to government agencies, management, and others.

Businesses with many employees often hire a person who is responsible for preparing the payroll. This person is called a **payroll clerk.** The payroll clerk makes sure that employees are paid on time, employees are paid the correct amounts, payroll records are completed, payroll reports are filed, and payroll taxes are paid.

All payroll systems have certain tasks in common. Each payroll system includes: (1) the calculation of earnings, (2) the calculation of deductions, (3) the recording of these amounts in the employer's payroll and accounting records, (4) the preparation of payroll checks, and (5) the reporting of employee earnings information to federal and state governments. In this and the next chapter, you will learn about these common payroll tasks.

Calculating Gross Earnings

Most employees are paid for the specific amount of time they have worked during a pay period. The total amount of money earned by an employee in a pay period is the employee's **gross earnings.** Gross earnings can be calculated in several ways. Some employees are paid on a salary basis; others are paid hourly wages, piece rates, or commissions. Employees may also be paid on a salary-plus-commission basis. In addition, if employees work extra hours during a pay period, the amount of overtime pay must be included in the calculation of gross earnings. Let's look at each of these ways of calculating gross earnings.

Salary

ACCOUNTING *Notes*....·

Salt was used as money in Roman times. Our word *salary* comes from the Latin word for "salt."

One common method of paying employees, especially those who are managers or supervisors, is by salary. A **salary** is a fixed amount of money paid to an employee for each pay period. In other words, an employee who is paid a salary is paid a fixed amount regardless of the number of hours worked during the pay period. The amount of the salary is the same as gross earnings, so no additional computations are needed. For example, Paula is paid a salary of $2,000 a month. Her gross earnings are thus $2,000 for each monthly pay period. Paula may work 160 hours one month and 180 hours the next, but her gross earnings will remain at $2,000 a month.

The hourly wage paid to some employees may be governed by a contract between the employer and a union.

Hourly Wage

Another common way of determining gross earnings is the hourly wage. A **wage** is an amount of money paid to an employee at a specified rate per hour worked. The number of hours worked multiplied by the hourly wage equals the gross earnings for the pay period. For example, Karen Nielson is paid $4.45 per hour. Last week she worked 36 hours. Karen's gross earnings were thus $160.20 (see the calculations in the margin).

```
$   4.45
×     36
    26.70
   133.5
 $160.20
```

R — E — M — E — M — B — E — R

Gross earnings are calculated by multiplying the hourly rate by the total hours worked.

No. _11_
Name _Karen Nielson_
Soc. Sec. No. _045-68-5733_
Week Ending _6/30/--_

DAY	IN	OUT	IN	OUT	IN	OUT	TOTAL
M	7:58	12:25	1:32	4:18			7¼
T	8:00	12:00	12:45	4:00			7¼
W	7:56	12:01	1:10	4:15			7
Th	8:01	11:55	1:02	4:16			7¼
F	7:45	12:02	1:05	3:58			7¼
S							
S							
					TOTAL HOURS		36

	Hours	Rate	Amount
REGULAR	36	$4.45	$160.20
OVERTIME	0		
		TOTAL EARNINGS	$160.20

Figure 11-1 A Time Card Completed by an Employee

To keep accurate records of the number of hours worked during each pay period, many businesses have their employees complete time cards. A **time card** is a record of the time an employee arrives at work each day, the time the employee leaves, and the total number of hours worked each day. The times may be recorded manually or by a time clock that registers each employee's arrival and departure times. For example, look at the time card Karen Nielson completed, shown in Figure 11-1.

Employee arrival and departure times are seldom exactly on the hour. As a result, most companies compute arrival and departure times to the nearest quarter hour (15 minutes). A quarter hour begins or ends on the hour, 15 minutes after the hour, 30 minutes after the hour, and 45 minutes after the hour. With this system, employees are paid for working to the nearest quarter hour, regardless of the time they enter and leave work. For example, on Monday Karen arrived for work at 7:58, left for lunch at 12:25, returned from lunch at 1:32, and left work at 4:18. Karen will be paid for working from 8:00 to 12:30 and from 1:30 to 4:15.

R E M E M B E R

When determining the number of hours worked, round arrival and departure times to the nearest quarter hour.

Some businesses are using computer technology at the point where employees enter and leave. This is done by **electronic badge readers.** Each employee's time card or identification badge has a magnetic strip on which is encoded certain employee information. When the time card is entered, the badge reader scans the magnetic strip. The identity of the employee, the department or area in which the employee works, and the arrival or departure time are entered directly into the computer. This electronic equipment enables a business to prepare a daily printout on employee work hours.

Regardless of how records on employee work hours are prepared, most companies have supervisors check the accuracy of the labor costs.

Piece Rate

$$\begin{array}{r} \$ \ 4.60 \\ \times \quad 40 \\ \hline \$184.00 \end{array} \qquad \begin{array}{r} \$ \ 535 \\ \times \quad .12 \\ \hline \$64.20 \end{array}$$

$$\begin{array}{r} \$184.00 \\ + \ \ 64.20 \\ \hline \$248.20 \end{array}$$

In many factories and manufacturing plants, employees are paid a specific amount of money for each item, or piece, they produce during a pay period. The amount paid for each piece produced is called the **piece rate.** Most companies also pay an hourly wage in addition to the piece rate. For example, Leon is paid an hourly rate of $4.60 plus 12¢ for each piece he produces. Leon worked 40 hours last week and produced 535 items. His gross earnings for the week were $248.20 (see the calculations in the margin).

Commission

$$\begin{array}{r} \$ \ 7,184 \\ \times \quad .05 \\ \hline \$359.20 \end{array}$$

A **commission** is an amount paid to an employee based on a percentage of the employee's sales. Many companies pay their sales employees a commission to encourage them to increase their sales. For example, Kate is paid a 5% commission on all her sales. Last week Kate's total sales were $7,184.00. Kate's gross earnings for the week were thus $359.20.

Salary Plus Commission or Bonus

$$\begin{array}{r} \$ \ 4,640 \\ \times \quad .03 \\ \hline \$139.20 \\ +200.00 \\ \hline \$339.20 \end{array}$$

Some companies pay their salespeople a base salary plus a commission or a bonus on the amount of their sales. For example, Jerry is paid a salary of $200.00 per week plus a commission of 3% of his sales. Jerry's sales were $4,640.00 last week. His gross earnings were thus $339.20.

```
$   4.60
×     40
$184.00

$   6.90
×      3
$  20.70
+184.00
$204.70
```

Overtime Pay

The number of hours an employee may work in a weekly pay period is regulated by state and federal laws. Generally, these laws require employers to pay overtime for all hours over 40 per work week. The **overtime rate,** set by the Fair Labor Standards Act of 1938, is $1\frac{1}{2}$ times the employee's regular hourly rate of pay. For example, Ben worked 43 hours last week; his hourly rate of pay is $4.60. Ben was paid for 40 hours at his regular rate of $4.60. He was also paid for the additional 3 hours at a rate of $6.90 ($4.60 × 1.5). Ben's gross earnings for the week were thus $204.70.

Employees who are paid a salary may also be entitled to overtime pay. If a salaried employee is to be paid overtime, the employee's hourly rate of pay must be determined. For example, Ellen's salary is $600.00 per week for a 40-hour week. Her hourly rate is determined by dividing $600.00 by 40 ($600.00 ÷ 40 = $15.00 per hour). Ellen's gross earnings for a 44-hour week would be $600.00 plus $90.00 for the 4 overtime hours at $22.50 per hour ($15.00 × 1.5), for a total of $690.00.

R — E — M — E — M — B — E — R

Employees who work more than 40 hours per work week must be paid overtime. The overtime rate is $1\frac{1}{2}$ times the employee's regular hourly rate of pay.

Before continuing, complete the following activity to check your understanding of the material you have just studied.

Check Your Learning

Use notebook paper to calculate the answers to the following questions.

1. If an employee is paid $4.68 per hour and is paid overtime for all hours worked over 40, what is the gross pay for each of the following?
   a. 37 hours   **b.** 42 hours   **c.** 49 hours
2. Tom is paid a salary of $200.00 per week plus a commission of 7% on sales. Tom's total sales last week were $3,450.00. What were his gross earnings?
3. Clare earns $4.75 per hour plus 10¢ for each item she produces. If Clare produced 371 items last week and worked 40 hours, what were her gross earnings?

Compare your answers to those in the answers section. Re-read the preceding part of the chapter to find the correct answers to any questions you may have missed.

Determining Deductions from Gross Earnings

The first time you received a paycheck, you may have been surprised to see that the amount of the check was not the same as the amount of your gross earnings. Various amounts are taken out of all employees' gross earnings. An amount that is subtracted from gross earnings is called a **deduction.** Deductions include those required by law and those an employee voluntarily wishes to have withheld from earnings.

Deductions Required by Law

An employer is required by law to withhold payroll taxes on its employees' gross earnings. These taxes include the federal income tax and the social security tax. In addition, many cities and states require employers to withhold city or state income taxes.

▲ **Federal Income Tax**   Most people who work must pay the federal government a tax based on their annual incomes. To ensure that taxpayers have the funds to pay their taxes, employers are required to withhold a certain amount of money from each employee's earnings. In other words, the employer acts as a collection agent for the federal government. The employer periodically sends the money that has been withheld from all employees' earnings to the Internal Revenue Service (IRS).

The amount of taxes withheld from each employee's paycheck is an estimate of the amount the employee will owe in taxes at the end of the tax year. The exact amount of taxes is determined when the employee prepares a tax return. If too much money has been withheld, the IRS will refund the amount of the overpayment. If too little money has been withheld, the employee is required to pay the additional amount when the income tax return is filed. Generally, to avoid penalties, an employee must pay in at least 90% of the actual taxes owed.

The amount withheld for federal income taxes each pay period depends on three things: (1) the employee's marital status, (2) the number of exemptions claimed by the employee, and (3) the employee's gross earnings. The first two items of information are found on each employee's Form W-4. This

Employees who earn a stated amount of money for each item sold or a percent of the total value of their sales are paid a "straight" commission.

form, called the Employee's Withholding Allowance Certificate, must be filled out by each employee upon starting a job. A new W-4 form should also be filed if the employee's marital status or exemptions change. Employers are required to keep a current Form W-4 on file for each employee.

Karen Nielson's completed Form W-4 is shown in Figure 11-2. As you can see, an employee must include her or his name, address, social security number, and marital status. In addition, the employee must list the number of exemptions claimed (see line 4 on the form). An **exemption** is an allowance claimed by a taxpayer that reduces the amount of taxes that must be paid. Usually, a taxpayer is allowed one personal exemption and one exemption for each person the taxpayer supports, such as a child or an elderly parent. The greater the number of exemptions claimed by a taxpayer, the lower the amount deducted from earnings for federal income taxes.

Figure 11-2 Employee's Withholding Allowance Certificate

A few employees may not be required to pay federal or state income taxes in a given year. To qualify as an "exempt" employee, a person must have paid no federal income tax the previous year and state that no tax is expected to be paid in the current year. A person cannot claim to be exempt if he or she is claimed as a dependent by another person, has any nonwage income, or expects to have more than $500 in income. If a person writes "Exempt" on Form W-4, the employer will not withhold amounts for federal or state income taxes.

An employee's gross earnings also affect the amount withheld for federal income taxes. Once gross earnings have been calculated, most employers use tax tables supplied by the IRS each year to calculate the amount of federal tax to withhold from each employee's earnings. The partial tax tables shown in Figure 11-3 (pages 220-221) are for use with single and married persons who are paid weekly. Other tax tables are also available.

Let's look at an example of how tax tables are used to calculate the amount of tax to be withheld. Karen Nielson is married and claims two exemptions. One week she earned $160.20. This amount falls between $160 and $165 on the tax table for married persons. Reading across this line to the column for two withholding allowances, you find that $3.00 is to be withheld from Karen's gross earnings for the week for federal taxes.

The amount withheld for federal income taxes is affected by the employee's marital status, exemptions claimed, and gross earnings.

▲ **Social Security Tax**   In addition to withholding employees' federal income taxes, employers must also collect social security taxes for the federal government. The present social security system was established by the Federal Insurance Contributions Act (FICA) in 1935. The social security system finances programs that provide income to certain individuals.

1. The old-age and disability insurance programs provide income to retired and disabled persons and their dependent children.
2. The survivors benefits program provides income to the spouse and dependent children of a deceased worker.
3. The Medicare program provides certain health insurance benefits for the elderly.

Under the Tax Reform Act of 1986, most individuals over the age of five should have a social security number. A person has the same social security number for life. This number is used when reporting an employee's earnings to federal and state governments. The employee's lifetime earnings — as well as all social security taxes paid — are recorded by her or his social security number. A taxpayer must use her or his social security number when filing federal or state income tax returns.

The social security tax is an exact tax rather than an estimated tax. The FICA tax rate is a percentage of the gross earnings of each employee. For example, the current tax rate is 7.65% of gross earnings. The social security tax rate is set by Congress, which has the power to change the rate at any time. Most employees must pay social security taxes, even those who claim an exemption from federal income taxes.

Social security taxes are deducted from each employee's earnings each pay period until the maximum taxable amount for the year is reached. Currently, the maximum earnings on which FICA taxes are deducted are

$$
\begin{array}{r}
\$\ 51,300 \\
\times\quad .0765 \\
\hline
\$3,924.45
\end{array}
$$

$51,300. Thus, the maximum amount of FICA taxes that may be withheld is $3,924.45. The maximum taxable amount may also be changed by Congress at any time.

▲ **State and Local Income Taxes**   Most states also have an income tax on earnings to provide funds for the state. Many cities tax the incomes of the people who live or work in the city. In some areas, state and/or city tax rates are set as a percentage of gross earnings. In other areas, the tax amounts to be deducted are calculated using tax tables similar to the ones used by the federal government.

Voluntary Deductions

Most employers agree to deduct other amounts from their employees' paychecks. Once the employee asks that deductions be made, they are withheld from each paycheck until the employee notifies the employer to stop.

SINGLE Persons—WEEKLY Payroll Period

And the wages are—		And the number of withholding allowances claimed is—										
At least	But less than	0	1	2	3	4	5	6	7	8	9	10
		The amount of income tax to be withheld shall be—										
145	150	19	13	7	1	0	0	0	0	0	0	0
150	155	19	14	8	2	0	0	0	0	0	0	0
155	160	20	14	8	2	0	0	0	0	0	0	0
160	165	21	15	9	3	0	0	0	0	0	0	0
165	170	22	16	10	4	0	0	0	0	0	0	0
170	175	22	17	11	5	0	0	0	0	0	0	0
175	180	23	17	11	5	0	0	0	0	0	0	0
180	185	24	18	12	6	0	0	0	0	0	0	0
185	190	25	19	13	7	1	0	0	0	0	0	0
190	195	25	20	14	8	2	0	0	0	0	0	0
195	200	26	20	14	8	3	0	0	0	0	0	0
200	210	27	21	15	10	4	0	0	0	0	0	0
210	220	29	23	17	11	5	0	0	0	0	0	0
220	230	30	24	18	13	7	1	0	0	0	0	0
230	240	32	26	20	14	8	2	0	0	0	0	0
240	250	33	27	21	16	10	4	0	0	0	0	0
250	260	35	29	23	17	11	5	0	0	0	0	0
260	270	36	30	24	19	13	7	1	0	0	0	0
270	280	38	32	26	20	14	8	2	0	0	0	0
280	290	39	33	27	22	16	10	4	0	0	0	0
290	300	41	35	29	23	17	11	5	0	0	0	0
300	310	42	36	30	25	19	13	7	1	0	0	0
310	320	44	38	32	26	20	14	8	2	0	0	0
320	330	45	39	33	28	22	16	10	4	0	0	0
330	340	47	41	35	29	23	17	11	5	0	0	0
340	350	48	42	36	31	25	19	13	7	1	0	0
350	360	50	44	38	32	26	20	14	8	2	0	0
360	370	51	45	39	34	28	22	16	10	4	0	0
370	380	53	47	41	35	29	23	17	11	5	0	0
380	390	54	48	42	37	31	25	19	13	7	1	0
390	400	56	50	44	38	32	26	20	14	8	3	0
400	410	58	51	45	40	34	28	22	16	10	4	0
410	420	61	53	47	41	35	29	23	17	11	6	0
420	430	64	54	48	43	37	31	25	19	13	7	1
430	440	67	56	50	44	38	32	26	20	14	9	3
440	450	70	58	51	46	40	34	28	22	16	10	4
450	460	72	61	53	47	41	35	29	23	17	12	6
460	470	75	64	54	49	43	37	31	25	19	13	7
470	480	78	67	56	50	44	38	32	26	20	15	9
480	490	81	70	59	52	46	40	34	28	22	16	10
490	500	84	72	61	53	47	41	35	29	23	18	12
500	510	86	75	64	55	49	43	37	31	25	19	13
510	520	89	78	67	56	50	44	38	32	26	21	15
520	530	92	81	70	59	52	46	40	34	28	22	16
530	540	95	84	73	62	53	47	41	35	29	24	18
$540	$550	$98	$86	$75	$64	$55	$49	$43	$37	$31	$25	$19
550	560	100	89	78	67	56	50	44	38	32	27	21
560	570	103	92	81	70	59	52	46	40	34	28	22
570	580	106	95	84	73	62	53	47	41	35	30	24
580	590	109	98	87	76	65	55	49	43	37	31	25
590	600	112	100	89	78	67	56	50	44	38	33	27
600	610	114	103	92	81	70	59	52	46	40	34	28
610	620	117	106	95	84	73	62	53	47	41	36	30
620	630	120	109	98	87	76	65	55	49	43	37	31
630	640	123	112	101	90	79	68	56	50	44	39	33
640	650	126	114	103	92	81	70	59	52	46	40	34
650	660	128	117	106	95	84	73	62	53	47	42	36
660	670	131	120	109	98	87	76	65	55	49	43	37
670	680	134	123	112	101	90	79	68	57	50	45	39
680	690	137	126	115	104	93	82	70	59	52	46	40
690	700	140	128	117	106	95	84	73	62	53	48	42
700	710	142	131	120	109	98	87	76	65	55	49	43
710	720	145	134	123	112	101	90	79	68	57	51	45
720	730	148	137	126	115	104	93	82	71	60	52	46
730	740	151	140	129	118	107	96	84	73	62	54	48
740	750	154	142	131	120	109	98	87	76	65	55	49
750	760	156	145	134	123	112	101	90	79	68	57	51
760	770	159	148	137	126	115	104	93	82	71	60	52
770	780	162	151	140	129	118	107	96	85	74	63	54
780	790	165	154	143	132	121	110	98	87	76	65	55
790	800	168	156	145	134	123	112	101	90	79	68	57
800	810	170	159	148	137	126	115	104	93	82	71	60
810	820	173	162	151	140	129	118	107	96	85	74	63
820	830	176	165	154	143	132	121	110	99	88	77	66
830	840	179	168	157	146	135	124	112	101	90	79	68
840	850	182	170	159	148	137	126	115	104	93	82	71
850	860	184	173	162	151	140	129	118	107	96	85	74
860	870	187	176	165	154	143	132	121	110	99	88	77
870	880	190	179	168	157	146	135	124	113	102	91	80
880	890	193	182	171	160	149	138	126	115	104	93	82
890	900	196	184	173	162	151	140	129	118	107	96	85
900	910	198	187	176	165	154	143	132	121	110	99	88
910	920	201	190	179	168	157	146	135	124	113	102	91
920	930	204	193	182	171	160	149	138	127	116	105	94
930	940	207	196	185	174	163	152	140	129	118	107	96

Figure 11-3 IRS Tax Tables

UNIT 3 Accounting for a Payroll System

MARRIED Persons—WEEKLY Payroll Period

And the wages are—		And the number of withholding allowances claimed is—										
At least	But less than	0	1	2	3	4	5	6	7	8	9	10
		The amount of income tax to be withheld shall be—										
140	145	12	6	0	0	0	0	0	0	0	0	0
145	150	12	6	0	0	0	0	0	0	0	0	0
150	155	13	7	1	0	0	0	0	0	0	0	0
155	160	14	8	2	0	0	0	0	0	0	0	0
160	165	15	9	3	0	0	0	0	0	0	0	0
165	170	15	9	3	0	0	0	0	0	0	0	0
170	175	16	10	4	0	0	0	0	0	0	0	0
175	180	17	11	5	0	0	0	0	0	0	0	0
180	185	18	12	6	0	0	0	0	0	0	0	0
185	190	18	12	6	1	0	0	0	0	0	0	0
190	195	19	13	7	1	0	0	0	0	0	0	0
195	200	20	14	8	2	0	0	0	0	0	0	0
200	210	21	15	9	3	0	0	0	0	0	0	0
210	220	22	17	11	5	0	0	0	0	0	0	0
220	230	24	18	12	6	0	0	0	0	0	0	0
230	240	25	20	14	8	2	0	0	0	0	0	0
240	250	27	21	15	9	3	0	0	0	0	0	0
250	260	28	23	17	11	5	0	0	0	0	0	0
260	270	30	24	18	12	6	0	0	0	0	0	0
270	280	31	26	20	14	8	2	0	0	0	0	0
280	290	33	27	21	15	9	3	0	0	0	0	0
290	300	34	29	23	17	11	5	0	0	0	0	0
300	310	36	30	24	18	12	6	0	0	0	0	0
310	320	37	32	26	20	14	8	2	0	0	0	0
320	330	39	33	27	21	15	9	3	0	0	0	0
330	340	40	35	29	23	17	11	5	0	0	0	0
340	350	42	36	30	24	18	12	6	1	0	0	0
350	360	43	38	32	26	20	14	8	2	0	0	0
360	370	45	39	33	27	21	15	9	4	0	0	0
370	380	46	41	35	29	23	17	11	5	0	0	0
380	390	48	42	36	30	24	18	12	7	1	0	0
390	400	49	44	38	32	26	20	14	8	2	0	0
400	410	51	45	39	33	27	21	15	10	4	0	0
410	420	52	47	41	35	29	23	17	11	5	1	0
420	430	54	48	42	36	30	24	18	13	7	1	0
530	540	70	65	59	53	47	41	35	29	23	17	11
540	550	72	66	60	54	48	42	36	31	25	19	13
550	560	73	68	62	56	50	44	38	32	26	20	14
560	570	75	69	63	57	51	45	39	34	28	22	16
570	580	76	71	65	59	53	47	41	35	29	23	17
580	590	78	72	66	60	54	48	42	37	31	25	19
590	600	79	74	68	62	56	50	44	38	32	26	20
600	610	81	75	69	63	57	51	45	40	34	28	22
610	620	82	77	71	65	59	53	47	41	35	29	23
620	630	84	78	72	66	60	54	48	43	37	31	25
880	890	148	137	126	115	104	93	87	82	76	70	64
890	900	151	140	129	118	107	96	89	83	77	71	65
900	910	154	143	132	121	110	99	90	85	79	73	67
910	920	157	146	135	124	113	102	92	86	80	74	68
920	930	160	149	137	126	115	104	93	88	82	76	70
930	940	162	151	140	129	118	107	96	89	83	77	71
940	950	165	154	143	132	121	110	99	91	85	79	73
950	960	168	157	146	135	124	113	102	92	86	80	74
960	970	171	160	149	138	127	116	105	94	88	82	76
970	980	174	163	151	140	129	118	107	96	89	83	77
980	990	176	165	154	143	132	121	110	99	91	85	79
990	1,000	179	168	157	146	135	124	113	102	92	86	80
1,000	1,010	182	171	160	149	138	127	116	105	94	88	82
1,010	1,020	185	174	163	152	141	130	119	107	96	89	83
1,020	1,030	188	177	165	154	143	132	121	110	99	91	85
1,030	1,040	190	179	168	157	146	135	124	113	102	92	86
1,040	1,050	193	182	171	160	149	138	127	116	105	94	88
1,050	1,060	196	185	174	163	152	141	130	119	108	97	89
1,060	1,070	199	188	177	166	155	144	133	121	110	99	91
1,070	1,080	202	191	179	168	157	146	135	124	113	102	92
1,080	1,090	204	193	182	171	160	149	138	127	116	105	94
1,090	1,100	207	196	185	174	163	152	141	130	119	108	97
1,100	1,110	210	199	188	177	166	155	144	133	122	111	100
1,110	1,120	213	202	191	180	169	158	147	135	124	113	102
1,120	1,130	216	205	193	182	171	160	149	138	127	116	105
1,130	1,140	218	207	196	185	174	163	152	141	130	119	108
1,140	1,150	221	210	199	188	177	166	155	144	133	122	111
1,150	1,160	224	213	202	191	180	169	158	147	136	125	114
1,160	1,170	227	216	205	194	183	172	161	149	138	127	116
1,170	1,180	230	219	207	196	185	174	163	152	141	130	119

Figure 11-3   IRS Tax Tables (Concluded)

Some common voluntary deductions include those for union dues, health insurance payments, life insurance payments, pension fund contributions, credit union deposits and payments, and charitable contributions.

Before continuing, complete the following activity to check your understanding of deductions from gross earnings.

Check Your Learning

Use notebook paper to write the answers to the questions that follow.

1. List three deductions from employee earnings that are required by law.
2. What two items of information for computing federal income taxes are recorded on an employee's Form W-4?
3. Using the tax tables on pages 220-221, find the amount of taxes for these employees.
    a. Employee 1: Married; claims 2 exemptions; gross weekly earnings, $224.
    b. Employee 2: Single; claims 1 exemption; gross weekly earnings, $162.
4. Calculate the amount of social security tax that each employee in Question 3 must pay.

Compare your answers to those in the answers section. Re-read the preceding part of the chapter to find the correct answers to any questions you may have missed.

Completing the Payroll Register

We mentioned earlier that federal and state laws require businesses to keep accurate records of the amounts paid to employees. A payroll register is one form that is used. The **payroll register** is a form that summarizes information about employees' earnings for each pay period. The payroll clerk is usually responsible for preparing the payroll register.

The payroll register shown in Figure 11-4 is used by Lenker Consulting Service. As you can see, each employee's I.D. number and name are listed along with her or his marital status and the number of exemptions claimed. Refer to this illustration as you read the following descriptions of the other columns in the payroll register.

1. Total Hours Column. The information in this column is taken from each employee's time card. Regular and overtime hours are added together and the total number of hours entered in this column.
2. Rate Column. The employee's current rate of pay is written in this column. The employee's earnings record is the source of information for each employee's rate of pay.
3. Earnings Columns. The earnings section of the payroll register is divided into three columns: regular earnings, overtime earnings, and total earnings. To complete these columns, the payroll clerk must multiply the employee's total hours worked by the employee's hourly rate.

PAY PERIOD ENDING _June 30_   19 _--_   DATE OF PAYMENT _June 30, 19--_

EMPLOYEE NUMBER	NAME	MAR STATUS	EXEMP	TOTAL HOURS	RATE	EARNINGS			DEDUCTIONS						NET PAY	CK. NO.
						REGULAR	OVERTIME	TOTAL	FICA	FED. INC. TAX	STATE INC. TAX	HOSP. INS.	OTHER	TOTAL		
012	Cropp, B.	M	1	39	4.25	165 75		165 75	12 68	9 00	4 97	3 20	(B)5 00	34 85	130 90	183
014	Lee, V.	S	0	43	4.10	164 00	18 45	182 45	13 96	24 00	6 57			44 53	137 92	184
017	Moore, L.	S	0	41	4.45	178 00	6 67	184 67	14 13	24 00	6 65	2 10		46 88	137 79	185
011	Nielson, K.	M	2	36	4.45	160 20		160 20	12 26	3 00	4 77	3 20		23 23	136 97	186
018	Thornton, S.	M	3	31	4.25	131 75		131 75	10 08	0 00	2 74	3 20	(B)5 00	21 02	110 73	187
25					TOTALS	799 70	25 12	824 82	63 11	60 00	25 70	11 70	(B)10 00	170 51	654 31	25

Other Deductions: Write the appropriate code letter to the left of the amount: B—U.S. Savings Bonds; C—Credit Union; UD—Union Dues; UW—United Way.

Figure 11-4   Payroll Register

$ 4.25
× 39
$165.75

$164.00
+ 18.45
$182.45

$12.68
9.00
4.97
3.20
+ 5.00
$34.85

$165.75
− 34.85
$130.90

For example, Employee 12 worked 39 hours during the week ended June 30. Employee 12, whose hourly rate is $4.25, earned $165.75 for the week. Since no overtime hours were worked, regular earnings and total earnings are the same.

If an employee works overtime, the overtime earnings are entered in the middle column. Employee 14, for example, worked 3 overtime hours, earning $18.45. That employee's regular and overtime earnings are added and entered in the total earnings column.

4. Deductions Columns. On this payroll register, the deductions section is divided into six columns. (The number of columns in this section varies from company to company.) Look at the deductions recorded for Employee 12. The deductions include those required by law—FICA tax, federal income tax, and state income tax—and voluntary deductions for hospital insurance and U.S. savings bonds. After the amount of each deduction is calculated for an employee, the amounts are added and the total is entered in the total deductions column.

5. Net Pay Column. **Net pay** is the amount of money left after all deductions are subtracted from gross earnings. For example, Employee 12's net pay is $130.90.

6. Check Number Column. Most employees are paid by check. After the payroll checks have been prepared, the check numbers are recorded in this column.

Notice also that each amount column is totaled and the totals entered on the last line of the payroll register. The totals recorded for earnings, deductions, and net pay should be cross-checked to verify the amounts.

R — E — M — E — M — B — E — R

Gross (total) earnings minus deductions equals net pay.

Preparing Payroll Checks

Once the payroll register has been checked for accuracy, a paycheck is prepared for each employee. Most businesses prefer to pay their employees

by check as a means of cash control. When a company has only a few employees, paychecks are often written on the company's regular checking account. Companies with several employees, however, generally have a separate checking account for payroll.

When a separate payroll account is used, funds must be put into this payroll account each pay period. This is usually done by writing a check on the company's regular checking account for the amount of the total net pay. This check is then deposited in the payroll checking account.

The payroll register is the source of information for preparing the paychecks. Along with the paycheck, each employee must be given a written explanation showing how the employee's net pay was calculated. A payroll check has an additional stub that is used for this purpose. A typical payroll check and stub are shown in Figure 11-5. Notice that the amounts recorded on the stub are the same as the amounts recorded in the payroll register for that employee. After each paycheck is written, its number is recorded in the payroll register.

LENKER CONSULTING SERVICE 382 Jefferson Street Newton, Utah 84327	No. 186
	June 30 19 -- 11-890 / 1210
Pay to the Order of Karen Nielson	$ 136.97
One hundred thirty-six and 97/100	Dollars
SECOND NATIONAL BANK Newton, Utah	Matthew Lenker
⑆121008901⑆ 233 576 0001 ⑈ 8986	

Employee Pay Statement
Detach and retain this statement.   No. 186

Period Ending	Earnings			Deductions						Net Pay
	Regular	Overtime	Total	FICA	Federal Income Tax	State Income Tax	Hosp. Ins.	Other	Total	
6/30/--	$160.20	—	$160.20	$12.26	$3.00	$4.77	$3.20		$23.23	$136.97

Figure 11-5 Completed Payroll Check and Stub

Some companies offer their employees the option of direct deposit of their paychecks. With **direct deposit,** the employee's net pay is deposited in her or his personal bank account. No paycheck is prepared. The employee does receive a record of the amount of money deposited and the amounts withheld for taxes and other deductions. Direct deposits are usually made through electronic funds transfer. With this system, the employer provides the employee's bank with a computer tape or card showing the wages that should be added to the employee's account. When the tape or card is run through the bank's computer system, the balance in the employee's account is automatically increased.

The Employee's Earnings Record

In addition to the payroll register, the employer must keep an individual payroll record for each employee. This payroll record is kept on a form called an **employee's earnings record.** An example of an employee's earnings record appears in Figure 11-6. The same amount columns that appear on the payroll register appear on the earnings record. In addition, there is a column on the earnings record for the employee's accumulated earnings. **Accumulated earnings** are each employee's year-to-date gross earnings, the employee's gross earnings from the beginning of the year through each pay period. For example, Karen Nielson's accumulated earnings as of June 30 are determined by adding her gross earnings for this pay period ($160.20) to her accumulated earnings for the previous pay period ($4,423.41).

$4,423.41
+ 160.20
$4,583.61

The earnings records are kept on a quarterly basis. This makes it easier for a business to complete government reports that are often required each quarter. At the end of each quarter, the amount columns on the earnings record are totaled. The final amount in the accumulated earnings column is carried forward to the top of the employee's earnings record for the next quarter, as shown in Figure 11-6.

EMPLOYEE'S EARNINGS RECORD FOR QUARTER ENDING __June 30, 19 ——__

Nielson, Karen L.
Last Name / First / Initial
Address 419 East Main Street
Kingston, UT 84743

EMPLOYEE NO. 11   MARITAL STATUS M   EXEMPTIONS 2
POSITION Office Clerk
RATE OF PAY $4.45   SOC. SEC. NO. 045-68-5733

| PAY PERIOD | | EARNINGS | | | DEDUCTIONS | | | | | | | NET PAY | ACCUMULATED EARNINGS |
NO.	ENDED	REGULAR	OVERTIME	TOTAL	FICA	FED. INC. TAX	STATE INC. TAX	HOSP. INS.	OTHER		TOTAL		2309 14
1	4/7/--	178 00		178 00	13 62	5 00	5 16	3 20			26 98	151 02	2487 14
2	4/14/--	175 77		175 77	13 45	5 00	5 10	3 20			26 75	149 02	2662 91
3	4/21/--	178 00		178 00	13 62	5 00	5 16	3 20	(B) 5 00		31 98	146 02	2840 91
4	4/28/--	178 00	13 34	191 34	14 64	7 00	5 55	3 20			30 39	160 95	3032 25
5	5/5/--	166 87		166 87	12 77	3 00	4 84	3 20			23 81	143 06	3199 12
6	5/12/--	178 00		178 00	13 62	5 00	5 16	3 20			26 98	151 02	3377 12
7	5/19/--	175 77		175 77	13 45	5 00	5 10	3 20	(B) 5 00		31 75	144 02	3552 89
8	5/26/--	178 00		178 00	13 62	5 00	5 16	3 20			26 98	151 02	3730 89
9	6/2/--	178 00	11 67	189 67	14 51	6 00	5 50	3 20			29 21	160 46	3920 56
10	6/9/--	151 30		151 30	11 57	1 00	4 39	3 20			20 16	131 14	4071 86
11	6/16/--	178 00		178 00	13 62	5 00	5 16	3 20	(B) 5 00		31 98	146 02	4249 86
12	6/23/--	173 55		173 55	13 28	4 00	5 03	3 20			25 51	148 04	4423 41
13	6/30/--	160 20		160 20	12 26	3 00	4 77	3 20			23 23	136 97	4583 61
QUARTERLY TOTALS		2249 46	25 01	2274 47	174 03	59 00	66 08	41 60	15 00		355 71	1,918 76	

Other Deductions: B—U.S. Savings Bonds; C—Credit Union; UD—Union Dues; UW—United Way.

EMPLOYEE'S EARNINGS RECORD FOR QUARTER ENDING __. September 30, 19 ——__

Nielson, Karen L.
Last Name / First / Initial
Address 419 East Main Street
Kingston, UT 84743

EMPLOYEE NO. 11   MARITAL STATUS M   EXEMPTIONS 2
POSITION Office Clerk
RATE OF PAY $4.45   SOC. SEC. NO. 045-68-5733

| PAY PERIOD | | EARNINGS | | | DEDUCTIONS | | | | | | | NET PAY | ACCUMULATED EARNINGS |
NO.	ENDED	REGULAR	OVERTIME	TOTAL	FICA	FED. INC. TAX	STATE INC. TAX	HOSP. INS.	OTHER		TOTAL		4583 61
1													

Figure 11-6 Employee's Earnings Record

A Computerized Payroll System

In recent years, computers have become an important part of payroll preparation and reporting for many businesses. Computers can process large quantities of payroll information quickly and accurately, thus helping to ensure that employees are paid on time and that their paychecks are accurate. Many businesses purchase their own computers, while others hire outside firms to process their payrolls for them.

When a company uses a computerized payroll system, basic information about each employee is stored in the computer's files. This information includes the employee's identification number, name, social security number, and method of calculating gross earnings. A payroll clerk normally inputs each employee's I.D. number and the number of hours worked during the pay period. The computer uses this information, along with the stored data on each employee's deductions and exemptions, to compute gross earnings, deductions, and net pay. The computer then prepares the payroll register.

The computer will also print the paychecks and the earnings information on the check stubs. If the employee is paid by direct deposit, the computer prepares the tape listing the amount of each employee's wages. The computer also prints the written record of earnings that each employee receives. The computer then prepares the employee's earnings records.

Many companies have their payrolls prepared by banks that use computerized payroll systems. When the payroll is prepared by a bank, information about each employee is stored in the bank's computers. When it is time for the payroll to be prepared, the number of hours worked by each employee must be communicated to the bank. The bank prepares the paychecks and sends the company a record of its employees' earnings for use in recording payroll information in the accounting system.

SUMMARY OF KEY POINTS

1. Most employers have a payroll system to ensure that employees are paid on time and that their paychecks and payroll records are accurate. Employers are required to keep accurate records of all payroll information.
2. Gross earnings may be calculated by various methods: salary, hourly wage, piece rate, commission, or a combination of these methods.
3. An employee who works more than 40 hours per work week must be paid overtime. The overtime rate is $1\frac{1}{2}$ times the regular rate of pay.
4. Deductions from gross earnings are those required by law—such as federal income taxes, FICA taxes, and city or state income taxes—and those requested by the employee—such as union dues, insurance payments, and charitable contributions.
5. A payroll register is prepared for each pay period to summarize the payroll information for all employees. In addition, an individual earnings record is kept for each employee and updated each pay period.
6. Computers are used in many businesses for payroll preparation. In a computerized payroll system, the computer does all the calculations and prints the payroll register, the employee paychecks and stubs, and the employee's earnings records.

REVIEW AND APPLICATIONS

Building Your Accounting Vocabulary

In your own words, write the definition of each of the following accounting terms. Use complete sentences for your definitions.

accumulated earnings
commission
deduction
direct deposit
electronic badge reader

employee's earnings record
exemption
gross earnings
net pay
overtime rate
pay period

payroll
payroll clerk
payroll register
piece rate
salary
time card
wage

Reviewing Your Accounting Knowledge

1. What are the two goals of a payroll system?
2. What five tasks are included in a payroll system?
3. What is the difference between a salary and a wage?
4. Why do some businesses pay their employees on a commission basis?
5. What two federal taxes are businesses required to withhold from employees' wages?
6. List three things that determine the amount withheld from employee earnings each pay period for federal income taxes.
7. What is a Form W-4?
8. Describe the programs that are financed by the social security system.
9. Explain the statement "the social security tax is an exact tax."
10. Name some common voluntary deductions that are withheld from employee paychecks.

Improving Your Human Relations Skills

Lenny Alvarez has a part-time job at a local department store. One of his classmates, Paul Tuan, also works at the same store after school and on weekends. One day Paul found Lenny between classes and told him that he would be half an hour late for work that evening. Paul asked Lenny to take his time card and punch in for him so that he would not lose pay for being late. Lenny believes that it is dishonest to punch in for Paul but he wants to remain friendly with him. What should Lenny say to Paul?

Applying Accounting Principles

Exercise 11-1   Calculating Total Hours Worked

Instructions: Part of a time card appears on page 228. Determine the total number of hours worked for the week. Use the form provided in the working papers.

DAY	IN	OUT	IN	OUT
M	8:03	12:30	1:30	5:10
T	7:49	12:07	12:59	5:05
W	7:58	12:15	12:45	4:30
TH	8:30	12:02	12:35	5:15
F	7:59	12:04	1:04	5:30

Exercise 11-2 Calculating Gross Earnings

Heywood Music Center has five employees. They are paid on a weekly basis with overtime for all hours worked over 40 per week. The overtime rate is $1\frac{1}{2}$ times the regular rate of pay. Employee names and other payroll information are given below.

David Brown: Single; 1 exemption; rate per hour, $4.95
Tonya Lutz: Single; 1 exemption; rate per hour, $5.25
Pat Lynch: Single; 2 exemptions; rate per hour, $4.80
Betty Quinn: Married; 2 exemptions; rate per hour, $4.90
Richard Sell: Married; 3 exemptions; rate per hour, $4.90

The time cards show that the total hours worked by each employee for the week ended July 17 are as follows:

Brown: $33\frac{1}{2}$ hours   Quinn: $44\frac{1}{4}$ hours
Lutz: 38 hours   Sell: $39\frac{1}{2}$ hours
Lynch: 43 hours

Instructions: Use a form similar to the one that follows. Calculate the amount of regular earnings, overtime earnings, and gross earnings for each employee. The first employee's earnings have been completed as an example.

Employee	Total Hours	Pay Rate	Regular Earnings	Overtime Earnings	Gross Earnings
Brown, David	$33\frac{1}{2}$	$4.95	$165.83	—	$165.83

Exercise 11-3 Determining Taxes on Gross Earnings

Use the gross earnings computed in Exercise 11-2 to complete this exercise.

Instructions: Determine the amounts to be withheld from each employee's gross earnings for FICA and income taxes. Use the tax charts on pages 220-221 for the federal income tax. The state income tax is 1.5% of gross earnings. The present FICA tax rate is 7.65% of earnings. Use the form provided in the working papers.

Problem 11-1 Preparing a Payroll Register

Win's Sport Shop has four employees. They are paid on a weekly basis with overtime paid for all hours over 38. The overtime rate is $1\frac{1}{2}$ times the regular rate of pay. The employee names and other information needed to prepare the payroll are as follows.

Megan Berg: Single; 0 exemptions; rate per hour, $4.95; employee no. 108
Don Holt: Married; 1 exemption; rate per hour, $5.25; employee no. 112; union member
Lisa Roberts: Married; 2 exemptions; rate per hour, $5.70; employee no. 102; union member
Steven Varga: Single; 1 exemption; rate per hour, $4.80; employee no. 109; union member

During the week ended July 7, Berg worked 39 hours, Holt worked 41 hours, and Varga and Roberts each worked 35 hours.

Instructions:

(1) Prepare a payroll register. List employees in alphabetical order by *last* name. Use the tax charts on pages 220-221 to determine the federal income taxes. There is no state income tax. Compute FICA taxes at 7.65% of gross earnings. Union members pay weekly dues of $3.80.

(2) After the payroll information is entered in the payroll register, total the columns and check the accuracy of the totals.

Problem 11-2   Preparing Payroll Checks and Employee's Earnings Records

Use the payroll register from Problem 11-1 to complete this problem.

Instructions:

(1) Prepare a paycheck and stub for each employee. Record the paycheck numbers in the payroll register.

(2) Record the payroll information in the employee's earnings records.

Problem 11-3   Preparing the Payroll

Dan's Audio Center has a total of six employees and pays its employees on a weekly basis. Hourly employees are paid overtime for all hours over 40. The overtime rate is $1\frac{1}{2}$ times the regular rate of pay.

Dan's Audio Center pays its employees by one of three methods: hourly rate, salary, or salary plus a 5% commission on total sales. The following table lists the employees and the method by which their wages are computed.

Employee	Method of Computing Earnings		
	Hourly	Salary	Salary Plus Commission
Chris Carroll		$270.00	
Pat Cashin	$4.95		
Tyler Davis			$160.00 plus 5%
Debbie Strong			$140.00 plus 5%
Jason Witty	$4.65		
Steven Wong			$140.00 plus 5%

Employee deductions include federal income taxes (use the charts on pages 220-221), FICA taxes at 7.65% of earnings, state income taxes of 1.5% of earnings, and a hospital insurance premium of $2.43 for single employees and $4.37 for married employees. Also, Steven Wong and Tyler Davis have $6.00 withheld each week for the purchase of U.S. savings bonds.

During the pay period ended October 14, the salespeople at Dan's Audio Center sold the following amounts of merchandise: Debbie Strong, $1,925.80; Steven Wong, $2,135.65; and Tyler Davis, $1,204.76. The hourly employees completed the following time cards.

No. 73							
Name _Jason Witty_							
Soc. Sec. No. _093-48-7423_							
Week Ending _10/14/--_							

DAY	IN	OUT	IN	OUT	IN	OUT	TO
M	8:58	12:03	12:55	5:09			
T	8:55	11:55	1:00	4:00			
W	9:30	12:10	1:04	3:30			
Th	8:57	12:03	12:59	6:00			
F	8:58	12:00	1:00	6:05			
S	9:00	12:00					
S							
					TOTAL HOURS		

	Hours	Rate	Amo
REGULAR			
OVERTIME			
	TOTAL EARNINGS		

No. 92							
Name _Pat Cashin_							
Soc. Sec. No. _087-46-3875_							
Week Ending _10/14/--_							

DAY	IN	OUT	IN	OUT	IN	OUT	TOTAL
M	8:55	12:06	1:01	5:35			
T	7:58	11:01	12:03	6:38			
W	9:03	1:10	2:00	6:00			
Th	7:59	11:55	1:10	4:51			
F	9:01	12:06	1:05	3:47			
S	9:00	12:03					
S							
					TOTAL HOURS		

	Hours	Rate	Amount
REGULAR			
OVERTIME			
	TOTAL EARNINGS		

Instructions:

(1) Prepare a payroll register for the week ended October 14. The date of payment is also October 14. Each employee's I.D. number, marital status, and number of exemptions claimed is listed on her or his employee's earnings record.

(2) Prepare a payroll check and stub for each employee.

(3) Record the payroll information for each employee on her or his employee's earnings record.

Problem 11-4   Preparing the Payroll Register

North Shore Office Products has seven employees who are paid weekly. The hourly employees are paid overtime for all hours worked over 40, at a rate $1\frac{1}{2}$ times their regular rate of pay. The payroll information for each employee is listed below.

Lynn Ferchi:	Married; 2 exemptions; employee no. 105
Judy Fox:	Married; 2 exemptions; employee no. 137
John French:	Single; 1 exemption; employee no. 135
Sonya Knox:	Married; 4 exemptions; employee no. 141
David Kovic:	Single; 0 exemptions; employee no. 139
Pat Printer:	Single; 1 exemption; employee no. 113
Guy Whitten:	Married; 3 exemptions; employee no. 129

Lynn Ferchi is the store manager and is paid a salary of $300.00 per week plus 1% of all sales made in the store. Judy Fox and John French are salespeople who are paid a salary of $200.00 per week plus a 6% commission on all sales over $500.00 per week. Sonya Knox and David Kovic are office workers and are paid an hourly wage of $5.20. Pat Printer is the assistant manager of the store and is paid a weekly salary of $295.00. Guy Whitten is a stock person who is paid $4.40 per hour.

The payroll deductions include federal income tax, FICA tax of 7.65%, and state income tax of 1.8%. Sonya Knox and Guy Whitten have $12.50 deducted each week for hospital insurance.

During the week ended March 24, Judy Fox had sales of $2,184.90 and John French had sales of $2,341.70. During the week, Sonya Knox worked 41 hours, David Kovic worked 38½ hours, and Guy Whitten worked 34 hours.

Instructions: Prepare a payroll register for the week ended March 24. Use the tax tables provided in the chapter.

Problem 11-5 Preparing the Payroll Register

Belco Products, Inc., is a small manufacturer of plastic products. The company has 10 employees, all of whom are paid weekly. Overtime is paid at a rate of 1½ times the regular rate of pay for all hours worked over 40. Production employees are paid an hourly rate plus 20¢ for each piece over 300 produced per week. The payroll information for each employee appears below.

	Emp. No.	Marital Status	No. of Exemp.	Method of Payment
Lee Chan	108	M	1	Salary $52,520 a year
Rita Cortez	116	S	0	$5.75 per hour
Stanley Garfield	137	S	2	$6.00 per hour plus piece rate
Jan Hunt	144	M	3	$5.90 per hour plus piece rate
John McGarrell	156	S	1	$5.50 per hour
Pat Ritzmann	173	M	6	Salary $59,800 a year
Sarah Schoenle	178	M	1	$6.20 per hour plus piece rate
Peggy Sellers	186	M	4	$6.20 per hour plus piece rate
Carol Stack	189	S	2	Salary $500 a week
Gary Wright	192	M	3	Salary $275 a week plus 3% of sales

Additional information needed to complete the payroll for the week ended December 21 follows.

	Hours Worked	Pieces Produced	Sales	Accumulated Earnings
Lee Chan				$50,500.00
Rita Cortez	43			12,750.00
Stanley Garfield	40	356		13,016.75
Jan Hunt	35	269		8,610.90
John McGarrell	41			11,350.50
Pat Ritzmann				57,500.00
Sarah Schoenle	42	402		16,400.50
Peggy Sellers	40	325		14,982.19
Carol Stack				25,000.00
Gary Wright			$21,025.00	44,394.25

The payroll deductions include federal income tax, FICA tax of 7.65%, and state income tax of 1.5%. The maximum taxable earnings for FICA are $51,300. All employees have hospital insurance deductions of $5.25 for single employees and $7.50 for married employees.

Instructions: Prepare a payroll register for the week ended December 21.

Computers

Computers can perform calculations quickly and accurately. The Cray Supercomputer, shown here, can perform 600 million calculations per *second.*

Computers in Government

Imagine what it's like for the federal government to keep track of all its citizens, property, services, and legislation; enforce its laws; monitor its businesses; or protect its borders.

While it's not known exactly how much data the federal government maintains, here's one statistic that will help to put things in perspective. The computer archives of government agencies keep an average of 18 files on every living citizen. Without the aid of computers, the paperwork and people needed to process it would be out of control.

The United States government is the biggest computer user in the world. Here are some examples of how computers help

various agencies within our federal government function.

The *Internal Revenue Service* processes over 95 million tax returns a year. They're sorted at the rate of 30,000 an hour, thanks to high-speed bar code readers; checked by computers; and stored on magnetic tape.

In 1890 Herman Hollerith's tabulating machine helped the *U.S. Census Bureau* count the population. It took six weeks to tabulate a population of 62,622,250. Today, computers keep a *running* count of our population, deaths, and births.

The *Securities and Exchange Commission* processes 6 million pages of documents every year to regulate the transactions of public corporations. And it can retrieve instantly any data filed by the 10,000 corporations it regulates.

The *Social Security Administration* keeps records on 100 million workers and issues monthly checks to 36 million people. Without the help of computers, these tasks would require the efforts of thousands of clerks.

The *Federal Bureau of Investigation (FBI)* stores a database of over 8 million records. These records are accessed by local police at the rate of 540,000 calls every day.

The *U.S. Forestry Service* operates in a shared information environment. All full-time personnel are computer literate. They use electronic mail, manage fires and supplies, and prepare environmental impact statements on computers.

Computers help our government manage a mountain of data.

Payroll and Tax Records

In Chapter 11, you learned that employers use a payroll system to ensure that their employees are paid on time and that the amounts they are paid are accurate. Many businesses hire a payroll clerk whose sole responsibility is to prepare the payroll.

You also learned in Chapter 11 that various amounts are withheld from employees' earnings for taxes and other voluntary deductions. Employers are also required to pay taxes on their employees' earnings. You will learn about those taxes in this chapter. You'll also learn how to record the various journal entries affecting payroll in the business's accounting records.

LEARNING OBJECTIVES

When you have completed this chapter, you should be able to

1. Record payroll information in the general journal.
2. Describe and calculate the employer's payroll taxes.
3. Record the employer's payroll taxes in the general journal.
4. Identify tax reports that are prepared regularly by the employer.
5. Define the accounting terms new to this chapter.

NEW Terms

unemployment taxes • federal tax deposit coupon • Form 941 • Form W-2 • Form W-3 • Form 940

Journalizing and Posting the Payroll

In Chapter 11, you learned that a check is written to transfer the total net pay amount from the business's regular checking account to the business's payroll checking account. For Lenker Consulting Service, the check written on June 30 was for $654.31. The check is deposited in the payroll account and all paychecks for the period are drawn on this payroll account. When that check is recorded in the general journal, the payroll transaction amounts are entered into the employer's accounting system. The payroll register contains all the information needed to make the journal entry to record the payroll.

Analyzing the Payroll Transaction

Let's analyze the effect of the payment of the payroll on the employer's accounting system. Each pay period, the business pays out a certain amount of money to its employees in the form of wages. Employee wages are a normal operating expense of a business. The expense account used to record employees' earnings is often called Salaries Expense.

Salaries Expense	
Dr.	Cr.
+	−
$824.82	

The payment of the payroll increases the expenses of the business. Thus, to increase the amount in Salaries Expense, the account is debited for the total gross earnings for the pay period. For example, the total amount of gross earnings shown on Lenker's payroll register for the week ended June 30 is $824.82 (see Figure 12-1 on page 236). This amount is recorded as a debit to Salaries Expense.

R　E　M　E　M　B　E　R

The total gross earnings each pay period is debited to Salaries Expense.

Various deductions, such as those for income and FICA taxes, are withheld from employees' gross earnings each pay period. The employer holds the amounts deducted from gross earnings until the specified times for paying them to the appropriate government agencies and businesses. These amounts are therefore *liabilities* of the employer since they are to be paid some time in the future.

Each type of payroll liability is recorded in a separate account. For example, total employees' federal income taxes withheld are recorded in Employees' Federal Income Tax Payable, employees' social security taxes are recorded in FICA Tax Payable, and so on. The liability accounts used by Lenker Consulting Service to record payroll deductions are:

Employees' Federal Income Tax Payable
Employees' State Income Tax Payable
FICA Tax Payable
Hospital Insurance Premiums Payable
U.S. Savings Bonds Payable

Amounts deducted from employees' earnings and held for payment by the employer are recorded as liabilities in the accounting records.

Let's look now at the credit part of the journal entry needed to record the payment of the payroll. The credit part of the journal entry is made up of several items. The largest item is for the amount of net pay. This is the amount actually paid out in cash by the employer to the employees. Therefore, Cash in Bank is credited for the total amount of net pay.

The difference between gross earnings and net pay equals the employer's payroll liabilities. Each payroll liability account is credited for its total amount shown on the payroll register. The following T accounts illustrate the effect of the payroll transaction. You can see that the credit part of the entry for Lenker Consulting Service is made up of six parts.

Cash in Bank		Employees' Federal Income Tax Payable		Employees' State Income Tax Payable	
Dr.	Cr.	Dr.	Cr.	Dr.	Cr.
+	−	−	+	−	+
	$654.31		$60.00		$25.70

FICA Tax Payable		Hospital Insurance Premiums Payable		U.S. Savings Bonds Payable	
Dr.	Cr.	Dr.	Cr.	Dr.	Cr.
−	+	−	+	−	+
	$63.11		$11.70		$10.00

$654.31
60.00
63.11
25.70
11.70
+ 10.00
$824.82

As you can see from these T accounts, the business has paid out $654.31 in cash (the total net pay). The business owes the federal government $60.00 for employees' federal income taxes and $63.11 for the employees' social security taxes. The business also owes employees' state income taxes of $25.70. The insurance company is owed $11.70. Finally, the federal government is owed $10.00 toward the purchase of U.S. savings bonds by the employees. The total of *all* these amounts is equal to the total gross earnings debited to Salaries Expense: $824.82.

Recording the Payroll

The totals line of the payroll register is the source of information for recording the payroll transaction. Figure 12-1 on page 236 illustrates this entry. The amount of total gross earnings is debited to Salaries Expense. Each of the payroll liability accounts is credited for its individual column total. (Several different types of deductions may be recorded in the Other Deductions column of the payroll register. If so, the total for each *type* of deduction is determined and credited to the liability account.) Cash in Bank is credited for the amount of net pay.

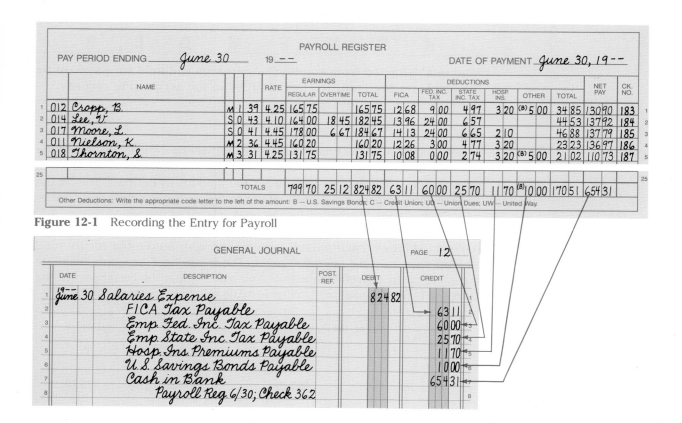

Figure 12-1 Recording the Entry for Payroll

Posting the Payroll Entry to the General Ledger

As you remember, entries in the general journal are posted to the general ledger accounts periodically. The posting of the journal entry for the payroll is shown in Figure 12-2.

Before reading any further, do the following activity to check your understanding of the journal entry made to record the payroll.

Check Your Learning

Write your answers to the following questions on notebook paper.

1. The amount recorded and posted to the Salaries Expense account is the total ___?___ for the pay period.
2. The amounts deducted from the gross earnings of the employees are considered ___?___ of the business until they are paid.
3. Cash in Bank is credited for the total ___?___ for the period.
4. The amount of the check written for the payroll is equal to the ___?___ amount.

Compare your answers to those in the answers section. Re-read the preceding part of the chapter to find the correct answers to any questions you may have missed.

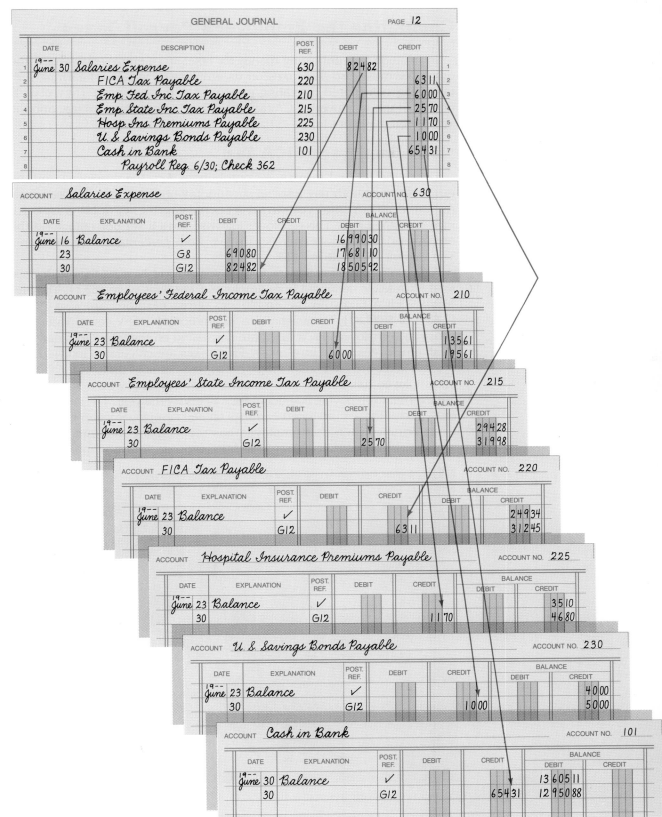

Figure 12-2 Posting the Payroll Entry to the General Ledger

Computing the Employer's Payroll Taxes

In addition to withholding money for taxes from employees' wages, the employer must also *pay* taxes on its employees' wages. The employer's taxes are considered operating expenses of the business. They usually consist of the employer's FICA tax, the federal unemployment tax, and the state unemployment tax.

The Employer's FICA Tax

Under the Federal Insurance Contributions Act, the employee and the employer must both pay a social security tax on the employee's earnings. As you recall, an employee pays a set percentage of her or his gross earnings for FICA taxes. The employer likewise pays a set percentage on the employees' total gross earnings as a tax. Both percentages are the same. The current FICA rate is 7.65%.

At Lenker Consulting Service for the week ended June 30, the employees' total FICA taxes deducted from employees' earnings were $63.11. The employer's FICA taxes on the employees' gross earnings are also $63.11 (7.65% of $824.82). Occasionally, a difference of a few cents results because the employer's FICA taxes are calculated on the total gross earnings of all employees while employees' FICA taxes are calculated individually.

FICA taxes are paid on an employee's gross earnings up to $51,300. After an employee has earned that amount, both the employee and employer are exempt from paying additional FICA taxes for the year. The payroll clerk must check the accumulated earnings on each employee's earnings record to determine when that employee has reached the maximum taxable amount. If the payroll is prepared by computer, the maximum taxable

Payroll records are frequently the first of a business's accounting records to be computerized.

amount is entered into the computer memory at the beginning of the year. When an employee reaches the limit, the computer automatically drops the FICA tax for that employee.

R — E — M — E — M — B — E — R

Both employees and employers pay FICA taxes on employees' gross earnings. The same percentage rate is used for both calculations.

Federal and State Unemployment Taxes

The Federal Unemployment Tax Act (FUTA) requires employers to pay unemployment taxes, which are based on a percentage of their employees' gross earnings. **Unemployment taxes** are collected to provide funds for workers who are temporarily out of work. For example, workers who lose their jobs during an economic recession are paid unemployment compensation to help them live until they can find other jobs.

The employer must pay both a federal unemployment tax and a state unemployment tax. The maximum federal unemployment tax is 6.2% on the first $7,000 of an employee's annual wages. The percentage rates for state unemployment taxes vary among states, as do maximum taxable amounts. Employers are allowed to deduct up to 5.4% of their state unemployment taxes from federal unemployment taxes. Most employers then pay a federal tax of .8% (6.2% − 5.4%).

R — E — M — E — M — B — E — R

Federal unemployment taxes are calculated on only the first $7,000 of an employee's gross earnings.

$824.82
× .008
$ 6.60
$824.82
× .054
$ 44.54

For Lenker Consulting Service, the federal unemployment tax for the week ended June 30 is found by multiplying the total gross earnings of $824.82 by .8%. Lenker's federal unemployment taxes are $6.60.

The state unemployment tax for the week ended June 30 is determined by multiplying the total gross earnings by 5.4%. Lenker's state unemployment taxes are $44.54.

In a few states, employees are required to pay unemployment taxes. The percentage amounts vary from one state to another.

Journalizing the Employer's Payroll Taxes

The payroll taxes that are paid by the employer are considered to be expenses of doing business. The total payroll taxes are therefore recorded in the expense account Payroll Tax Expense. Like the taxes and other deductions withheld from employees' earnings, the employer's taxes are collected and held until they are required to be paid. The employer's payroll taxes thus represent *liabilities* of the business.

$ 63.11
6.60
+ 44.54
$114.25

The FICA Tax Payable account is used to record both the employees' FICA taxes and the employer's FICA taxes. The employer's unemployment taxes are recorded in the accounts Federal Unemployment Tax Payable and State Unemployment Tax Payable.

T accounts can be used to analyze the debit and credit parts of the entry for payroll taxes. The following T accounts illustrate the entry for Lenker Consulting Service's payroll taxes.

Payroll Tax Expense			FICA Tax Payable	
Dr.	Cr.		Dr.	Cr.
+	−		−	+
$114.25				Bal. $63.11
				63.11

Federal Unemployment Tax Payable			State Unemployment Tax Payable	
Dr.	Cr.		Dr.	Cr.
−	+		−	+
	$6.60			$44.54

Since no check is being written at this time, the employer's payroll tax liabilities are recorded in the general journal. The source document for the journal entry is the payroll register. This general journal entry is shown in Figure 12-3.

GENERAL JOURNAL   PAGE 12

DATE	DESCRIPTION	POST. REF.	DEBIT	CREDIT
19--				
June 30	Payroll Tax Expense		1 1 4 25	
	FICA Tax Payable			63 11
	Fed. Unemploy. Tax Payable			6 60
	State Unemploy. Tax Payable			44 54
	Payroll Register 6/30			

Figure 12-3 Recording the Entry for the Employer's Payroll Taxes

The date used for this journal entry is the same as the ending date of the pay period. The Payroll Tax Expense account is debited for the total amount of the employer's taxes. The individual payroll tax liability accounts are credited for the amount of each tax.

Posting Payroll Taxes to the General Ledger

After the journal entry has been made to record the payroll tax amounts, these amounts are posted to the appropriate general ledger accounts. The posting of the employer's payroll taxes is shown in Figure 12-4.

Notice that the FICA Tax Payable account has two entries for the June 30 payroll. The first entry is the amount of the FICA taxes withheld from the *employees'* earnings. The second entry is the amount of FICA taxes paid by the *employer* on the employees' total gross earnings.

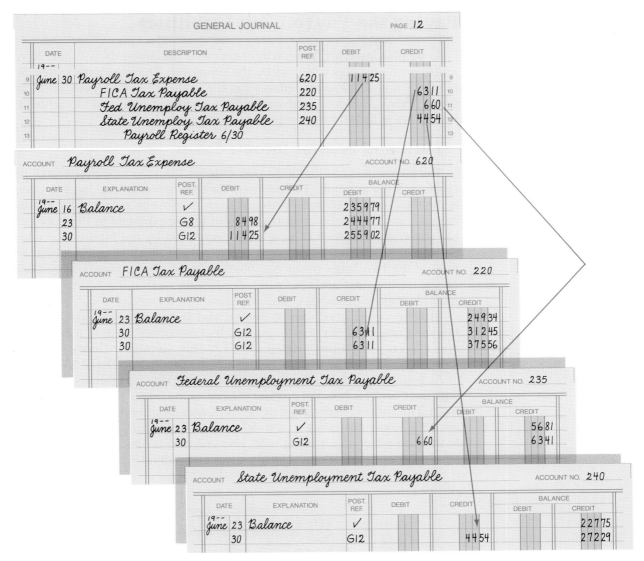

Figure 12-4 Posting Payroll Taxes to the General Ledger

Check Your Learning

Use notebook paper to write your answers to the following questions.

1. If the federal unemployment tax rate is .8%, what were the federal unemployment taxes on accumulated earnings of $14,264.91?
2. Name the liability accounts used to record the employer's payroll taxes.
3. Payroll taxes are usually paid only by the ____?____ .
4. Using the FICA tax rate of 7.65%, what is the amount of the employer's social security taxes on employees' gross earnings of $33,468.92?

Compare your answers to those in the answers section. Re-read the preceding part of the chapter to find the answers to any questions you missed.

Paying the Payroll Tax Liabilities

At regular intervals, the payroll taxes and the amounts withheld from employees' earnings are paid by the employer. These amounts include: (1) FICA and employees' federal income taxes, (2) employees' state income taxes, (3) federal and state unemployment taxes, and (4) amounts voluntarily withheld from employees' earnings.

FICA and Federal Income Taxes

The payment made for FICA taxes includes both the employees' and the employer's tax amounts. The payment for employees' federal income taxes is the total amount of taxes withheld from employees' earnings for federal income tax. These two amounts are sent in one payment to the appropriate government agency or to a bank designated by the Internal Revenue Service to receive such payments. The payment must be made when the total of the two taxes owed is $500.00 or more. The business writes one check for the total amount owed. For Lenker Consulting Service, this is monthly. Larger businesses may pay these taxes weekly.

After recording the June 30 payroll and the employer's payroll taxes, Lenker Consulting Service found that its employees' federal income tax and FICA tax liabilities totaled $571.17. This amount included the employees' federal income taxes of $195.61 and the FICA taxes of $375.56.

A **federal tax deposit coupon** (Form 8109) is also prepared and sent with the check to show the amount of taxes being sent to the federal government. The Form 8109 prepared by Lenker Consulting Service is shown in Figure 12-5. Notice the ovals on the right side of the form. One oval is filled in to indicate which tax is being paid, and one oval is filled in to indicate the tax period covered. The oval for the FICA and federal income tax payment is the one labeled "941."

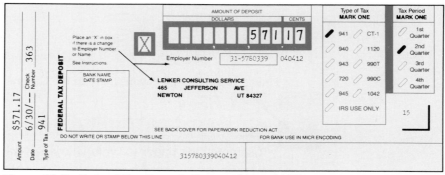

Figure 12-5   Federal Tax Deposit Coupon (Form 8109)

The check written to pay FICA and employees' federal income taxes is recorded in the general journal. The entry is shown on lines 14-17 in Figure 12-6. Since the liability accounts Employees' Federal Income Tax Payable and FICA Tax Payable are being decreased by the payment, those accounts are debited. Employees' Federal Income Tax Payable is debited for $195.61

and FICA Tax Payable is debited for $375.56. Cash in Bank is also being decreased by the payment, so that account is credited for the total amount being paid out, $571.17.

	DATE	DESCRIPTION	POST. REF.	DEBIT	CREDIT	
		GENERAL JOURNAL			PAGE 12	
	19--					
14	June 30	Emp. Fed. Inc. Tax Payable		195 61		14
15		FICA Tax Payable		375 56		15
16		Cash in Bank			571 17	16
17		Check 363				17
18	30	Emp. State Inc. Tax Payable		319 98		18
19		Cash in Bank			319 98	19
20		Check 364				20
21	30	Fed. Unemploy. Tax Payable		63 41		21
22		Cash in Bank			63 41	22
23		Check 365				23
24	30	State Unemploy. Tax Payable		272 29		24
25		Cash in Bank			272 29	25
26		Check 366				26
27	30	Hosp. Ins. Premiums Payable		46 80		27
28		Cash in Bank			46 80	28
29		Check 367				29
30	30	U. S. Savings Bonds Payable		50 00		30
31		Cash in Bank			50 00	31
32		Check 368				32
33						33
34						34

Figure 12-6 Recording the Journal Entries for the Payment of Payroll Liabilities

State Income Taxes

The amounts withheld by the employer for employees' state income taxes are also paid regularly. The entry to record the payment of a state income tax liability is shown on lines 18-20 in Figure 12-6.

Federal and State Unemployment Taxes

Most businesses pay the federal unemployment tax quarterly. If a business has accumulated federal unemployment taxes of less than $100 for the year, only one annual payment is necessary. A federal tax deposit coupon (Form 8109) is also prepared and sent with the check for federal unemployment taxes. The oval filled in for this payment is labeled "940," which is the number assigned to FUTA taxes. The journal entry made to record the payment of federal unemployment taxes is shown on lines 21-23 in Figure 12-6.

State unemployment taxes are also paid on a quarterly basis. The requirements for paying unemployment taxes vary from state to state. The journal entry to record the payment of the state employment taxes is shown on lines 24-26 in Figure 12-6.

Other Liability Amounts

In addition to the payments for taxes, an employer is also responsible for making payments to appropriate organizations for all voluntary deductions from employees' earnings. For Lenker Consulting Service, these deductions are for insurance premiums and U.S. savings bonds. Other companies may withhold amounts from employees' earnings for union dues, charitable contributions, and so on.

On June 30, Lenker Consulting Service prepared checks to pay the amounts withheld for employees' insurance premiums ($46.80) and the amounts withheld for the employees' purchase of U.S. savings bonds ($50.00). The journal entries for these two cash payments are shown on lines 27-32 in Figure 12-6.

Posting the Journal Entries for Payment of Payroll Liabilities

After all the payments for the employer's payroll liabilities have been recorded, the entries are posted to the appropriate general ledger accounts. The postings made to Lenker Consulting Service's general ledger accounts are shown in Figure 12-7 on pages 245-246.

R E M E M B E R

The employer's payroll taxes are recorded as liabilities in the business's accounting records.

Before continuing, complete the following activity to check your understanding of the material you have just studied.

Check Your Learning

Use Figure 12-7 to answer the following questions.

1. How many different entries were made on June 30 to record the checks written by Lenker Consulting Service to pay its payroll liabilities?
2. Why wasn't just one check written to pay all the payroll liabilities?
3. What was the amount of the check written to pay the FICA and employees' federal income taxes?
4. What was the total liability for unemployment taxes for the June 30 payroll?
5. How much cash did Lenker Consulting Service pay out on June 30 for its payroll liabilities?
6. What is the balance of Hospital Insurance Premiums Payable after all entries have been posted for June 30?

Compare your answers with those in the answers section. Re-read the preceding part of the chapter to find the correct answers to any questions you may have missed.

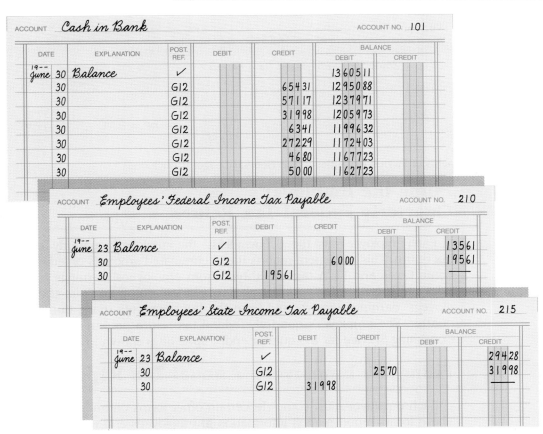

GENERAL JOURNAL   PAGE _12_

	DATE	DESCRIPTION	POST. REF.	DEBIT	CREDIT	
	19--					
14	June 30	Emp. Fed. Inc. Tax Payable	210	195 61		14
15		FICA Tax Payable	220	375 56		15
16		Cash in Bank	101		571 17	16
17		Check 363				17
18	30	Emp. State Inc. Tax Payable	215	319 98		18
19		Cash in Bank	101		319 98	19
20		Check 364				20
21	30	Fed. Unemploy. Tax Payable	235	63 41		21
22		Cash in Bank	101		63 41	22
23		Check 365				23
24	30	State Unemploy. Tax Payable	240	272 29		24
25		Cash in Bank	101		272 29	25
26		Check 366				26
27	30	Hosp. Ins. Premiums Payable	225	46 80		27
28		Cash in Bank	101		46 80	28
29		Check 367				29
30	30	U. S. Savings Bonds Payable	230	50 00		30
31		Cash in Bank	101		50 00	31
32		Check 368				32
33						33
34						34

ACCOUNT _Cash in Bank_   ACCOUNT NO. _101_

DATE	EXPLANATION	POST. REF.	DEBIT	CREDIT	BALANCE DEBIT	BALANCE CREDIT
19-- June 30	Balance	✓			13 605 11	
30		G12		654 31	12 950 88	
30		G12		571 17	12 379 71	
30		G12		319 98	12 059 73	
30		G12		63 41	11 996 32	
30		G12		272 29	11 724 03	
30		G12		46 80	11 677 23	
30		G12		50 00	11 627 23	

ACCOUNT _Employees' Federal Income Tax Payable_   ACCOUNT NO. _210_

DATE	EXPLANATION	POST. REF.	DEBIT	CREDIT	BALANCE DEBIT	BALANCE CREDIT
19-- June 23	Balance	✓				135 61
30		G12		60 00		195 61
30		G12	195 61			—

ACCOUNT _Employees' State Income Tax Payable_   ACCOUNT NO. _215_

DATE	EXPLANATION	POST. REF.	DEBIT	CREDIT	BALANCE DEBIT	BALANCE CREDIT
19-- June 23	Balance	✓				294 28
30		G12		25 70		319 98
30		G12	319 98			—

Figure 12-7   Posting the Payments of Payroll Liabilities to the General Ledger

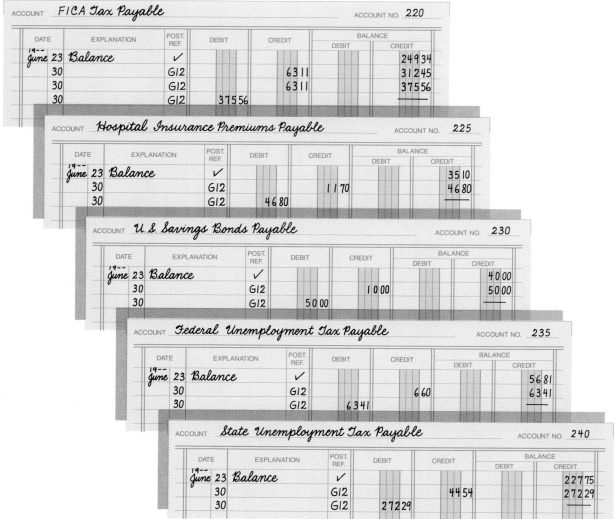

Figure 12-7 Posting the Payments of Payroll Liabilities to the General Ledger (Concluded)

Filing the Employer's Quarterly Federal Tax Return

Each employer must file a **Form 941,** the employer's quarterly federal tax return. This document reports the accumulated amounts of federal income taxes and FICA taxes withheld from employees' earnings for the quarter. The data for completing Form 941 is obtained from the employees' earnings records and from the tax payments made during the quarter. The employer's quarterly federal tax return prepared by Lenker Consulting Service for the quarter ended June 30 is shown in Figure 12-8.

Filing the Employer's Annual Tax Reports

Each employer must complete certain other forms on an annual basis. These forms report payroll information to employees and to various government agencies. The most common forms prepared are the wage and

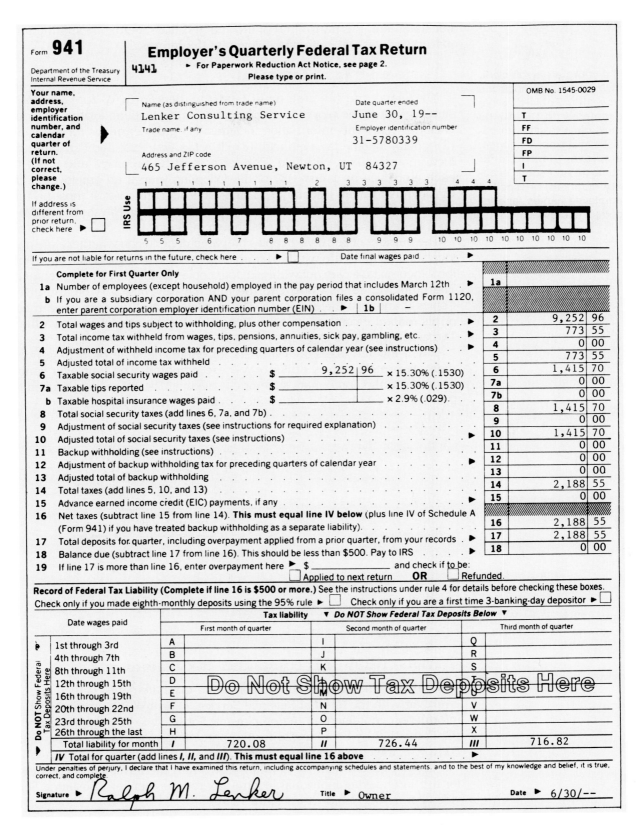

Figure 12-8 Form 941, Employer's Quarterly Federal Tax Return

If you're a payroll clerk, always double-check the obvious. The IRS says problems on tax filings most often result from obvious mistakes — incorrect employer identification numbers and social security numbers, misspelled employee names, and incorrect addresses.

tax statement, the transmittal of income and tax statements, and the employer's federal and state unemployment tax returns.

Wage and Tax Statement

The wage and tax statement is also called Form W-2. **Form W-2** summarizes an employee's earnings and tax deductions for the previous calendar year. This information includes: (1) gross earnings for the year, (2) federal income tax withheld, (3) FICA tax withheld, and (4) state and local income taxes withheld. The form must be prepared and given to each employee by January 31 of the following year. If an employee ends employment before December 31 and requests Form W-2, it must be furnished to the employee within 30 days. A copy of Karen Nielson's Form W-2 from Lenker Consulting Service is shown in Figure 12-9.

The number of Form W-2 copies prepared depends on whether state and local income taxes are withheld from employees' earnings. When state and local income taxes are *not* withheld, four copies (A through D) are prepared. The employer sends Copy A to the Internal Revenue Service and gives Copies B and C to the employee. The employee must file Copy B with her or his federal income tax return; Copy C is for the employee's own files. The employer keeps Copy D.

When income taxes are withheld for either the state or local government, two more copies of Form W-2 are prepared. The employer sends one copy to the appropriate state or city agency. The other copy is given to the employee to be filed with state or city income tax returns.

1 Control number	22222	For Paperwork Reduction Act Notice, see back of Copy D. OMB No. 1545-0008	For Official Use Only ▶		
2 Employer's name, address, and ZIP code			3 Employer's identification number 31-5780339		4 Employer's state I.D. number 475087
Lenker Consulting Service 465 Jefferson Avenue Newton, UT 84327			5 Statutory employee ☐ Deceased ☐ Pension plan ☐ Legal rep. ☐	942 emp. ☐ Subtotal ☐ Deferred compensation ☐	Void ☐
			6 Allocated tips		7 Advance EIC payment
8 Employee's social security number 045-68-5733	9 Federal income tax withheld 358.80		10 Wages, tips, other compensation 7,394.40		11 Social security tax withheld 565.67
12 Employee's name (first, middle, last) Karen L. Nielson			13 Social security wages 7,394.40		14 Social security tips
			16 (See Instr. for Forms W-2/W-2P)		16a Fringe benefits incl. in Box 10
419 East Main Street Kingston, UT 84743			17 State income tax 233.48	18 State wages, tips, etc. 7,394.40	19 Name of state Utah
15 Employee's address and ZIP code			20 Local income tax	21 Local wages, tips, etc.	22 Name of locality

Form **W-2 Wage and Tax Statement**

Copy A For Social Security Administration   Dept. of the Treasury—IRS

Figure 12-9 Form W-2, Wage and Tax Statement

Transmittal of Income and Tax Statements

Form W-3, the transmittal of income and tax statements, is filed by the employer with the Internal Revenue Service. **Form W-3** summarizes the information contained on the employees' Forms W-2. The employer must file Form W-3 by February 28 for the preceding year's taxes. Along with Form W-3, the employer must include Copy A of each employee's Form W-2. The federal government feeds information from the forms into computers for use in checking individual income tax returns. Lenker Consulting Service's Form W-3 is shown in Figure 12-10.

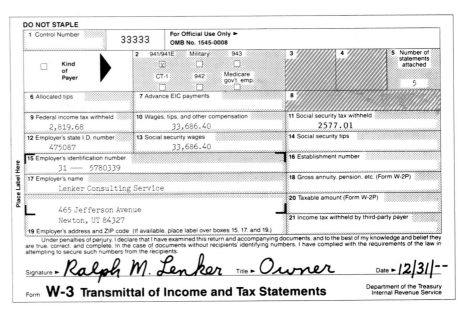

DO NOT STAPLE							
1 Control Number 33333		For Official Use Only ▶ OMB No. 1545-0008					

Figure 12-10 Form W-3, Transmittal of Income and Tax Statements

Within the form:

- 1 Control Number: 33333
- For Official Use Only ▶ OMB No. 1545-0008
- Kind of Payer
- 2 941/941E [x]   Military □   943 □   CT-1 □   942 □   Medicare gov't. emp. □
- 3   4   5 Number of statements attached: 5
- 6 Allocated tips
- 7 Advance EIC payments
- 8
- 9 Federal income tax withheld: 2,819.68
- 10 Wages, tips, and other compensation: 33,686.40
- 11 Social security tax withheld: 2577.01
- 12 Employer's state I.D. number: 475087
- 13 Social security wages: 33,686.40
- 14 Social security tips
- 15 Employer's identification number: 31 — 5780339
- 16 Establishment number
- 17 Employer's name: Lenker Consulting Service
- 465 Jefferson Avenue Newton, UT 84327
- 18 Gross annuity, pension, etc. (Form W-2P)
- 20 Taxable amount (Form W-2P)
- 21 Income tax withheld by third-party payer
- 19 Employer's address and ZIP code (If available, place label over boxes 15, 17, and 19.)
- Place Label Here

Under penalties of perjury, I declare that I have examined this return and accompanying documents, and to the best of my knowledge and belief they are true, correct, and complete. In the case of documents without recipients' identifying numbers, I have complied with the requirements of the law in attempting to secure such numbers from the recipients.

Signature ▶ *Ralph M. Lenker*   Title ▶ *Owner*   Date ▶ 12/31/--

Form **W-3 Transmittal of Income and Tax Statements**   Department of the Treasury Internal Revenue Service

Employer's Unemployment Tax Returns

Each employer is also responsible for filing **Form 940,** an employer's annual unemployment tax return. The information on this return includes both federal and state unemployment taxes paid during the year. This form must be filed by January 31 for the preceding calendar year. The requirements for filing state unemployment tax returns vary from state to state.

SUMMARY OF KEY POINTS

1. The payroll register is the source of information for preparing the entry to record the payment of the payroll.
2. Employees' wages are considered to be a normal operating expense for the business. The amount of the total gross earnings is debited to the Salaries Expense account.
3. Amounts deducted from employees' earnings and held by the employer are liabilities of the business. The employer must make regular payments of the amounts withheld to the appropriate government agencies or to other businesses or organizations.
4. Employers are required to pay taxes on the total amount of their employees' gross earnings. These amounts are operating expenses of the business. Employer's payroll taxes include FICA taxes, federal unemployment taxes, and state unemployment taxes.
5. FICA taxes are paid by both the employee and the employer. The same percentage used to calculate employees' deductions is also used to determine the employer's FICA tax. The employer's FICA tax is calculated on the total gross earnings amount.
6. Employers must report earnings and tax information to employees once a year on Form W-2.
7. Each employer is required to file quarterly and annual tax reports on employee earnings and on taxes paid by the employee and the employer.

REVIEW AND APPLICATIONS

Building Your Accounting Vocabulary

In your own words, write the definition of each of the following accounting terms. Use complete sentences for your definitions.

federal tax deposit
   coupon
Form W-2

Form W-3
Form 940
Form 941

unemployment
   taxes

Reviewing Your Accounting Knowledge

1. Why is the amount of the total gross earnings rather than total net pay charged to the Salaries Expense account?
2. Why are the amounts withheld from employees' paychecks liabilities of the employer?
3. What account is credited for the total amount of the employees' net pay?
4. How is the amount owed by the employer for FICA taxes determined?
5. Why do few employers pay the full 6.2% federal unemployment taxes?
6. Why is the employer's share of payroll taxes recorded in Payroll Tax Expense?
7. What is the source of information for preparing Form 941?
8. When do employees receive Form W-2 from their employers?
9. Explain how an employee uses the different copies of Form W-2.
10. Why does the federal government require the employer to submit copies of the employees' Forms W-2 with Form W-3?

Improving Your Communications Skills

In business communications, courtesy makes a good impression on people and encourages them to respond favorably. Courteous messages are stated in polite, positive words and use the "you" approach whenever possible. Rewrite the following sentences, changing them to courteous statements.

1. Give us more information if you want us to act on your complaint.
2. You will not get the discount unless you pay the bill in 10 days.
3. We cannot extend to you more than a $200 line of credit just now.
4. Send us your check or we can't ship your order.
5. We cannot deliver your order because our plant is closed until July 15.

Applying Accounting Procedures

Exercise 12-1 Calculating Employee Tax Deductions

Instructions: Use the form provided in the working papers. For each of the following gross earnings amounts, determine: (1) employees' federal income tax to be withheld (use the tax tables on pages 220-221 of the textbook); (2) FICA tax to be withheld (the FICA tax rate is 7.65%); (3) state income tax to be withheld (the state tax rate is 1.5%).

	Marital Status	Exemptions	Gross Earnings
1.	M	2	$183.74
2.	S	0	$216.48
3.	S	1	$243.84
4.	M	1	$162.80
5.	S	1	$149.99

Exercise 12-2 Calculating Employer's Payroll Taxes

Instructions: Use the form provided in the working papers. For each of the following total gross earnings amounts, determine the employer's FICA tax (rate 7.65%), the federal unemployment tax (rate .8%), and the state unemployment tax (rate 5.4%).

1. $ 914.80
2. $1,113.73
3. $2,201.38
4. $ 791.02
5. $1,245.75

Exercise 12-3 Identifying Entries for Payroll Liabilities

The following list includes several common payroll-related items. These items are included either in the entry to record the payment of the payroll or the entry to record the employer's payroll taxes.

Employees' federal income taxes
State unemployment tax
U.S. savings bonds
Employer's FICA tax
Federal unemployment tax

Employees' state income taxes
Union dues
Employees' FICA taxes
Life insurance premiums

Instructions: Use the form provided in the workbook. Place a check mark in the column that describes the entry in which the item is recorded.

Problem 12-1 Recording the Payment of the Payroll

The totals of the payroll register for Aurora Garden Shop are shown below. On November 30, the accountant wrote Check 731 to pay the payroll.

			PAYROLL REGISTER							
PAY PERIOD ENDING _November 30_ 19 --						DATE OF PAYMENT _November 30, 19--_				

			EARNINGS			DEDUCTIONS						NET PAY	CK. NO.
NAME		RATE	REGULAR	OVERTIME	TOTAL	FICA	FED. INC. TAX	STATE INC. TAX	HOSP. INS.	OTHER	TOTAL		
TOTALS			943 10	87 56	1030 66	78 85	161 00	62 93	17 42	——	320 20	710 46	

Other Deductions: Write the appropriate code letter to the left of the amount: B — U.S. Savings Bonds; C — Credit Union; UD — Union Dues; UW — United Way.

Instructions:

(1) Record the payroll entry in the general journal.

(2) Post the entry to the general ledger accounts.

Problem 12-2 Journalizing Payroll Transactions

The Potter Company's payroll register for the week ended June 28 appears on the next page.

	NAME				RATE	EARNINGS			DEDUCTIONS						NET PAY	CK. NO.
						REGULAR	OVERTIME	TOTAL	FICA	FED. INC. TAX	STATE INC. TAX	HOSP. INS.	OTHER	TOTAL		

PAYROLL REGISTER
PAY PERIOD ENDING __June 28__ 19-- DATE OF PAYMENT __June 28, 19--__

	NAME	M/S	Allow.	Rate Hrs	RATE	REGULAR	OVERTIME	TOTAL	FICA	FED. INC. TAX	STATE INC. TAX	HOSP. INS.	OTHER	TOTAL	NET PAY	CK. NO.
1	12 Blondi, M.	M	1	38	4.95	188 10		188 10	14 39	12 00	3 76		(UD) 4 65	34 80	153 30	1
2	14 Dilloway, S.	S	1	41	4.90	196 00	7 35	203 35	15 56	21 00	4 07			40 63	162 72	2
3	19 Lake, M.	S	0	42½	5.60	224 00	21 00	245 00	18 74	33 00	4 90		(UD) 4 65	61 29	183 71	3
4	13 Lapolla, J.	M	2	36	5.25	189 00		189 00	14 46	6 00	3 78		(UD) 4 65	28 89	160 11	4
5	18 Zeoli, N.	S	1	26	5.40	140 40		140 40	10 74	12 00	2 81		(UD) 4 65	30 20	110 20	5
25																25
	TOTALS					937 50	28 35	965 85	73 89	84 00	19 32	—	18 60	195 81	770 04	

Other Deductions: Write the appropriate code letter to the left of the amount: B — U.S. Savings Bonds; C — Credit Union; UD — Union Dues; UW — United Way.

Instructions:

(1) Record the entry for the payment of the payroll on page 15 of the general journal. Check 573 was written on June 28 to pay the payroll.

(2) Use the information in the payroll register to compute the employer's payroll taxes. These include FICA taxes (7.65%) and federal (.8%) and state (5.4%) unemployment taxes.

(3) Record the entry for the employer's payroll taxes.

Problem 12-3 Recording and Posting Payroll Transactions

The Clune Marina completed the following payroll transactions during the first two weeks of May. Clune's pays its employees on a biweekly basis.

Instructions:

(1) Record the May 13 transactions in the general journal (page 14).

(2) Post the entries to the appropriate general ledger accounts.

(3) Journalize and post the May 16 transactions.

Transactions:

May 13 Wrote Check 636 to pay the payroll of $3,840.58 (gross earnings) for the pay period ended May 13. The following amounts were withheld: FICA taxes, $293.80; employees' federal income taxes, $639.00; employees' state income taxes, $96.02; insurance premium, $21.00; U.S. savings bonds, $20.00.

13 Recorded the employer's payroll taxes (FICA tax rate, 7.65%; federal unemployment tax rate, 0.8%; state unemployment tax rate, 5.4%).

16 Paid the amounts owed to the federal government for employees' federal income taxes and FICA taxes, Check 637.

16 Purchased U.S. savings bonds for employees for $100.00, Check 638.

16 Paid $148.00 to the American Insurance Company for employees' insurance, Check 639.

Problem 12-4 Recording and Posting Payroll Transactions

The Book Worm pays its employees twice a month. Employee earnings and tax amounts for the pay period ended March 31 are listed below.

Gross Earnings	FICA Tax	Emp. Fed. Inc. Tax	Emp. State Inc. Tax
$12,183.40	$932.03	$679.00	$239.20

Instructions:

(1) Prepare Check 713 (payable to "Book Worm Payroll Account") to transfer the net pay amount to the payroll checking account.

(2) Journalize and post the payroll transaction. Use general journal page 19.

(3) Journalize and post the entry to record the employer's payroll taxes. The FICA tax rate is 7.65%; the state unemployment tax rate is 5.4%; and the federal unemployment tax rate is .8%.

(4) Prepare checks dated March 31 to pay the following payroll liabilities.

    (a) federal unemployment taxes, payable to First City Bank (Check 714)

    (b) state unemployment taxes, payable to the State of Missouri (Check 715)

    (c) employee's federal income taxes and FICA taxes, payable to First City Bank (Check 716)

(5) Journalize and post the entries for the payment of the payroll liabilities.

(6) Prepare Forms 8109 for the two federal tax deposits made in #4.

Problem 12-5 Recording Payroll Transactions

The Wiesel Company pays its employees each week. The payroll register for the week ended September 16 is shown below.

PAYROLL REGISTER

PAY PERIOD ENDING September 16, 19--   DATE OF PAYMENT September 16, 19--

	NAME				RATE	EARNINGS			DEDUCTIONS						NET PAY	CK. NO.
						REGULAR	OVERTIME	TOTAL	FICA	FED. INC. TAX	STATE INC. TAX	HOSP. INS.	OTHER	TOTAL		
1	102 Abbott, D.	M	2	39	5.20	202 80		202 80	15 51	9 00	4 06	3 80	(C) 5 00	37 37	165 43	1
2	116 Concannon, A.	S	0	42	4.80	192 00	14 40	206 40	15 79	27 00	4 13	2 45	(B) 5 00	54 37	152 03	2
3	109 Flowers, D.	M	1	41	5.35	214 00	8 03	222 03	16 99	18 00	4 44	3 80		43 23	178 80	3
4	121 Jackson, P.	S	1	36	4.95	178 20		178 20	13 63	17 00	3 56	2 45	(C) 10 00	46 64	131 56	4
5	117 Oller, W.	S	0	31	5.10	158 10		158 10	12 09	20 00	3 16	2 45	(B) 5 00	42 70	115 40	5
6	123 Repicky, J.	S	1	40	5.10	204 00		204 00	15 61	21 00	4 08	2 45	(C) 15 00	58 14	145 86	6
7	141 Toomey, B.	M	2	33	5.35	176 55		176 55	13 51	5 00	3 53	3 80		25 84	150 71	7
8	139 Welsh, J.	S	0	41	5.10	204 00	7 65	211 65	16 19	29 00	4 23	2 45	(UW) 3 00	54 87	156 78	8
25	TOTALS					1,529 65	30 08	1,559 73	119 32	146 00	31 19	23 65	B 10 00 UW 3 00 C 30 00	363 16	1,196 57	25

Other Deductions: Write the appropriate code letter to the left of the amount: B — U.S. Savings Bonds; C — Credit Union; UD — Union Dues; UW — United Way.

Instructions:

(1) Record the payment of the payroll on page 16 of the general journal. Check 831 was written on September 16 to pay the payroll.

(2) Compute the employer's payroll taxes (FICA tax rate, 7.65%; state unemployment tax rate, 5.4%; federal unemployment tax rate, 0.8%). The following employees have accumulated earnings of $7,000 or more: Abbott, Concannon, Flowers, Repicky, and Welsh. Assume $7,000 is the maximum taxable wage for both federal and state purposes. Record the entry for the employer's payroll taxes.

(3) Record the payment of FICA and employees' federal income taxes, Check 832. The previous account balances were: Employees' Federal Income Tax Payable, $139.00, and FICA Tax Payable, $236.40.

(4) Record the income tax payment to the state, Check 833. The balance in the account Employees' State Income Tax Payable before the September 16 payroll was $178.40.

(5) Record the payments for amounts withheld from employees' paychecks:

    (a) Check 834 to Tri-County Credit Union (previous balance, $270.00).

    (b) Check 835 for hospital insurance (previous balance, $260.15).

Computers

Computers have dramatically increased the amount of data that can be collected, processed, and stored.

Data Access vs. Privacy: A Delicate Balance

Scenario #1: It's 10:00 p.m. on a Friday evening. Early the next morning, Sandy is going camping with some friends. "Oh, no! I forgot to go to the bank."

No problem. The automatic teller machine (ATM) is always up and running. Sandy drives to the nearest bank, slips in her card, keys in her secret code number and the amount she wants, and—presto!—instant money. This machine knew who Sandy was, how much money she had in her account, and the new balance in her account after the transaction—in seconds.

Scenario #2: Company's coming for dinner in one hour. The carpet is covered with dog hairs. Your mother heads for the broom closet. "Oh, no! The vacuum cleaner isn't here. I forgot to pick it up at the repair shop."

No problem. You offer to go get it. Your mother gives you her credit card and you drive into town. The vacuum cleaner is ready. You hand your mother's credit card to the repair person, who validates it by sliding it through a little machine. The digital readout gives its approval in seconds. You get home just in time to race the cleaner across the rug.

In this fast-paced world, time is of the essence, and computers help us accomplish many time-consuming tasks efficiently. But in order for organizations, businesses, and government agencies to accomplish their objectives, they must have access to a lot of personal data. And that, to some, is a threat to our right of privacy.

Information about our credit, health, and employment history could be embarrassing. And it could even be harmful if confidentiality is not respected, if the information is incorrect, or if those who use it don't exercise good judgment and fairness.

So while accessible databases save hours and dollars, they must be carefully guarded so they're used with our approval and with the right to review and to challenge incorrect facts.

There will likely be many debates on the issue of accessibility vs. privacy. Can we have it both ways?

Payroll Accounting

In Unit 3, you studied the procedures involved in a payroll system — from determining and recording employees' earnings to preparing employers' tax reports. Now you will have the opportunity to review and apply what you have learned as you prepare the payroll and maintain payroll records for a business called The Greens.

When you have completed this activity, you will have

1. calculated employees' gross earnings
2. determined deductions from employees' gross earnings
3. calculated employees' net pay
4. prepared a payroll register
5. written payroll checks and stubs for employees
6. recorded payroll information on employees' earnings records
7. journalized and posted the payroll transaction
8. calculated the employer's payroll taxes
9. journalized and posted the employer's payroll tax transaction
10. journalized and posted the payment of FICA taxes and federal income taxes
11. prepared Form 8109
12. journalized and posted the payment of a monthly insurance premium

The Greens

The Greens is a golf shop located in Concord, Massachusetts. It is a merchandising business, organized as a corporation, owned and operated by the Jackson family. The store has been in operation for almost five years. During that time, its sales have increased each year, and the business is now showing a good profit.

Payroll Information

The store presently employs eight people. A Form W-4 is on file for each employee. The list that follows summarizes the data on those documents.

Chris Carroll:	Single; claims 1 exemption
Ralph DeLuca:	Single; claims 1 exemption
Christina Frei:	Single; claims 1 exemption
Gary Gula:	Single; claims 0 exemptions
Anne Holland:	Married; claims 2 exemptions
Marcy Jackson:	Married; claims 2 exemptions
Betty Quinn:	Married; claims 3 exemptions
Yourself:	Single; claims 1 exemption

The business pays its employees on a weekly basis. Overtime is paid at the rate of $1\frac{1}{2}$ times the regular rate of pay for all hours worked over 40. The weekly pay period runs from Monday through Saturday, with employees being paid on Saturday for that week's work. The store is closed for business on Sunday.

The employees are paid by one of three methods: hourly rate, salary, or salary plus a 10% commission on the amount of merchandise sold. The following table lists the employees, the method by which their wages are computed, and other pertinent information.

Employee	Emp. No.	Position	Employee Status	Rate of Pay
Marcy Jackson	010	Manager	Full-time	$500.00/week
Anne Holland	011	Salesperson	Full-time	$175.00/week plus 10% commission
Christina Frei	012	Accounting clerk	Part-time	$200.00/week
Gary Gula	013	Stock clerk	Full-time	$4.95/hour
Betty Quinn	016	Salesclerk	Full-time	$5.15/hour
Ralph DeLuca	018	Salesclerk	Full-time	$5.15/hour
Chris Carroll	019	Stock clerk	Part-time	$4.90/hour
Yourself	022	Accounting clerk	Part-time	$200.00/week

Federal and state tax tables are used to determine income taxes to be withheld. These tables are included in the working papers that accompany this textbook. The current rates for other taxes are as follows.

FICA: 7.65% employee contribution
           7.65% employer contribution
State unemployment tax: 5.4%
Federal unemployment tax: 0.8%

Preparing the Payroll for The Greens

The business entered the third quarter of its fiscal year at the beginning of July. It is presently the last week of July. Christina Frei, the accounting clerk, is on vacation. In her absence, you are to prepare this week's payroll.

Today is Saturday, July 29. The time cards for the employees who are paid on an hourly basis are included in the working papers accompanying this textbook. The hours worked by those employees are listed below and on the following page.

Chris Carroll

	IN	OUT	IN	OUT
M	2:00	5:00		
T	2:00	6:00		
W	3:00	5:00		
TH	2:00	6:00		
F	2:00	6:00		
S	9:00	2:00		

Ralph DeLuca

	IN	OUT	IN	OUT
M	9:00	12:00	12:30	5:00
T	9:00	11:30	12:00	5:00
W	9:00	1:00		
TH	9:00	12:00	12:30	4:00
F	8:30	1:00	1:30	3:00
S	9:00	1:30		

Gary Gula

	IN	OUT	IN	OUT
M	9:00	12:00	1:00	3:00
T	9:00	12:00	1:00	5:00
W	8:00	12:00	1:00	5:00
TH	9:00	12:00	1:00	3:30
F	9:00	12:00	1:00	4:00
S	9:00	12:00		

Betty Quinn

	IN	OUT	IN	OUT
M	9:00	12:00	12:30	5:00
T	9:00	12:30	1:00	6:00
W	9:00	12:00	1:00	4:30
TH	8:30	12:30	1:00	5:00
F	9:00	11:30	12:00	5:00
S	9:00	1:00		

Instructions:

(1) Complete the time cards for the four hourly employees. Enter the total hours worked at the bottom of each card.

(2) Anne Holland recorded sales this week of $1,241.00. Calculate her commission and add it to her salary to determine her gross earnings.

(3) Enter the payroll information for all employees in the payroll register. Each employee was recently assigned an employee number because Marcy Jackson is planning to computerize the payroll system. Since this payroll is being prepared manually, list the employees in the payroll register in alphabetical order by *last name*.

(4) Use the following information to complete the payroll register.
- **(a)** Use the federal and state tax charts to determine income tax amounts to be withheld.
- **(b)** Chris Carroll, Ralph DeLuca, Gary Gula, and Anne Holland each have a $5.00 deduction for the purchase of U.S. savings bonds.
- **(c)** Christina Frei, Marcy Jackson, and Betty Quinn each have $3.00 deducted for donations to the United Way.
- **(d)** All employees pay an insurance premium each week. Married employees pay $4.55 and single employees pay $2.75.
- **(e)** None of The Greens' employees has reached the maximum taxable amount for the FICA tax.

(5) Calculate the net pay for each employee.

(6) Total all amount columns in the payroll register. Prove the accuracy of the totals.

(7) Write Check 972 on the business's regular checking account for the amount of the total net pay. Make the check payable to The Greens Payroll Account. In Christina's absence, Marcy Jackson will sign the check for you. Complete the deposit slip for the payroll account.

(8) Record the payroll transaction in the general journal, page 19. Use information contained in the payroll register and Check 972 as the source documents. Post the transaction to the general ledger accounts.

(9) Write the paychecks for the employees. Use the information in the payroll register to complete the check stubs. After a check has been written for an employee, enter the check number in the payroll register.

(10) Enter this week's payroll information on the employee's earnings records for Chris Carroll and Anne Holland only. Be sure to add the current gross earnings amount to the accumulated total.

(11) Calculate and record the employer's taxes for this pay period. The source of information is the payroll register.

Only one employee, Marcy Jackson, has reached the maximum for federal and state unemployment taxes. The business is not required to pay these taxes on Marcy's earnings for the rest of the year.

(12) Make a deposit for the taxes owed to the federal government. The total includes the amounts withheld for employees' federal income tax and for FICA tax. Complete Form 8109 by entering the amount owed. Write Check 973, payable to the First Federal Bank of Boston, for the taxes.

(13) Enter the transaction in the general journal.

(14) Pay the monthly insurance premium by writing Check 974 to Yankee Insurance Company for $164.40. Record the payment in the general journal.

(15) Complete the posting from the general journal.

Appendix
Optional Reinforcement Problems

This appendix does not include an optional activity for Chapter 1.

Chapter 2, Problem 2A Determining the Effects of Business Transactions on the Accounting Equation

Ashley Moore has set up a business for herself as an accountant.

Instructions: Use a form similar to the one below. For each of the following transactions,

(1) Identify the accounts affected.
(2) Write the amount of the increase or decrease in the space provided.
(3) Determine the new balance for each account.

| Trans. | ASSETS | | | | | = | LIABILITIES | + | OWNER'S EQUITY |
	Cash in Bank	Accts. Rec.	Office Supp.	Comp. Equip.	Office Equip.	=	Accounts Payable	+	A. Moore, Capital
1									

Transactions:

1. Ashley Moore, the owner, opened a checking account for the business by depositing $48,000 of her personal funds.
2. Paid the monthly rent of $1,500.
3. Bought office supplies on account for $1,000.
4. Ashley Moore invested $3,000 of office equipment in the business.
5. Paid cash for a new computer for the business, $5,000.
6. Paid for an advertisement in the local newspaper, $200.
7. Completed accounting services for a client and sent a bill for $800.
8. Paid $700 on account for the office supplies bought earlier.
9. Received $500 on account from a client.
10. Ashley Moore withdrew $1,000 from the business for personal use.

Chapter 3, Problem 3A Analyzing Transactions into Debit and Credit Parts

Paul Morales owns a cleaning service. The accounts he uses to record and report business transactions are listed on the following page.

Cash in Bank	Store Equipment
Accounts Receivable	Van
Cleaning Supplies	Accounts Payable
Cleaning Equipment	Paul Morales, Capital

Instructions:

(1) Prepare a T account for each account listed above.
(2) Analyze and record each of the following business transactions in the appropriate T accounts. Identify each transaction by number.
(3) After recording all transactions, compute and record the account balance on the normal balance side of each T account.
(4) Add the balances of those accounts with normal debit balances.
(5) Add the balances of those accounts with normal credit balances.
(6) Compare the two totals. Are they the same?

Transactions:

1. Paul Morales invested $30,000 from his savings into the business.
2. Invested cleaning equipment, valued at $650, in the business.
3. Bought a van on account from Westside Motors for $19,360.
4. Bought cleaning supplies for $550, Check 100.
5. Bought a new rug shampooer on account from Harris Equipment for $1,250.
6. As a favor, sold some cleaning supplies on credit to a neighboring business, $50.
7. Purchased storage shelves for the business for $650, Check 101.
8. Paid $500 on account to Harris Equipment, Check 102.
9. Bought cleaning supplies for $175, Check 103.
10. Paid $1,250 on account to Westside Motors, Check 104.

Chapter 4, Problem 4A   Analyzing Transactions

Jane Black owns the Arbor Landscaping Service. She plans to use the following accounts for recording and reporting business transactions.

Cash in Bank	Jane Black, Withdrawals
Accounts Receivable	Landscaping Fees
Equipment	Maintenance Expense
Accounts Payable	Rent Expense
Jane Black, Capital	Utilities Expense

Instructions:

(1) Prepare a T account for each account listed above.
(2) Analyze and record each of the following transactions, using the appropriate T accounts. Identify each transaction by number.
(3) After recording all transactions, compute a balance for each account.
(4) Test for the equality of debits and credits.

Transactions:

1. Jane Black invested $25,000 cash in the business.
2. Bought a new lawnmower on account from Mason Lawn Products, Inc., for $1,400.
3. Jane Black invested equipment valued at $125 in the business.
4. Paid the rent for the month of $350, Check 101.
5. Wrote Check 102 for $20 for minor repairs to the equipment.
6. Completed landscaping for a customer and sent a bill for $350.

7. Paid the utility bill of $75, Check 103.
8. Deposited the daily receipts for landscaping services, $175.
9. Sent Check 104 for $500 to Mason Lawn Products as a payment on account.
10. Received $150 from a charge customer on account.
11. Ms. Black withdrew $150 for her personal use, Check 105.
12. Paid the telephone bill of $35, Check 106.
13. Deposited the daily receipts of $600 for landscaping services.

Chapter 5, Problem 5A   Recording Transactions in the General Journal

Six months ago, Jack Wiley opened his own engineering company. He uses the following accounts to record the business's transactions.

Cash in Bank	Accounts Payable—Engineering Suppliers
Accounts Receivable— Hempfield Township	Accounts Payable—Mohawk Van Dealers
Accounts Receivable— Unity Township	Jack Wiley, Capital
	Jack Wiley, Withdrawals
Engineering Supplies	Professional Fees
Surveying Equipment	Advertising Expense
Blueprint Equipment	Rent Expense
Motor Vehicles	Utilities Expense

Instructions: Record the following transactions on page 6 of a general journal.

Transactions:

June 1   Jack Wiley invested surveying equipment valued at $800 in the business, Memorandum 202.

      3   Wrote Check 150 to New Town Press for advertisements, $125.

      6   Completed services for Hempfield Township and sent a bill for $750, Invoice 91.

      8   Paid the $85 utility bill, Check 151.

   15   Purchased $160 in engineering supplies from Engineering Suppliers on account, Invoice 1161.

   18   Received a check for $375 from Hempfield Township to apply on account, Receipt 123.

   20   Sent a bill for $900 to Unity Township for engineering services performed on account, Invoice 92.

   22   Sent Check 152 for $160 to Engineering Suppliers on account.

   25   Jack Wiley withdrew $15 in engineering supplies for personal use, Memorandum 203.

   28   Received $500 from Unity Township on account, Receipt 124.

   30   Purchased a $16,000 van from Mohawk Van Dealers on account, Invoice 553.

Chapter 6, Problem 6A   Posting Business Transactions

Bruno Ciani started a business to provide dental services to the community. The accounts used by the business, Bruno Ciani, D.D.S., have been opened and are included in the working papers accompanying this textbook. The general journal entries for the May business transactions are also included in the working papers.

Instructions:

(1) Post each journal entry to the appropriate accounts in the ledger.
(2) Prove the ledger by preparing a trial balance.

Chapter 7, Problem 7A   Preparing a Six-Column Work Sheet

The final balances in the general ledger of the Bodyworks Fitness Center at the end of July are as follows.

101	Cash in Bank	$16,095.50
105	Accounts Receivable — R. D. Best	350.00
110	Supplies	612.00
115	Exercise Equipment	15,090.00
120	Office Equipment	2,600.00
125	Office Furniture	3,200.00
201	Accounts Payable — Lake Co.	688.00
205	Accounts Payable — Pro Equipment Co.	2,405.95
210	Accounts Payable — Walton Supply Co.	620.50
301	Lynn Foster, Capital	31,679.55
305	Lynn Foster, Withdrawals	1,500.00
310	Income Summary	0.00
401	Membership Fees	10,500.00
405	Class Fees	8,400.00
501	Advertising Expense	1,250.00
505	Maintenance Expense	1,619.00
510	Miscellaneous Expense	515.00
515	Rent Expense	1,900.00
520	Salaries Expense	6,100.00
525	Utilities Expense	3,462.50

Instructions: Prepare a work sheet for the month ended July 31.

Chapter 8, Problem 8A   Preparing Financial Statements

The work sheet for the A-1 Driving School appears below.

A-1 Driving School
Work Sheet
For the Quarter Ended September 30, 19--

ACCT. NO.	ACCOUNT NAME	TRIAL BALANCE DEBIT	TRIAL BALANCE CREDIT	INCOME STATEMENT DEBIT	INCOME STATEMENT CREDIT	BALANCE SHEET DEBIT	BALANCE SHEET CREDIT	
101	Cash in Bank	6 107 00				6 107 00		1
105	Accts. Rec.- Andover Pub. Schools	450 00				450 00		2
110	Accts. Rec.- Taunton Pub. Schools	1 600 00				1 600 00		3
115	Office Equipment	2 510 00				2 510 00		4
120	Motor Vehicles	30 600 00				30 600 00		5
201	Accts. Pay.- Bay State Motors		15 423 00				15 423 00	6
205	Accts. Pay.- Tappley Co.		1 629 00				1 629 00	7
301	Mark O'Keefe, Capital		18 516 00				18 516 00	8
305	Mark O'Keefe, Withdrawals	3 600 00				3 600 00		9
310	Income Summary							10
401	Instruction Fees		15 960 00		15 960 00			11
501	Advertising Expense	2 000 00		2 000 00				12
505	Fuel Expense	1 656 00		1 656 00				13
510	Maintenance Expense	1 800 00		1 800 00				14
515	Rent Expense	900 00		900 00				15
520	Utilities Expense	305 00		305 00				16
		51 528 00	51 528 00	6 661 00	15 960 00	44 867 00	35 568 00	17
	Net Income			9 299 00			9 299 00	18
				15 960 00	15 960 00	44 867 00	44 867 00	19

Instructions:

(1) Prepare an income statement for the quarter ended September 30.

(2) Prepare a statement of changes in owner's equity. Mark O'Keefe made no additional investments during the period.

(3) Prepare a balance sheet in report form.

Chapter 9, Problem 9A   Preparing Closing Entries

The following information appeared on the work sheet of Young Air Conditioning Repair for the year ended June 30.

	Income Statement		Balance Sheet	
	Debit	Credit	Debit	Credit
Harold Young, Capital				38,000.00
Harold Young, Withdrawals			8,000.00	
Income Summary	—	—		
Repair Service Fees		37,000.00		
Advertising Expense	2,000.00			
Miscellaneous Expense	1,500.00			
Rent Expense	12,000.00			
Telephone Expense	1,200.00			
Utilities Expense	3,600.00			
	20,300.00	37,000.00	56,419.00	39,719.00
Net Income	16,700.00			16,700.00
	37,000.00	37,000.00	56,419.00	56,419.00

Instructions: Using the information above, prepare the four journal entries to close the temporary capital accounts. Use journal page 19.

Chapter 10, Problem 10A   Reconciling the Bank Statement

On April 30, the accounting clerk for Horizon Movers received the bank statement dated April 28. After comparing the company's checkbook with the bank statement, the accounting clerk found:

1. The checkbook balance on April 30 was $13,462.96.

2. The ending bank statement balance was $13,883.80.

3. The bank statement showed a service charge of $17.50.

4. Deposits of $675.00 on April 28 and $925.00 on April 29 did not appear on the bank statement.

5. The following checks were outstanding:

Check 1266	$125.00	Check 1270	$1,462.19
Check 1268	69.42	Check 1271	381.73

Instructions:

(1) Record the bank service charge in the checkbook.

(2) Reconcile the bank statement for Horizon Movers.

(3) Record the entry for the bank service charge on general journal page 13.

(4) Post the bank service charge to the appropriate ledger accounts.

Chapter 11, Problem 11A   Preparing a Payroll Register

Kelly's Supermarket has four employees. They are paid on a weekly basis with overtime paid for all hours worked over 40. The overtime rate is $1\frac{1}{2}$

times the regular rate of pay. The employee names and other information needed to prepare the payroll are as follows.

Don Bell: Married; 3 exemptions; rate per hour, $6.50; employee no. 106
Alice Kerr: Single; 1 exemption; rate per hour, $5.75; employee no. 112; union member
Eric Sullivan: Married; 2 exemptions, rate per hour, $5.25; employee no. 117; union member
Carol Vinton: Single; 0 exemptions; rate per hour, $5.90; employee no. 119; union member

During the week ended May 6, Bell worked 44 hours, Kerr and Vinton each worked 40 hours, and Sullivan worked 41 hours.

Instructions:

(1) Prepare a payroll register. The date of payment is May 6. List employees in alphabetical order by last name.
  (a) Compute FICA taxes at 7.65% of gross earnings.
  (b) Use the tax charts on pages 220-221 to determine federal income taxes. There is no state income tax.
  (c) All four employees have deductions for hospital insurance: $3.70 for single employees and $5.10 for married employees.
  (d) Union members pay weekly dues of $2.50.

(2) After the payroll information is entered in the payroll register, total the columns and check the accuracy of the totals.

Chapter 12, Problem 12A   Recording Payroll Transactions

The payroll register of Star Bakery for the week ended March 31 appears below.

PAY PERIOD ENDING March 31, 19-- — PAYROLL REGISTER — DATE OF PAYMENT March 31,19--

	NAME				RATE	EARNINGS REGULAR	OVERTIME	TOTAL	DEDUCTIONS FICA	FED. INC. TAX	STATE INC. TAX	HOSP. INS.	OTHER		TOTAL	NET PAY	CK. NO.
1	13 Austin, Corrine	S	1	39	6.25	243 75		243 75	18 65	27 00	9 75	4 50			59 90	183 85	1
2	16 Fisher, Paul	M	4	40	7.00	280 00		280 00	21 42	9 00	11 20	5 25	UW	3 85	50 72	229 28	2
3	19 Lopez, Lisa	S	1	25	5.80	145 00		145 00	11 09	13 00	5 80	4 50			34 39	110 61	3
4	23 Rutherford, Amy	S	0	43	6.80	272 00	30 60	302 60	23 15	42 00	12 10	4 50	UW	3 00	84 75	217 85	4
5	26 Willams, Randy	S	2	35	6.50	227 50		227 50	17 40	18 00	9 10	4 50	C	5 00	54 00	173 50	5
6	27 Wong, Cynthia	M	3	43	590	236 00	26 55	262 55	20 09	12 00	10 50	5 25	UW	2 25	50 09	212 46	6
25					TOTALS	1,404 25	57 15	1,461 40	111 80	121 00	58 45	28 50		14 10	333 85	1,127 55	25

Other Deductions: Write the appropriate code letter to the left of the amount: B — U.S. Savings Bonds; C — Credit Union; UD — Union Dues; UW — United Way.

Instructions: Record the following transactions in the general journal (page 11).

Transactions:

Mar. 31   Wrote Check 603 to pay the payroll for the period ended March 31.
  31   Recorded the employer's payroll taxes (FICA tax rate, 7.65%; federal unemployment tax rate, 0.8%; state unemployment tax rate, 5.4%).

31   Issued Check 604 for the amounts owed to the federal government for employees' federal income taxes ($252.00) and FICA taxes ($435.04).

31   Paid $114.00 to the Mutual Insurance Company for the employees' hospital insurance, Check 605.

Answers to "Check Your Learning" Activities

Chapter 2, Page 19
1. a. $7,000; b. $1,500; c. $8,000
2. $40
3. $20
4. $14,000

Chapter 2, Page 21
1. $25,000
2. liabilities
3. $158,000

Chapter 2, Page 27
1. Cash in Bank, +$30,000; Jan Swift, Capital, +$30,000
2. Office Furniture, +$700; Jan Swift, Capital, +$700
3. Delivery Equipment, +$10,000; Cash in Bank, −$10,000
4. Office Furniture, +$5,000; Accounts Payable, +$5,000
5. Accounts Receivable, +$700; Office Furniture, −$700
6. Accounts Payable, −$2,000; Cash in Bank, −$2,000
   Ending Balances: Assets, $33,700 = Liabilities, $3,000 + Owner's Equity, $30,700

Chapter 2, Page 30
1. Jan Swift, Capital, −$50; Cash in Bank, −$50
2. Cash in Bank, +$1,000; Jan Swift, Capital, +$1,000
3. Jan Swift, Capital, −$600; Cash in Bank, −$600
4. Jan Swift, Capital, −$800; Cash in Bank, −$800
5. Cash in Bank, +$200; Accounts Receivable, −$200
   Ending Balances: Assets, $33,250 = Liabilities, $3,000 + Owner's Equity, $30,250

Chapter 3, Page 44
1. debit
2. credit
3. debit
4.

Office Equipment

Debit	Credit
+	−
$2,000	$500
1,500	
Bal. $3,000	

The balance of $3,000 is recorded on the debit side.

Chapter 3, Page 46
1. right
2. left
3. credit
4.

Accounts Payable

Debit	Credit
−	+
$600	$700
200	500
400	300
	Bal. $300

The balance of $300 is recorded on the credit side.

5.

Patrick Vance, Capital

Debit	Credit
−	+
$1,500	$ 9,000
700	3,000
	1,500
	Bal. $11,300

The balance of $11,300 is recorded on the credit side.

Chapter 4, Page 66
1. The normal balance side of any account is the side on which increases are recorded in that account.
2. A debit increases an expense account.
3. The normal balance for a revenue account is a credit balance.
4. A credit increases a revenue account.
5. A debit balance is the normal balance for an expense account.
6. A credit decreases the withdrawals account.
7. A debit balance is the normal balance for a withdrawals account.

Chapter 4, Page 75
1. Cash in Bank; Rent Expense
2. Cash in Bank is an asset account; Rent Expense is an expense account.
3. Cash in Bank is decreased; Rent Expense is increased.
4. Rent Expense is debited for $2,000.
5. Cash in Bank is credited for $2,000.
6. Rent Expense is debited for $2,000 and Cash in Bank is credited for $2,000.

Rent Expense

Debit	Credit
+	−
$2,000	

Cash in Bank

Debit	Credit
+	−
	$2,000

Chapter 5, Page 88
1. fiscal period
2. cycle; fiscal period
3. source documents
4. general journal

Chapter 5, Page 91
1. September 12
2. Office Supplies, $125
3. Cash in Bank, $125
4. Check 424

Chapter 5, Page 97
1. Advertising Expense
2. 9
3. Memorandum 2

4. October 15
5. 2
6. Global Travel completed services for Burton Company and billed them $450, Invoice 1000.

Chapter 5, Page 100
1. a. assets; b. assets; c. owner's equity; d. expenses; e. revenue; f. liabilities; g. expenses
2. a. Cash in Bank; b. Accounts Receivable — Martinez Company; c. Accounts Payable — Podaski Co.; d. B. Watson, Capital; e. Membership Fees; f. Maintenance Expense; g. Miscellaneous Expense
3. a. 1; b. 1; c. 3; d. 5; e. 4; f. 2; g. 5

Chapter 6, Page 112
1. the date: June 6, 19 —
2. Accounts Payable — Monroe Products
3. $250; credit balance
4. 101

Chapter 6, Page 117
1. the letter and page number of the journal entry
2. $4,200
3. a zero balance
4. to indicate that an amount is not being posted from a journal
5. Credit Balance column

Chapter 7, Page 135
1. heading
2. Accounts appear in the same order as they appear in the chart of accounts.
3. A dash is entered in the normal balance amount column.

Chapter 7, Page 140
1. Balance Sheet
2. net income or net loss
3. capital
4. Check to see that all debit and credit balances have been extended properly. If all balances have been extended, check the addition and subtraction.

Chapter 8, Page 154
1. Who? What? When?
2. For the Quarter Ended June 30, 19 —
3. individual account balances; totals
4. net income; $236

Chapter 8, Page 157

1. capital account
2. income statement
3. $23,200
4. balance sheet

Chapter 8, Page 160

1. October 31, 19 —
2. heading, assets section, and liabilities and owner's equity sections
3. in the same order as they appear in the Balance Sheet section of the work sheet
4. statement of changes in owner's equity

Chapter 9, Page 173

1. a. Ticket Revenue; b. Income Summary; c. $6,000; $6,000
2. a. June 30, 19 — ; b. Income Summary; c. $3,100; d. Gas and Oil Expense, Miscellaneous Expense, Utilities Expense; e. $700, $600, $1,800

Chapter 9, Page 176

1. work sheet
2. 4
3. Income Summary
4. increased
5. 3

Chapter 10, Page 194

1. Global Travel Agency
2. Hilda G. Burton; Patriot Bank
3. ABA
4. account

Chapter 10, Page 199

1. $2,938.95
2. $635.00
3. $782.00
4. $2,938.95
5. Yes

Chapter 11, Page 216

1. a. $173.16; b. $201.24; c. $250.38
2. $441.50
3. $227.10

Chapter 11, Page 222

1. federal income tax; social security tax; city or state income tax
2. marital status; number of exemptions
3. a. $12.00; b. $15.00
4. a. $17.14; b. $12.39

Chapter 12, Page 236

1. gross earnings
2. liabilities
3. net pay
4. net pay

Chapter 12, Page 242

1. $56.00
2. FICA Tax Payable; Federal Unemployment Tax Payable; State Unemployment Tax Payable
3. employer
4. $2,560.37

Chapter 12, Page 244

1. 6
2. the payments were made to different government agencies and businesses
3. $571.17
4. $51.14
5. $1,323.65
6. $0

Glossary

a

account subdivision under the three sections of the basic accounting equation used to summarize increases and decreases in assets, liabilities, and owner's equity

accountant a person who handles a broad range of jobs related to the making of choices and decisions about the design of a business's accounting system and the preparation and explanation of financial reports

accounting clerk entry-level job that can vary with the size of the company from specialization in one part of the system to a wide range of recordkeeping tasks

accounting cycle a full range of activities that help a business keep its accounting records in an orderly fashion

accounting system a systematic process of recording and reporting the financial information resulting from business transactions

accounts payable an amount owed to a creditor for goods or services bought on credit

accounts receivable an amount to be received from a customer for goods or services sold on credit

accumulated earnings an employee's year-to-date gross earnings

assets property or economic resources owned by a business or individual

b

balance sheet a report of the final balances in all asset, liability, and owner's equity accounts at a specific time

balance side the same side of an account as the side used to increase that account

bank service charge a fee charged by the bank for maintaining bank records and processing bank statement items for the depositor

bank statement an itemized record of all transactions occurring in a depositor's account over a given period, usually a month

basic accounting equation assets = liabilities + owner's equity; shows the relationship between assets and total equities

business entity an organization that exists independently of its owner's personal holdings

business transaction a business event, such as the buying, selling, or exchange of goods, that causes a change in the assets, liabilities, or owner's equity of a business

c

canceled checks checks paid by the bank and deducted from the depositor's account

capital the money invested in a business by an owner; the owner's equity in a business; the owner's claim or right to a business's assets

certified public accountant (CPA) a public accountant who has passed the licensing exam on accounting theory, practice, auditing, and business law

chart of accounts a list of all the accounts used in journalizing a business's transactions

charter a written permission to operate as a corporation; it spells out the rules under which a business must operate

check a written order from a depositor telling the bank to pay cash to the person or business named on the check

check stub the portion remaining after a check has been detached from a checkbook; the check stub contains details of the cash payment

checking account a bank account that allows a bank customer to deposit cash and to write checks against the account balance

closing entries journal entries made to close out, or reduce to zero, the balances in the temporary capital accounts and to transfer the net income or loss for the period to the capital account

commission an amount paid to an employee based on a percentage of the employee's sales

compound entry a journal entry having two or more debits or credits

computerized accounting system a system in which financial information is recorded by entering it into a computer

corporation a business organization legally recognized to have a life of its own

correcting entry an entry made to correct an error in a journal entry discovered after posting

credit an agreement to pay for a purchase at a later time; an entry to the right side of a T account

creditor a person or business that has a claim to the assets of a business; a person or business to which money is owed

d

debit an entry made to the left side of a T account

deduction (payroll) an amount that is subtracted from an employee's gross earnings

deposit slip a bank form on which the currency (bills and coins) and checks to be deposited are listed

depositor a person or business that has cash on deposit in a bank

direct deposit the depositing of an employee's net pay directly into her or his personal bank account; usually made through electronic funds transfer

double-entry accounting a financial recordkeeping system in which each transaction affects at least two accounts; for each debit there must be an equal credit

drawee the bank on which a check is written

drawer the person who signs a check

e

electronic badge reader computerized equipment that reads a magnetic strip on an employee's time card and automatically records the employee's arrival or departure time

electronic funds transfer system a system that enables banks to transfer funds from the account of one depositor to the account of another without the immediate exchange of checks

employee's earnings record an individual payroll record prepared for each employee; includes data on earnings, deductions, net pay, and accumulated earnings

endorsement an authorized signature written or stamped on the back of a check

equity the total financial claims to the assets, or property, of a business

exemption an allowance claimed by a taxpayer that reduces the amount of taxes that must be paid

expense the cost of the goods or services that are used to operate a business; expenses decrease owner's equity

external controls those controls provided outside a business (for example, controls maintained by banks to protect deposits)

f

federal tax deposit coupon (Form 8109) a form sent with the payment for FICA and federal income taxes or federal unemployment taxes to indicate the total amount of taxes being paid

financial statements reports prepared to summarize the changes resulting from business transactions that have occurred during the fiscal period

fiscal period the time covered by an accounting report (usually one year)

Form 940 the employer's unemployment tax return; it includes both federal and state unemployment taxes paid during the year

Form 941 the employer's quarterly federal tax return; it reports the accumulated amounts of FICA and federal income tax withheld from employees' earnings for the quarter as well as FICA tax owed by the employer

Form W-2 a form that provides the employee with a summary of earnings and amounts withheld for federal, state, and local taxes; also called a wage and tax statement

Form W-3 a summary of the information contained on the employees' Forms W-2; also called a transmittal of income and tax statements

g

general bookkeeper one person who keeps all the accounting records, usually for a small- or medium-sized business

general journal an all-purpose journal in which all transactions may be recorded

general ledger the group of accounts used by a business

going concern the assumption that a business entity will continue to operate for an indefinite time

gross earnings the total amount of money earned by an employee during a pay period

i

income statement a report of the net income or net loss for a fiscal period; sometimes called a "profit and loss" statement

Income Summary account the account in the general ledger used to summarize the revenue and expenses for the fiscal period

internal controls steps a business takes to protect cash (for example, limiting the number of persons handling cash)

invoice a bill; a form that lists the quantity, description, unit price, and total cost of the items sold and shipped to a buyer

j

journal a chronological record of a business's transactions

journalizing the process of recording business transactions in a journal

l

ledger a book or file containing a separate page for each business account; serves as a permanent record of financial transactions

ledger account form the accounting stationery used to record financial information about a specific account

liabilities amounts owed to creditors; the claims of creditors to the assets of the business

liquidity ease with which an asset can be converted to cash

loss the result of a company's spending more than it receives in revenue

m

managerial accounting accounting within a business firm to provide financial information to management

manual accounting system a system in which accounting information is processed by hand

manufacturing business a business that transforms raw materials into finished products through the use of labor and machinery

matching principle principle stating that expenses are compared to revenues for the same period

memorandum a brief written description of a transaction that takes place within a business

merchandising business a business that buys goods (for example, books or clothing) and then sells those goods for a profit

n

net income the amount left after expenses for the period have been subtracted from revenue for the same period

net loss the amount by which total expenses exceed total revenue

Glossary

net pay the amount of money left after all deductions have been subtracted from gross earnings

normal balance the increase side of an account: assets, debit side; liabilities and capital, credit side

not-for-profit organization an organization that does not operate for the purpose of making a profit

NSF check a check returned by the bank because there are not sufficient funds in the drawer's checking account to cover the amount of the check

o

on account buying on credit; agreeing to pay for an item later

outstanding checks checks that have been written but not yet presented to the bank for payment

outstanding deposits deposits that have been made and recorded in the checkbook but that do not appear on the bank statement

overtime rate a rate of pay $1\frac{1}{2}$ times an employee's regular rate of pay; overtime is paid for all hours worked over 40 per week

owner's equity the owner's claims to or investment in the assets of the business

p

partnership a type of business ownership in which two or more persons agree to operate the business as co-owners

pay period the amount of time for which an employee is paid

payee the person or business to whom a check is written; the person or business to whom a promissory note is payable

payroll a list of the employees of a business that shows the payments due to each employee for a specific pay period

payroll clerk a person whose responsibility is the preparation of the payroll

payroll register a form that summarizes information about employees' earnings for each pay period

permanent accounts accounts that are continuous from one accounting period to the next; balances are carried forward to the next period (for example, assets, liabilities, and owner's capital accounts)

piece rate the amount paid to an employee for each item, or piece, produced

post-closing trial balance the trial balance prepared after the closing entries have been journalized and posted

posting the process of transferring information in a journal entry to accounts in a ledger

private enterprise economy an economy in which people are free to produce the goods and services they choose

profit the amount of revenue earned above the expenses incurred to operate the business

property items of value that are owned or controlled by a business; economic resources of a business

property rights creditors' and owners' financial claims to the assets of a business

proving cash the process of determining whether the amounts of cash recorded in a business's accounting records and in its checkbook agree

proving the ledger adding all debit balances and all credit balances of ledger accounts and then comparing the two totals to see whether they are equal

r

receipt a form that serves as a record of cash received

reconciling the bank statement the process of determining any differences between a bank statement balance and a checkbook balance

report form a format for preparing the balance sheet in which the classifications of accounts are one under another

restrictive endorsement a check endorsement that restricts or limits how a check may be handled (for example, "For Deposit Only")

revenue income earned by a business from its operations; revenue increases owner's equity

revenue principle accounting principle that states that revenue is recognized and recorded on the date it is earned

ruling a single line drawn under a column of figures to signify that the entries above the rule are to be added or subtracted; a double rule under an amount signifies a total

s

salary a fixed amount of money paid to an employee for each pay period

service business a business operated for profit that provides a needed service for a fee

signature card a card containing the signature(s) of the person(s) authorized to write checks on a checking account

slide accidental misplacement of a decimal point in an amount

sole proprietorship a business that has one owner

source document a paper prepared as evidence that a transaction occurred

statement of changes in owner's equity a financial statement prepared to summarize the effects of business transactions on the capital account

stop payment order a demand by the depositor that a bank not honor a certain check

t

T account an account shaped like a "T" that is used for analyzing transactions

temporary capital accounts accounts used to record information during the fiscal period that will be transferred to a permanent capital account at the end of the period

time card a record of the time an employee arrives at work, the time the employee leaves, and the total number of hours worked each day

transposition error the accidental reversal of two numbers

trial balance a proof of the equality of total debits and credits

u

unemployment taxes taxes collected to provide funds for workers who are temporarily out of work; usually paid only by the employer

v

voiding a check canceling a check by writing the word "Void" on the front of a check in ink

w

wage an amount of money paid to an employee at a specified rate per hour worked

withdrawal the removal of cash or another asset from the business by the owner for personal use

work sheet a working paper used to collect information from ledger accounts for use in completing end-of-fiscal-period work

Credits

Book design and production: Graphics etcetera
Technical art: Graphics etcetera
Calligraphy: Nancy Edwards

Photographs

1 © Peter L. Chapman
4 © Miro Vintoniv/Stock, Boston
8 © Jay Freis/The Image Bank
16 © Gary Gladstone/The Image Bank
18 © Peter L. Chapman
29 © Charles Gupton/Stock, Boston
38 © The Stock Market/Gabe Palmer 1981
39 © Lawrence Migdale/Photo Researchers, Inc.
47 © Zao-Sulle/The Image Bank
50 © Susan Van Etten/THE PICTURE CUBE
59 © Lowell Georgia/Photo Researchers, Inc.
62 © Pictures Unlimited
71 © Richard Hutchings/Photo Researchers, Inc.
82 © Dan McCoy/Rainbow
98 © Peter L. Chapman
106 © Frank Siteman/THE PICTURE CUBE
109 © Michal Heron/Woodfin Camp & Associates
127 © The Stock Market/Gabe Palmer
132 © Richard Hutchings/Photo Researchers, Inc.
147 © Elliott V. Smith/Int'l Stock Photo
151 © The Stock Market/Ed Bock 1987
167 © Jen & Des Bartlett/BRUCE COLEMAN INC.
176 © Joseph Nettis/Photo Researchers, Inc.
186 © Dan McCoy/Rainbow
188 © Steve Dunwell/The Image Bank
195 © Elyse Lewin/The Image Bank
206 © The Stock Market/Randy Duchaine 1986
211 © Peter L. Chapman
214 © Jennifer Cogswell/THE PICTURE CUBE
217 © Robert Capece/Monkmeyer Press Photo Service
232 © Michael Abramson/Woodfin Camp & Associates
238 © Bonnie Freer/Photo Researchers, Inc.
254 © Robert Isear/Photo Researchers, Inc.

Index

a

ABA number, 190
account, *def.,* 21
　balance, 43
　cash received on, 52-53
　determining balance of, 43
　four-column form, 109-110
　normal balance of, 43, 45, 63,
　　64, 66
　number, 98-99, 133
　opening an, 110, 116-117
　payment on, 25-26, 51-52
　permanent, 62
　purchase on, 25, 49-51
　T, *def.,* 42
　temporary capital, 61
　title, 22
　zero balance in, 116
account number, 98-99
account title, 22
　on work sheet, 133
accountant, *def.,* 9-10; 38, 206
accounting, *def.,* 6
　assumptions, 7-8
　basic accounting equation, 20-21
　careers in, 9-10, 38, 127, 206
　computerized, 8-9, 30-31, 87,
　　96-97, 226
　cycle, steps in, 84-87
　debit and credit rules of, 42-46,
　　62-67
　double-entry, 42
　equation, 20-21
　financial claims in, 20-21
　managerial, 10

　not-for-profit, 10
　organizations, 10-11
　payroll, 212-226
　public, 10
　purpose of, 6
　and teaching, 10
　See also accounting system.
accounting clerk, *def.,* 9, 127
accounting cycle, *def.,* 84, *illus.,* 84
　for a service business, 128-129
　steps in, 84-87
accounting equation, *def.,* 20
　effects of business transactions
　　on, 22-30
accounting system, *def.,* 6, 42
　computerized, 8, 87, 96-97
　manual, 87
　recording transactions in an,
　　87, 88-96
accounts
　chart of, 68, 98
　classifying, 20-21, 99
　general ledger, 108-110
　listed on work sheet, 133
　numbering, 98-99
　opening, 110
　permanent, 62
　posting to, 111-116
　temporary capital, 61
accounts payable, *def.,* 22
　normal balance of, 45
accounts receivable, *def.,* 22
accumulated earnings, *def.,* 225
American Institute of Certified
　　Public Accountants, 11

assets, *def.,* 20
　in accounting equation, 20
　analyzing transactions affect-
　　ing, 46-53
　cash purchase of, 24-25
　classifying, 99
　rules of debit and credit for, 43-
　　44
　section of balance sheet, 158
assumptions, accounting, 7-8
automated accounting system.
　　See computerized account-
　　ing system.

b

balance sheet, *def.,* 157
　assets section of, 158
　computer-generated, 160-161
　illustrated, 159
　heading of, 157-158
　liabilities section of, 158-159
　owner's equity section of, 158-
　　159
　purpose of, 157
　section of work sheet, 135
　for sole proprietorship, 157-160
balance side, *def.,* 43
　for asset accounts, 43
　for expense accounts, 64-65
　for liabilities and owner's eq-
　　uity accounts, 44-45
　for revenue accounts, 63-64
　for withdrawals accounts, 66
bank service charges, *def.,* 197
　journalizing, 199

recording in checkbook, 197
bank statement, *def.,* 195; *illus.,* 196
  reconciling, 196-198
basic accounting equation, *def.,* 20-21. *See also* accounting equation.
bookkeeper, general, *def.,* 9
business
  not-for-profit, 3
  for profit, 3-5
business entity, 7
business organization, forms of, 5
business transaction, *def.,* 21
  effect on accounting equation, 22-30, 47-53
  journalizing, 87, 88-96, 96-97
  posting, 108, 111-116
  recording, 87
  steps in analyzing, 22-30, 46-53, 67-74, 86

c

canceled check, *def.,* 196
capital, *def.,* 3, 22
capital account, *def.,* 22
  analyzing transactions affecting, 47-49
  and closing entries, 173-175
  determining balance of, 155-156
  rules of debit and credit for, 44-45
  temporary, 61, 62-66
careers, in accounting, 9-10, 38, 127, 206
cash
  protecting, 188
  proving, 195
  purchases, 24-25, 48
cash payments, 24-25, 51-52
cash purchases, journalizing, 90-91
certified public accountant (CPA), *def.,* 10, 206
charter, corporate, 5
chart of accounts, *def.,* 98
  for sole proprietorship service business, 40, 68, 99
check, *def.,* 189; *illus.,* 190
  ABA number on, 190
  canceled, 196
  drawee, 193
  drawer, 193
  endorsing, 191-192
  MICR number on, 190
  NSF (not sufficient funds), 200
  outstanding, 197
  payee, 193

payroll, 223-224
  stopping payment on, 200
  voiding, 194
  writing, 192-194
check stub, *def.,* 85
  recording checks on, 192-193
  recording deposits on, 192
  recording service charges on, 197
  as source document, 85
checkbook, *illus.,* 190
  described, 190
  recording bank charges in, 197
  recording checks in, 192-193
  recording deposits in, 192
checking account, *def.,* 189
  and bank statement, 195-198
  deposits to, 191-192
  signature card for, 189
  writing checks, 192-194
  See also check.
closing entries, *def.,* 169
  in computerized system, 179
  for expense accounts, 172-173
  journalizing, 171-175
  need for, 169-170
  posting, 176-178
  for revenue accounts, 171-172
  for a sole proprietorship, 169-175
  for withdrawals account, 174-175
commission, *def.,* 215
compound entry, *def.,* 172
computer, 16
  in accounting, 30-31
  data access, 254
  and security, 106, 147
computer-generated reports
  balance sheet, 160-161
  post-closing trial balance, 179
computerized accounting system, 96-97
  closing entries in, 179
  financial statements, 160-161
  opening accounts in, 110
  for payroll, 226
  posting in a, 117
  See also accounting, accounting system.
controls, cash, 188
corporation, *def.,* 5
  charter, 5
correcting entries, *def.,* 119
  journalizing, 120-121
  for general ledger accounts, 120-121
credit, *def.,* 19, 42

buying on, 19, 25, 49-50
  rules of, 42-46, 63-67, 75
creditor, *def.,* 19

d

dates, of posting, 111
debit, *def.,* 42
  rules of, 42-46, 63-67, 75
deductions
  from gross earnings, 216-222
  section of payroll register, 223
  voluntary payroll, 219, 222
depositor, *def.,* 189
deposits
  making, 191-192
  outstanding, 197
  recording, in checkbook, 192
deposit slip, *def.,* 191
direct deposit, 224
dollar sign, in journal entries, 90
double-entry accounting, *def.,* 42
drawee, *def.,* 193
drawer, *def.,* 193

e

earnings
  accumulated, 225
  employee's record of, 224-225
  gross, 213
electronic badge readers, *def.,* 215
electronic funds transfer system (EFTS), 3, 200-201, 224
employee's earnings record, *def.,* 225
Employee's Withholding Allowance Certificate, 218
employer's payroll taxes, 238-239
  journalizing, 239-240
employer's quarterly federal tax return, 246, 247
endorsement, *def.,* 191
  restrictive, 192
equation, accounting. *See* accounting equation.
equity, *def.,* 20
  owner's, 20
  statement of changes in owner's, 155-156
errors
  correcting, in journal, 96
  correcting entries for, 119-121
  finding, on trial balance, 118-119
  finding, on work sheet, 134
exemption, *def.,* 218
expense, *def.,* 27
  cash payment of, 27-28

journalizing transactions, affecting, 93-95
and matching principle, 137
section of income statement, 153
expense accounts
analyzing transactions affecting, 27-28, 68-70, 72-73
closing, 172-173
rules of debit and credit for, 64-65
external controls, for cash, 188

f

federal income tax
payment of, 242-243
payroll deductions for, 217-218
tables, 220-221
withholding, 217-218
Federal Insurance Contributions Act, 219
federal tax deposit coupon, 242
federal unemployment tax, 238-239
paying, 243-244
Federal Unemployment Tax Act, 239
FICA taxes
employee's, 219
employer's, 238-239
payment of, 242-243
Financial Accounting Standards Board (FASB), 11
financial claims in accounting, 20-21
financial statements, *def.,* 149
balance sheet, 157-160
income statement, 150-154
prepared by computer, 160-161
purpose of, 149
for a sole proprietorship, 149-160
statement of changes in owner's equity, 155-156
fiscal period, *def.,* 8, 84
and closing entries, 169-170
on financial statements, 149
length of, 84
Form 8109, 242
Form 940, 249
Form 941, *def.,* 246; 247
Form W-2, *def.,* 248
Form W-3, *def.,* 248; 249
Form W-4, 218

g

general bookkeeper, 9
general journal, *def.,* 87; *illus.,* 88
closing entries in, 171-175

correcting entries, 120-121
employer's payroll taxes in, 240
payroll transactions in, 236
posting from, 111-116
recording transactions in, 88-96
general ledger, *def.,* 108
closing entries posted to, 176-178
opening accounts in, 110
posting from general journal, 111-116
proving the equality of, 117-118
going concern, 7
gross earnings, *def.,* 213
calculation of, 213-216
deductions from, 216-222

h

heading
on financial statements, 150, 157-158
on work sheet, 132-133
hourly wage, *def.,* 214
calculating, 214-215

i

income, net, 137
income statement, *def.,* 150
expenses section of, 153
heading for, 150
net income or loss on, 153-154
purpose of, 150
revenue section of, 151-153
section of work sheet, 136-137
for sole proprietorship, 150-160
Income Summary account, *def.,* 170
classification of, 170-171
closing, 173-174
and closing entries, 171-173
need for, 170-171
income tax. *See* federal income tax.
internal controls for cash, 188
Internal Revenue Service (IRS), 11
investments, by owner, 23-24, 47-49
invoice, *def.,* 85

j

journal, *def.,* 87
general, 87
journalizing, *def.,* 87; 88-96
closing entries, 171-175
correcting errors in, 96, 119-121
information required for, 87
payroll, 234-236

l

ledger, *def.,* 108
four-column form, 109-110
general, 108-110
opening accounts in, 110, 116-117
posting to, 109, 111-112, 117
proving equality of, 117-118
liabilities, *def.,* 20
analyzing transactions affecting, 46-53
payroll, 239-240, 242-244
rules of debit and credit for, 44-45
section of balance sheet, 158-159
liquidity, *def.,* 98
loss, *def.,* 3

m

managerial accounting, 10
manual accounting system, *def.,* 87
manufacturing business, 4
matching principle, 137
memorandum, *def.,* 85
merchandising business, *def.,* 4
MICR number, on check, 190

n

net income, *def.,* 137
closing entry for, 171-172
section of income statement, 153
on statement of changes in owner's equity, 155-156
on work sheet, 136-138
net loss, *def.,* 138
on income statement, 154
entering, on work sheet, 138-139
net pay, *def.,* 223
normal balance. *See* balance side.
not-for-profit accounting, 3, 10
NSF check, 200

o

organization, types of business, 3, 5
outstanding check, 197
outstanding deposit, 197
overtime rate, *def.,* 216
owner's equity, *def.,* 20
section of balance sheet, 158-159
statement of changes in, 155-156

p

partnership, *def.,* 5
pay period, *def.,* 213
payee, of check, 193
payroll, *def.,* 213
  accounting, 212-226
  checks, preparing, 223-224
  computerized system, 215, 226
  deductions, 216-222
  employer's taxes, 238-244
  journalizing, 234-236
  liabilities, 234-235
  posting transaction for, 236-237
  system, 213
payroll clerk, 213
payroll register, *def.,* 222
  completing, 222-223
  deductions section of, 223
  earnings section of, 222
  net pay section of, 223
payroll taxes
  computing, 238-239
  journalizing, 239-240
  paying, 242-244
  posting, 240-241, 244
permanent accounts, *def.,* 62
piece rate, *def.,* 215
post-closing trial balance, *def.,* 169
  preparing, 178-179
posting, *def.,* 108
  closing entries, 175-178
  in a computerized system, 117
  frequency of, 111
  to general ledger accounts, 109, 111-116
  payroll transaction, 236-237
  reference, 111-112
posting reference, 111-112
private enterprise economy, 3-5
profit, *def.,* 3
property, *def.,* 18
  rights, 18, 20-21
proprietorship. *See* sole proprietorship.
public accounting, 10
purchases
  on account, 49-50
  cash, 48

r

receipt, *def.,* 85
reconciling bank statements, 196-198
record of original entry. *See* journal.
report form, *def.,* 157
restrictive endorsement, *def.,* 191

revenue, *def.,* 27
  and matching principle, 137
  section of income statement, 151-152
revenue accounts
  analyzing transactions affecting, 27-28, 70-72
  closing entries for, 171-172
  rules of debit and credit for, 63-64
rights, property, 18
ruling, *def.,* 134
  work sheet, 134, 138

s

salary, *def.,* 213
Securities and Exchange Commission, 11
service business, 4
service charge, bank, 197
  journalizing, 199
signature card, *def.,* 189
slide error, 119
social security tax. *See* FICA tax.
sole proprietorship, *def.,* 5
  financial statements for, 149-160
  investments by owner of, 23-24, 27-30, 47, 49
  journalizing transactions for, 87-90
source document, *def.,* 85
  as evidence of business transaction, 86
  types of, 85
spreadsheet, computerized, 31
state income taxes, 219
  paying, 243
state unemployment taxes, 239
statement of changes in owner's equity, *def.,* 155
  preparing, 155-156
  purpose of, 155
stop payment order, 200

t

T account, *def.,* 42
taxes
  employee's federal income, 217-218
  employer's payroll, 238-239
  federal unemployment, 239
  FICA, 219, 238-239, 240, 242
  state income, 219, 243
  state unemployment, 239
  tables, 220-221
  tax rate, FICA, 219

temporary capital accounts, *def.,* 61
  closing, 170, 174-175
  rules of debit and credit for, 62-67
time period, 8. *See also* fiscal period.
time card, *def.,* 214
totaling work sheet, 134, 136, 355
transaction. *See* business transaction.
transmittal of income and tax statements (Form W-3), 249
transposition error, 119
trial balance, *def.,* 108; 76, 118
  post-closing, 169, 178-179
  section of work sheet, 133-134

u

unemployment taxes, *def.,* 239
  paying, 243
unit of measure, 8

v

voiding a check, 194

w

wage, hourly, *def.,* 214
  calculating, 214-215
wage and tax statement (Form W-2), 248
withdrawals, *def.,* 29
  analyzing transactions affecting, 29-30, 73-74
  closing into capital account, 174-175
  journalizing, 96
  by owner, 29-30, 73-74
  rules of debit and credit for owner's, 66
  on statement of changes in owner's equity, 155-156
withholding allowance certificate, 218
withholding taxes, 217-218
work sheet, *def.,* 131; *illus.,* 139
  balance sheet section of, 135
  extending amounts on, 135-136
  heading for, 132-133
  income statement section of, 136
  listing accounts on, 133
  net income on, 136-138, 140
  net loss on, 138-139
  ruling, 134, 138
  six-column, 131-140
  steps in preparing, 131-139, 140
  totaling, 136-139
  trial balance section of, 133-134